Question&Answer

CONSTITUTIONAL AND ADMINISTRATIVE LAW

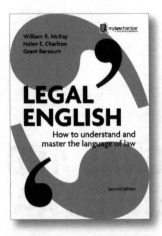

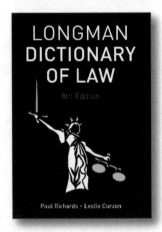
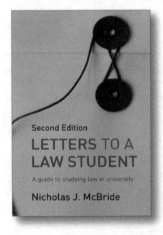

Law Express

Q&A

Question&Answer

CONSTITUTIONAL AND ADMINISTRATIVE LAW

Vicky Thirlaway
Senior Lecturer in Criminal and Public Law,
Leeds Metropolitan University

Longman
is an imprint of

Harlow, England • London • New York • Boston • San Francisco • Toronto • Sydney • Singapore • Hong Kong
Tokyo • Seoul • Taipei • New Delhi • Cape Town • Madrid • Mexico City • Amsterdam • Munich • Paris • Milan

Pearson Education Limited
Edinburgh Gate
Harlow
Essex CM20 2JE
England

and Associated Companies throughout the world

Visit us on the World Wide Web at:
www.pearsoned.co.uk

First published 2012

ISBN: 978-1-4082-4124-0

British Library Cataloguing-in-Publication Data
A catalogue record for this book is available from the British Library

Library of Congress Cataloging-in-Publication Data
A catalog record for this book is available from the Library of Congress.

10 9 8 7 6 5 4 3 2
15 14 13 12

Typeset in 10pt Helvetica Condensed by 30
Printed and bound in Great Britain by Henry Ling Limited, at the Dorset Press, Dorchester, DT1 1HD

Contents

Supporting resources

Visit the **LawExpress Question&Answer** series companion website at
www.pearson.co.uk/lawexpressqa to find valuable learning material including:

- Additional **essay and problem questions** arranged by topic for each chapter give you more opportunity to practise and hone your exam skills.
- **Diagram plans** for all additional questions assist you in structuring and writing your answers.
- **You be the marker** questions allow you to see through the eyes of the examiner by marking essay and problem questions on every topic covered in the book.
- Download and print all **Attack the question** diagrams and **Diagram plans** from the book.

Also: The companion website provides the following features:

- Search tool to help locate specific terms of content.
- Online help and support to assist with website usage and troubleshooting.

For more information please contact your local Pearson sales representative or visit www.pearsoned.co.uk/lawexpressqa

Acknowledgements

To my sister Katie.

Publisher's acknowledgements

Our thanks go to all reviewers who contributed to the development of this text, including students who participated in research and focus groups which helped to shape the series format.

The material in this guide is up-to-date and accurate as the law stood in April 2011, although some minor updating has been possible at later stages in production.

What you need to do for every question in Constitutional and Administrative Law

HOW TO USE THIS BOOK

Books in the *Question and Answer* series focus on the *why* of a good answer along side the *what,* thereby helping you to build your question answering skills and technique.

This guide should not be used as a substitute for learning the material thoroughly, your lecture notes or your textbook. It *will* help you to make the most out of what you have already learned when answering an exam or coursework question. Remember that the answers given here are not the *only* correct way of answering the question but serve to show you some good examples of how you *could* approach the question set.

Make sure that you refer regularly to your course syllabus, check which issues are covered (as well as to what extent they are covered) and whether they are usually examined with other topics. Remember that what is required in a good answer could change significantly with only a slight change in the wording of a question. Therefore, do not try to memorise the answers given here, instead use the answers and the other features to understand what goes into a good answer and why.

The study of the British constitution poses challenges for students, as there is seldom one 'correct' answer to a question. Essay questions demand that you will be able to analyse various competing theories about the nature of the constitution, and formulate a reasoned argument. In order to be persuasive, a legal argument must be supported by evidence and, therefore, you must ensure that you are able to point to examples of the operation of the constitution drawn from historical and current events, academic argument and judicial decisions. Where you are expressing a view or opinion of your own, remember that you still need supporting evidence to show the examiner why you have reached that conclusion. You need to be specific. Comments such as 'many have argued that ...' will not attract high marks. It is far more authoritative to say something like 'Dicey argued that ...', as this shows your examiner that there is a source for your opinion.

Make sure that you use the terminology correctly and consistently; it is important not to say 'government' if you mean 'Parliament', for example.

Constitutional and administrative law is changing at a rapid pace. The Labour administration instigated an extensive programme of legislative change and this seems set to continue under the Coalition government. To do well in this subject, you need to keep abreast of developments by paying attention to the press, the law reports, and journals.

A common mistake made by students is to see the examination as a memory test. Whilst you certainly do need to remember a lot of law, take care not to make the mistake of thinking you are only required to show how much law you remember. Many students submit answers (particularly to problem scenarios) that are too descriptive. Far higher marks are given to those students who have the confidence to select the legal provisions most relevant to the facts given in the question. You should concentrate on applying the law to the facts you have been given and using this to draw conclusions about the likely outcome for the party or parties you are asked to advise. Similarly, if your examiner sets an essay question about the rule of law, then there are no marks available for discussing parliamentary supremacy, unless you wish to argue there is a connection between the two theories.

Guided tour

What you need to do for every question in Constitutional and Administrative Law

What to do for every question – Find out the key things you should do and look for in any question and answer on the subject in order to give every one of your answers a great chance from the start.

1

Sources of the constitution

How this topic may come up in exams

Generally, examiners ask essay questions that require you to engage with the debate about the sources of the constitution and the ideas (doctrines) said to underpin it. Students sometimes struggle with this topic, as it does require some knowledge of history and of political theory. It can be difficult to find authorities to support arguments, and you will need to ensure that you can remember some key points made by theorists and academics. There will be considerable overlap between this part of the syllabus and the role of Parliament, especially when considering the doctrine of the separation of powers.

How this topic might come up in exams – Learn how to tackle any question on this topic by using the handy tips and advice relevant to both essay and problem questions. In-text symbols clearly identify each question type as they occur.

 Essay question

 Problem question

Attack the question – Attack attack attack! Use these diagrams as a step by step guide to help you confidently identify the main points covered in any question asked.

Answer plans and Diagram plans – Clear and concise answer plans and diagram plans support the planning and structuring of your answers whatever your preferred learning style.

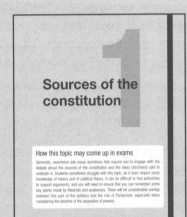

■ Attack the question

Does the question concern questioning a suspect who is not under arrest?

Yes / No

No duty to answer questions, no power to detain short of arrest

Does the question concern stop and search?

Yes / No

Reasonable suspicion Notification Art 5/II Trespass to person

Does the question concern powers of arrest?

No / Yes

Reasonable grounds

Diagram plan

Define 'conventions'

Provide examples of key conventions

Identify how some conventions have changed over time

Outline occasions on which particular conventions have been followed

Outline occasions particular con bee

Answer plan

→ Outline the definitions of conventions given by Dicey and Jennings.

→ Consider particular conventions and the consequences of breach.

→ Analyse how particular conventions could be said to lose their force.

→ Consider whether or not some conventions could be codified.

→ Draw some conclusions about the extent to which conventions are binding.

Answer with accompanying guidance – Make the most out of every question by using the guidance to recognise what makes a good answer and why. Answers are the length you could realistically hope to produce in an exam to show you how to gain marks quickly when under pressure.

[2]This is helpful, as it shows the marker that there will be a clear, logical structure.

[3]Whilst the answer could simply state that Parliament was entitled to legislate as it chose, the case is a useful illustration. The facts aren't required; the key point is the comment in the judgment that the moral content of a statute was constitutionally irrelevant.

[4]Credit will be given for giving a view, but this must be followed with some illustrative examples to support the

According to Dicey, the doctrine of Parliamentary supremacy encompasses three aspects. First, Parliament is free to legislate on any subject-matter. Secondly, Parliament cannot be bound by a predecessor or bind a successor. Lastly, no person or body can question the validity of an act of Parliament. The effect of the HRA can be evaluated against these precepts in turn.[2]

In the case of **Madzimbamuto v Lardner-Burke** [1969] AC 645, Lord Reid observed that there were no constitutional or legal mechanisms to prevent Parliament acting, even if morally or politically 'highly improper'.[3] The HRA requires Parliament to be mindful of the European Convention of Human Rights in respect of all legislation. Section 19 stipulates that a Minister introducing legislation must make a statement of compatibility prior to the second reading of the Bill. If it is not possible, then the Minister must confirm that government still wishes to proceed. It is not necessary to give reasons to support either position. It is submitted that the effect of s 19 is limited.[4] Since the HRA came into force in 2000, there has only been one instance of a Bill being laid before Parliament without a state-

[7]Again, the case of *Entick v Carrington* is central to this aspect of the topic so you need to show the examiner that you are aware of this.

[8]It is always important to demonstrate knowledge of two sides of a debate, but crucial to be able to find some examples to support each side of the argument.

[9]Many commentators refer to this as an important constitutional case, and it is a

The notion that 'no man is above the law' seems straightforward. Dicey cited **Entick v Carrington** as support for this proposition, declaring it to be one of many instances where government officials were called to account.[7] **M v Home Office** [1994] 1 AC 377 is an example of a government Minister being held in contempt of court after ignoring a court order. This would seem to suggest the truth of Dicey's statement. There are, though, examples of classes of persons who are not subject to the law in the same way such as those enjoying diplomatic immunity, or MPs protected from defamation in Parliament.[8] Part IV of the Anti Terror, Crime and Security Act of 2001 attempted to create a law to which only one class of persons, foreign nationals, would be subject. The court's opposition (**A v Secretary of State for the Home Department** [2004] UKHL 56[9]) can be used to support the argument that the judiciary play an important role in preserving the rule of law. If the statement

---

Case names clearly highlighted – Easy to spot bold text makes those all important case names stand out from the rest of the answer, ensuring they are much easier to remember in revision and in the exam.

Make your answer stand out – Really impress your examiners by including these additional points and further reading to illustrate your deeper knowledge of the subject, fully maximising your marks.

✓ Make your answer stand out

- By expanding the explanation of 'democracy' to explore how privilege is connected to the doctrines of separation of powers and the rule of law. You have touched on the fact that privilege allows the Commons to hold the executive to account by asking questions without fear of censure: this could be linked to Bagehot's view of the constitution, in which the ability to operate a system of checks and balances is central to democracy.

- By ensuring you are abreast of developments in this highly topical area of law. At the time of writing, for example, a number of Members of Parliament have sought to use privilege to protect them from legal action arising from the expenses scandal. If you can use these kind of examples in your answers, you will be rewarded because it will show current awareness.

- By incorporating reference to earlier calls for reform of privilege. You could consider, for example, Leopold's discussion, in 'Report of the Joint Committee on Parliamentary Privilege' (1999) Public Law 604.

Don't be Tempted to – Avoid common mistakes and losing easy marks by understanding where students most often trip up in exams.

! Don't be tempted to...

- Explain the relevant conventions without providing examples of how they operate. There is very little case law concerning conventions, but you still need to provide support for any propositions that you make.

- Write a generalised account of the operation of conventions in the constitution. Students who revise the topic assuming it will appear as an essay question can be wrong footed by a problem scenario; ensure that you use the knowledge you have about conventions to draw conclusions about the events described here.

- Ignore the fact that, when dealing with this topic, there are no clear answers. As the answer shows, it is possible to find examples supporting contrasting outcomes here; you will be rewarded for acknowledging this fact.

Bibliography – Use this list of further reading to really explore areas in more depth, enabling you to excel in exams.

Bibliography

Allan, T. R. S (2001) *Constitutional Justice: A Liberal Theory of the Rule of Law*. Oxford: Oxford University Press

Ashworth, A. (2010) '*Gillan and Quinton v United Kingdom*: human rights – article 5 – stop and search as deprivation of liberty', 5 Crim LR 415

Austin, R. (2007) 'The new powers of arrest: plus ça change: more of the same or major change?', Crim LR 459

Guided tour of the companion website

 Book resources are available to download. Print your own **Attack the question** and **Diagram plans**

 Additional **Essay and Problem questions** with **diagram plans** arranged by topic for each chapter give you more opportunity to practise and hone your exam skills. Print and email your answers.

 You be the marker gives you a chance to evaluate sample exam answers for different question types for each topic and understand how and why an examiner awards marks. Use the accompanying guidance to get the most out of every question and recognise what makes a good answer.

Table of cases and statutes

■ Cases

■ Statutes

Sources of the constitution

How this topic may come up in exams

Generally, examiners ask essay questions that require you to engage with the debate about the sources of the constitution and the ideas (doctrines) said to underpin it. Students sometimes struggle with this topic, as it does require some knowledge of history and of political theory. It can be difficult to find authorities to support arguments, and you will need to ensure that you can remember some key points made by theorists and academics. There will be considerable overlap between this part of the syllabus and the role of Parliament, especially when considering the doctrine of the separation of powers.

Attack the question

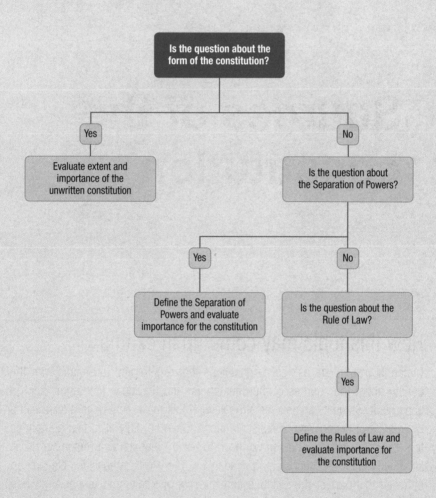

Question 1

The program of reform since 1997 means it is no longer appropriate to refer to the 'unwritten constitution'.

Discuss.

Answer plan

→ Explain the distinction between written and unwritten constitutions.

→ Discuss whether or not the constitution could have been described as wholly unwritten.

→ Identify and outline major changes post-1997.

→ Consider whether unwritten sources remain relevant.

→ Argue that a written constitution demands a higher form of law.

Diagram plan

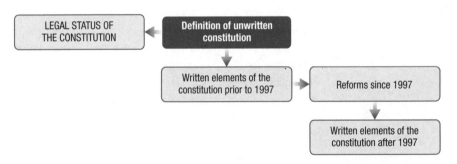

A printable version of this diagram is available from www.pearsoned.co.uk/lawexpressqa

Answer

[1]This definition is quite basic, but shows that you do recognise that the term constitution should be defined by its role, rather than the form it takes.

A constitution is described as a set of rules and practices that determine how power is divided within a state.[1] The UK constitution is sometimes described as 'unwritten', as there is no single written document codifying the relevant laws. This is unusual; the United Kingdom is one of only three nations without a written constitution. In 1997, the Labour government embarked on an ambitious programme of constitutional reform. Arguably, the proliferation of statutes that now define the workings of the state mean that it is now largely written. However, many aspects remain uncodified and, to understand the constitution, it is still necessary to refer to

3

[2]The focus of the argument will be that the distinction between 'written' and 'unwritten' constitutions is not about the format as much as the notion of a superior form of law.

[3]Discussion of change to the constitution does demand that you are able to outline the historical development of the United Kingdom's arrangements. However, it is important to keep this brief, so that the balance of your answer can concentrate on the main focus of the question which is the impact of change.

[4]As the question refers to 'rapid constitutional change', it is clearly important to be able to demonstrate knowledge of major areas of reform. These should be summarised as succinctly as possible to leave room for analysis; therefore, the paragraph following this sentence must be kept brief.

numerous sources. The term 'written constitution' also denotes a source of law superior to 'ordinary' law. In the United Kingdom, despite an increasing number of codified rules, the constitution has no special status.[2]

The UK constitution comes not from a single, revolutionary, point in history. Rather, the system of governance has evolved in piecemeal fashion over time.[3] It would be wrong, however, to suggest that the constitution prior to 1997 could be accurately characterised as entirely unwritten. As well as the unwritten sources of the constitution such as conventions and prerogative powers, there are important documents delineating the division of power. Statutes that could be mentioned include the Bill of Rights, which redefined the relationship between the monarch and the legislature; the various acts extending the franchise; the Parliament Acts of 1911 and 1949, which shifted the balance of power between the Commons and the Lords; and the European Communities Act, which made provision for community law to take effect in the domestic courts. Key judgments affected the role of the executive. In **Entick v Carrington** (1765) 19 St Tr 1029, the exercise of arbitrary government power was curtailed, and in **Council of Civil Service Unions v Minister for the Civil Service** [1985] AC 374 (the GCHQ case), the right of the judiciary to scrutinise the use of executive power was asserted. It is correct to say, however, that the operation of the state depended in large part on tradition, and practice, and the exercise of the historical powers of the prerogative.

It is undeniable that the period between 1997 and the present day has seen immense constitutional change.[4] Within the first five years of office, the Labour government steered though legislation to alter the composition of the House of Lords, devolve executive power to Northern Ireland, Scotland, and Wales, ensure that the European Convention on Human Rights can be enforced in the domestic courts, and to increase access to information regarding the state. Perhaps the most systematic alteration to constitutional structures came in the form of the Constitutional Reform Act 2005. The Act was designed to strengthen the separation of powers and the rule of law through a number of measures, including reform of the office of Lord Chancellor, and the separation of the Law Lords from the legislative assembly.

Despite an increase in written sources of constitutional power, unwritten sources also remain although the relevance of such sources is, perhaps, debatable. Prerogative powers, normally exercised by the executive in the name of the crown, can be abolished by the creation of statute (see, for example, **Attorney General v de Keyser's Royal Hotel Ltd** [1920] AC 508[5]). It could be argued that the prerogative no longer occupies a position of constitutional importance; the supervisory role of the judiciary now seems to be entrenched in the wake of the landmark ruling of the **GCHQ case**. In addition, it appears unlikely that any government could use the powers available without fear of political consequence. For example, in 2003, the decision to declare war on Iraq was reached following a vote in the House of Commons. Strictly speaking, this was unnecessary as declaration of war is a prerogative power. Giving evidence to the Liaison Committee, the then Prime Minister stated that it was 'inconceivable' that the power would be exercised without reference to Parliament. However, since that time, three Private Members Bills calling for the abolition of the prerogative have been tabled, and have failed to gather executive support. It is fair to say that in 2007 the government stated a commitment to reform of the prerogative but, save for the minor changes introduced by the Constitution and Governance Act 2010, no sustained or substantive change has materialised.[6]

Unwritten conventions remain part of the constitution.[7] Dicey[8] defined conventions as 'understanding habits and practices' which are considered to be binding, but have no legal force. Jennings, and others, consider that conventions are crucial to the operation of the constitution and must be followed, arguing that their unwritten nature allows for flexibility and change in accordance with developing societal and political norms. Those who suggest codification is desirable point to the lack of consequence when a convention is ignored. Loveland, for example, points to the Matrix Churchill affair of the 1990s when, in the absence of legally enforceable controls, the convention of ministerial 'responsibility' seemed to shift towards a less onerous concept of 'accountability'.

A commitment to codification of the prerogative has not been made, but there has at least been widespread acknowledgement of the need to consider the issue. However, there has been little commitment to

[9]This is a good point to make, as it is evidence that some aspects of the unwritten constitution appeared to enjoy continued support from a reforming government.

[10]This is the crux of the argument that was set out in the introduction.

[11]This is a solid conclusion, which sets out a clear point of view; showing confidence with the subject matter.

the codification of conventions. Indeed, the government endorsed the establishment of the Sewel convention when devolving power to the Scottish assembly and arguably, then, has supported some enlargement of the unwritten element of the constitution.[9]

The significance of these issues is not simply the question of whether constitutional arrangements are written or unwritten. They are, rather, symptomatic of the fact that there is no deference to constitutional principles which will take precedence over all other forms of law.[10] There is no method of forcing compliance with constitutional arrangements governed by convention, and still some reluctance by the courts to curtail the prerogative.

It cannot be said, then, that the proliferation of legislation reforming aspects of the constitution has resulted in a written constitution. It may be the case that there are a greater number of written sources of the constitution. Certainly, the Constitutional Reform Act 2005 was significant, as it expressly referred to the doctrines of the separation of powers, and to the rule of law. Constitutional lawyers have long argued that these doctrines are part of our constitution, but the Act placed this on a statutory, hence written, basis. As has been shown, however, informal, unwritten sources of power remain and these are subject to limited control. Nations described as possessing a written constitution are distinguishable not simply by the existence of a document, but rather by the acknowledgement that the constitution represents a superior form of legal power. This cannot be said to be the case in the United Kingdom, which does not afford the constitution such an elevated position.[11]

✓ Make your answer stand out

- By making reference to to KC. Wheare's classifications of constitutions as 'supreme' or 'subordinate'.
- By developing the argument regarding 'superior law' by outlining the difference between the powers of the new Supreme Court in the United Kingdom and that of the United States, which has the power to declare legislation 'unconstitutional'.
- By suggesting that 'superior law' is impossible in light of the doctrine of Parliamentary Supremacy. This will show the examiner that you are able to make connections between different topics in the syllabus.

! Don't be tempted to...

- Try to explain the workings of the constitution in great detail. There is no need to outline the various functions of the executive, legislature and judiciary here.
- Include a detailed list of all constitutional changes since 1997, as the question requires analysis of the impact of changes rather than a descriptive account.

📝 Question 2

'For the first time, we have a clear separation of powers between the legislature, the judiciary and the executive in the United Kingdom.' Lord Matravers, President of the Supreme Court.

To what extent has the Constitutional Reform Act 2005 been successful in achieving the aim of strengthening the separation of powers?

Answer plan

→ Explain the meaning of 'separation of powers'.

→ Describe the extent to which a separation of powers existed prior to the Act.

→ Outline the key provisions of the Act.

→ Consider how far there is a true separation of powers.

→ Consider whether or not a true separation of powers is possible.

Diagram plan

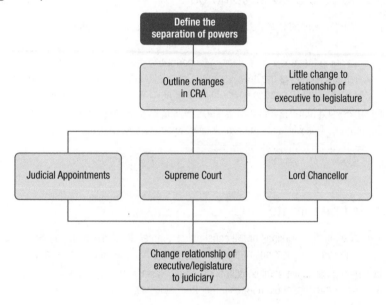

A printable version of this diagram is available from www.pearsoned.co.uk/lawexpressqa

Answer

[1]Reference to Montesquieu is essential, as it shows an awareness of the origins of the doctrine.

The doctrine of the separation of powers was first espoused by the political theorist Montesquieu in the eighteenth century.[1] The doctrine has been considered to be an important element of the constitution since that time. The Constitutional Reform Act (CRA) introduced changes intended to reinforce the importance of the doctrine of the separation of powers. In order to assess the impact of these changes it is necessary to first establish the pre-existing position. The success of the legislation can then be considered. It will be suggested that a complete separation of powers is neither desirable, nor possible. It will be argued that the establishment of the Supreme Court will have little impact, but that reforms to the office of Lord Chancellor are a significant step towards a greater separation of powers.[2]

[2]The introduction should outline the main argument to be adopted in the remainder of the essay; this will reassure the examiner that there will be a coherent structure to the argument.

[3]It is important to be able to succinctly explain what is meant by the term 'separation of powers' without spending too long outlining the development of the doctrine.

The state can be described as consisting of three bodies which perform distinct functions: the legislature; the executive; and the judiciary. The traditional doctrine of the separation of powers, states that there should be no overlap of personnel or functions between the institutions in order to prevent abuses of power.[3] If the separation of powers is understood in this way, then it is clear that Montesquieu must have been outlining an idealised position, for there has always been an overlap of personnel in the institutions of the United Kingdom. This does not inevitably mean that the doctrine should be dismissed, as there can still be separation of function, and a system of checks and balances between the institutions.

[4]It is not possible to deal with every aspect of the interaction between the powers in detail, so a more confident answer will highlight a few areas for discussion.

The examples of overlap prior to the CRA are numerous, but for the purpose of this discussion three will be considered.[4] First, the Law Lords sat in the House of Lords as part of the legislature. Secondly, the unique position of the Lord Chancellor who, as head of the judiciary, Speaker of the House of Lords, and a Cabinet Minister, occupied a position at the heart of all three institutions of the state. Lastly, and linked to the Lord Chancellor's office, was the system of senior judicial appointments which were made on his recommendation. This system had long been the subject of criticism and certainly, the fact of executive involvement in determining the composition of the judiciary posed a challenge to claims of the existence of a separation of powers. If one role of the judiciary is to restrain executive abuse of power, then even the hypothetical possibility of executive influence can be seen to threaten the integrity of the system.[5]

[5]It will be suggested later that the CRA focused primarily on judicial independence, so it is worth stating why this is seen as critical.

[6]The Constitutional Reform Act introduced many changes, so it is necessary to be able to focus on those relevant to the question, and be able to explain the effect on the office of Lord Chancellor and the House of Lords.

In 2003, the government unexpectedly announced plans to abolish the role of Lord Chancellor. The Constitutional Reform Act did not go as far as abolition, but instead severely curtailed the role (ss 2–22).[6] The Lord Chancellor now retains a role as government Minister but no longer sits as a judge, or acts as Speaker of the House of Lords. In addition, the Law Lords now sit as a Supreme Court, which, in a visible symbol of separation, is located outside of the Houses of Parliament. A new system for judicial appointments was introduced, to limit the possibility of accusations of executive influence (s 61). Indeed, the Act specifically charges the Lord Chancellor, and all Ministers, with a responsibility to uphold the independence of the judiciary, and not to seek to influence any decisions made in court proceedings (s 3).

The pronouncement made by Lord Matravers suggests that, prior to the establishment of the Supreme Court, not only was there a lack of separation, but, more particularly, that this was evidenced by the inclusion of senior judiciary in the legislature. It is, of course, true that the Law Lords were entitled to sit in the House of Lords, and to participate in debate. However, by convention, they declined to participate in proceedings concerning legislation that they might, in future, have to adjudicate upon. It is not clear that there was any real danger of the judiciary seeking to exercise a legislative function in the creation of statute. The Supreme Court is in its infancy, but there is no suggestion that its function will represent any constitutional departure from that previously exercised by the judicial branch of the House of Lords. The physical change of location and the alteration of title are perhaps better understood as being symbolic, representative of the desire to promote transparency in our constitutional arrangements.[7]

[7]Marks will be afforded for the ability to form a reasoned view about the impact of legislative change rather than simply stating the law.

Arguably, the alterations to the office of Lord Chancellor are a more systematic attempt to effect real constitutional change. At the beginning of Labour's programme of constitutional reform, Lord Irvine defended the role,[8] arguing that the unique function of the office was to allow there to be communication between the organs of state so each could understand the objectives of the other. The office was a clear example of what had been described by Bagehot in the nineteenth century as the almost 'complete fusion' between the institutions, which he considered to be the 'efficient secret' of the constitution.[9] Nonetheless, the numerous responsibilities of the Lord Chancellor in all areas of government led to the possibility of tensions between the various roles. Lord Woolf highlighted the need for statutory protection for judicial independence, rather than convention and reliance on mutual respect, and linked this to the preservation of the rule of law. The restriction of the Lord Chancellor's role, and the removal of his powers of judicial appointment, then, can be viewed as an acknowledgment of the truth of the famous maxim 'justice must not only be done, it must be seen to be done' (**R v Sussex Justices ex parte McCarthy** [1923] All ER 233).[10] The possibility of executive influence over the composition of the judiciary has, then, been diminished.

[8]This reference shows that you are familiar with the way that policy has shifted over time from defence of the office, towards reform.

[9]Inclusion of Bagehot here will be rewarded, as it shows ability to explore the topic a little more, by demonstrating awareness of the fact that it is arguable whether a separation of powers is desirable.

[10]The answer has tended towards suggesting that change has been largely cosmetic. Inclusion of this quote shows familiarity with the case, but more importantly, points towards an understanding that it is important that fairness is transparent in the organisation of the state.

The CRA focused on judicial independence. It did not address other aspects of the constitution which threaten the separation of powers such as the fact that government ministers sit as part of the legislature, or the quasi judicial function exercised by Parliament in the regulation of its own affairs.[11] It could be suggested that the judiciary had proved able to maintain independence despite their position in the Lords, under the supervision of the Lord Chancellor. There are many instances in which the Lords have been willing to

[11]In the interests of balance, it is useful to be able to point to evidence that contradicts the view given by Lord Matravers.

[12]It is important not to be too descriptive when using case law. Sometimes, as here, there is no need to include any of the facts. The reference to a specific point made in the judgment shows familiarity with, and understanding of, the case.

confront both the legislature and the executive (consider the rebuke Lord Hoffmann delivered in **A v Secretary of State for the Home Department** [2004] UKHL 56).[12] Although the CRA may be more concerned with form than substantive change, it is important to ensure that independence is protected and thus it must be seen as a step in the right direction. However, given the issues which pertain to the other institutions, the Act cannot be said to have significantly strengthened the separation of powers.

 Make your answer stand out

- By incorporating primary sources in the theoretical discussion. You could refer to additional cases in which the importance of a separation of powers has been sanctioned; see, for example, comments of Lord Diplock in *Duport Steels Ltd v Sirs [1980] 1 WLR 142*.

- You could argue that a view of the impact of the Act may depend on the definition of the separation of powers that is adopted. The answer has already indicated that Montesquieu and Bagehot saw the separation of powers differently, and development of this point would show the examiner that you have the ability to utilise theoretical perspectives to assess primary sources of law.

- If space allowed, reference could be made to other academic perspectives. Specifically, you could consider Marshall, who makes the point that there is no clear or consistent definition of the principle (Marshall, G., *Constitutional Theory* (1971) Oxford: Clarendon Press).

! Don't be tempted to...

- Become distracted by outlining the personnel and/or functions of the institutions. There is a temptation to show 'how much you know' about the operation of the constitution and students often begin this kind of answer by describing how the different institutions operate. This approach will not gather marks and it is more important to focus on analysing the impact of the Act mentioned in the question.

- Similarly, it is not enough to outline the provisions of the CRA here. An answer which sets out the key changes and then draws conclusions about the effect of the Act will appear quite weak. This question really does require you to show that you understand some of the academic and judicial comment on the issues covered by the Act. The conclusions you draw will then be supported by evidence.

Question 3

'In the mouth of a British Constitutional Lawyer, the term "rule of law" seems to mean primarily a corpus of basic principles and values, which together lend some stability and coherence to the legal order.' (T.R.S. Allan)

Discuss the relevance of the concept of the 'rule of law' to the United Kingdom Constitution.

Answer plan

→ Try to define the rule of law.

→ Acknowledge the variety of definitions.

→ Consider the current position with examples.

→ Argue that the rule of law is relevant as an ideal.

→ Argue that the rule of law needs clearer definition and protection.

Diagram plan

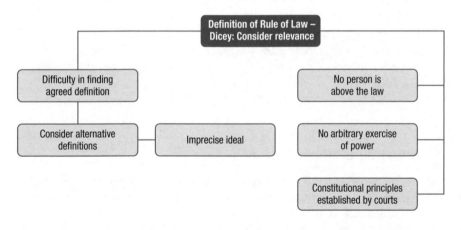

A printable version of this diagram is available from www.pearsoned.co.uk/lawexpressqa

Answer

The 'rule of law' is a term often invoked by politicians, judges and academics but the definition is far from certain. The lack of a clearly discernible meaning is problematic, as it has been said to underpin the organisation of the state. The Constitutional Reform Act formally recognises the importance of the rule of law (s 1). Dicey maintained that the rule of law was a key characteristic of the Constitution, giving a three part explanation of its meaning. To assess whether or not the rule of law retains its key position, it is appropriate to consider whether the elements described by Dicey are evident today. It is necessary to acknowledge competing definitions which may be more appropriate.[1]

[1]This question demands that you acknowledge the difficulty in defining the rule of law, but all questions dealing with the doctrine require demonstration of understanding of the Diceyean position.

Dicey saw the rule of law as embodying three concepts: no person should be punished except for a distinct breach of the law; no person is above the law; and constitutional principles are established in the common courts.[2] The contemporary relevance of each of these can be assessed in turn.

[2]You should be able to summarise Dicey's three 'rules' accurately and succinctly.

Dicey's first rule can be interpreted as expressing a need for protection from the arbitrary exercise of power. **Entick *v* Carrington** (1765) 2 Wils 275 articulated this principle of legality by holding that in the absence of statutory or common law authority, entry to a citizens home was unlawful.[3] It is worth noting that the requirement for legality as part of the rule of law does not necessarily mean that the judiciary will be concerned with the fairness of a particular provision. **IRC *v* Rossminster** [1980] AC 952 required the courts to consider powers of search and seizure that were, in the view of Lord Scarman, a 'breathtaking' interference with privacy and property.[4] As the lawful authority existed, the principle of legality was satisfied. Dicey was critical of the use of discretionary authority, and would undoubtedly be disturbed by the range of discretionary powers now afforded to the executive, for example; in the administration of the welfare state. In reading Dicey, it is important to remember he wrote at a time when the functions of government were few. This cannot be said to be the case in the complex society we now inhabit where the job of administration would be impossible if not for the exercise of discretion.[5] A modern explanation of this part of the principle of the rule of law would perhaps not require the absence of discretionary powers but rather a robust system to

[3]*Entick* v *Carrington* is a key constitutional case, as it is one of the first times that the judiciary articulated the principle of legality; therefore, it is important to be able to recognise the importance of the case in a discussion about the rule of law.

[4]This is a really useful authority to cite, especially alongside Entick. The two cases are, in a sense, two sides of the same coin. Whilst you should not set out the facts in any detail, you should provide enough information to demonstrate how the case shows that a law does not need to be fair.

[5]Dicey is sometimes dismissed by students as being outdated, which is a valid view, but there is a need to point to evidence of this.

[6] Here, the answer shows an ability to relate legal theory to the way the constitution operates in practice. This shows that you really understand the significance of the point Dicey was making by the first rule.

[7] Again, the case of *Entick* v *Carrington* is central to this aspect of the topic so you need to show the examiner that you are aware of this.

[8] It is always important to demonstrate knowledge of two sides of a debate, but crucial to be able to find some examples to support each side of the argument.

[9] Many commentators refer to this as an important constitutional case, and it is a useful one to be aware of for this topic area.

regulate the exercise of discretion.[6] Therefore, judicial review of executive action can be seen as central to the rule of law. Attempts to exclude the courts power of review have been rejected by the judiciary, in the important case **R (Cart) v Upper Tribunal; R (U and XC) v Special Immigration Appeals Commission** [2009] EWHC 3052 (Admin); it was held that judicial review was available, and further is a 'principle engine of the rule of law'.

The notion that 'no man is above the law' seems straightforward. Dicey cited **Entick v Carrington** as support for this proposition, declaring it to be one of many instances where government officials were called to account.[7] **M v Home Office** [1994] 1 AC 377 is an example of a government Minister being held in contempt of court after ignoring a court order. This would seem to suggest the truth of Dicey's statement. There are, though, examples of classes of persons who are not subject to the law in the same way such as those enjoying diplomatic immunity, or MPs protected from defamation in Parliament.[8] Part IV of the Anti Terror, Crime and Security Act of 2001 attempted to create a law to which only one class of persons, foreign nationals, would be subject. The court's opposition (**A v Secretary of State for the Home Department** [2004] UKHL 56[9]) can be used to support the argument that the judiciary play an important role in preserving the rule of law. If the statement suggests there should be equality before the law, then arguably, all citizens should be able to enforce their rights and there must be equal access to the courts. It is not clear that this is the case, for, despite a purported commitment to ensuring this (Access to Justice Act 1999), there have been extensive reductions in the availability of legal aid, and it is not certain that reliance on arrangements such as *pro bono* representation and no win no fee agreements can ensure that access is ensured for all.

The final element of Dicey's conception of the rule of law[10] expresses his belief that the common law was capable of protecting individual rights, obviating the need for a written constitution. The Human Rights Act 1998 incorporates the rights under the European Convention on Human Rights into domestic law, and therefore, arguably, the role of the courts is diminished.

There have been many other explanations of the rule of law.[11] Craig argues that there are two main schools of thought. One approach is the formal conception of the rule of law, which is concerned with the process of law making, and simply demands that laws are made according to an open clear process, and that obligations imposed by the law are prospective and clear. The rule of law, on this definition, is not concerned with the content of those laws. A substantive conception of the rule of law suggest the law embodies rights, and that distinctions can be drawn between good and bad laws. Raz notes that there are numerous definitions of the rule of law, but rejects efforts to imbue the doctrine with a moral ideology. He argues that some features are required including the requirement for clear, prospective laws, an independent judiciary, and review powers available to the courts. On this simple definition, it can be argued that the rule of law remains central to the constitution.[12] The CRA explicitly protects the independence of the judiciary (s 3) and, as discussed, powers of review remain. There are few examples of retrospective legislation. The War Damage Act is often referred to, but this was half a century ago and there are few other examples.[13] (The European Convention on Human Rights expressly prohibits retrospective criminal legislation.)

The rule of law is not a precise legal doctrine, and there are aspects of Dicey's description of its operation which seem less relevant in a modern context. If the key elements as suggested by Raz are accepted as broadly accurate, then it seems clear that the concept remains both relevant and central.[14]

✓ Make your answer stand out

■ By showing a knowledge of a broader range of academic theorists in this area. The answer references Raz and Craig, but there are many people you could mention. Some useful sources are as follows:

■ Allan, T.R.S., *Constitutional Justice: A Liberal Theory of the Rule of Law* (2001) Oxford: Oxford University Press.

■ Craig, P., 'Formal and substantive conceptions of the Rule of Law: an analytical framework' [1997] PL 467.

■ Jowell, J. and Oliver, D. (eds.), *The Changing Constitution* (4th edn) (2000) Oxford: Oxford University Press.

■ Raz, J., *The Authority of Law* (1979) Oxford: Oxford University Press.

■ By considering the relationship between the doctrine of the rule of law, and other principles said to underpin the constitution. This answer refers to the role of the judiciary; it could be argued that a functional separation of powers is necessary to uphold the rule of law. The examiner will be impressed by an answer that demonstrates understanding of how different topics considered on the syllabus overlap.

! Don't be tempted to...

■ Treat the question as an invitation to outline Dicey's theory and ignore other definitions of the rule of law. This is an area of the syllabus that students do tend to find very difficult; mainly because we would like there to be one 'correct' definition of the rule of law. If you are able to show that you understand that there are competing definitions, you will be rewarded.

■ Ignore primary sources. Although this is a very academic area of the syllabus, there are key cases that can, and should, be incorporated into your answer because they illustrate how the judiciary approach the rule of law. Weaker answers are often limited to mention of *Entick* v *Carrington*. Marks will be given to the answer that can refer to more recent cases such as *A* v *SSHD*.

Question 4

The United Kingdom constitution is underpinned by strong, clear principles which protect democracy.

Discuss.

Answer plan

→ Describe the form of the UK constitution.

→ Outline the principles that are said to underpin the constitution.

→ Debate whether or not the principles can be said to be 'strong' and 'clear'.

→ Consider whether or not these principles ensure 'democracy'.

Diagram plan

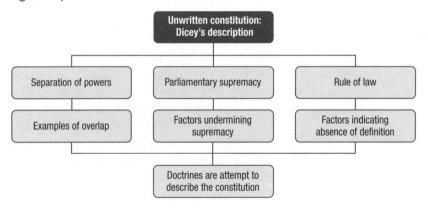

A printable version of this diagram is available from www.pearsoned.co.uk/lawexpressqa

Answer

It is often said that the UK constitution is unwritten, referring to the absence of a single, codified set of constitutional rules and regulations. The United Kingdom is almost unique in this respect. In the United Kingdom, the constitution is not the result of a single revolutionary moment, but has evolved across centuries. Commentators

[1]The potential scope of a question dealing with constitutional principles is vast, so you will need to have the confidence to limit the discussion, and explain the reasons for your choice in the introduction.

[2]The key conclusion to the answer will be that all definitions of constitutional doctrines are subjective and, by setting out the position here, the remainder of the essay can keep referring back to this central theme.

[3]The ability to explain the origins of the doctrine shows familiarity with political theory and will be rewarded. It is important to remain succinct.

[4]You have indicated in the introduction that the doctrines are unclear because of the various definitions that exist. Therefore, you must be able to reference a few different viewpoints.

[5]This argument is the central point of the answer that was highlighted at the outset. It is useful to refer back to this at the end of each section as this shows that there is a clear argument developing.

[6]There is no need to explain the provisions of the CRA in any great detail, but the brief reference demonstrates awareness of the key issues that relate to the separation of powers.

have nonetheless identified doctrinal principles which some maintain ensure consistency and safeguard democratic values. It is beyond the scope of this essay to consider in detail the extent to which each remains central to the operation of the modern day constitution. However, it will be argued that to describe any as 'strong' or 'clear' is an oversimplification.[1]

A. V. Dicey, writing in the nineteenth century, described the UK constitution as based upon three key principles: the Separation of Powers; the Rule of Law; and Parliamentary Sovereignty. Arguably, however, Dicey's description of the constitution was informed and shaped by his own ideological viewpoint. Indeed, the same can be said of all constitutional theorists; leading to difficulty in accurately identifying the core elements of each doctrine.[2]

Most democratic states place great emphasis on the principle of the separation of powers. For example, the US constitution imposes a clear and rigid demarcation of responsibilities and power between the three institutions of government. The theory can be traced back to Aristotle, but the work of Montesquieu, writing about the English constitution, forms the basis of the modern doctrine.[3] Montesquieu maintained that any overlap between function and personnel would lead to tyranny, and it is the prevention of the abuse of power which is the key to any understanding of the separation of powers. However, Montesquieu's work cannot be regarded as an accurate depiction of the English government in the late eighteenth century, as there has never been the pure separation he espoused. Indeed, Bagehot argued that the almost 'complete fusion' between legislature, executive and judiciary, was the 'efficient secret' of the UK constitution. Blackstone argued that to protect democracy by preventing abuse, the separation of powers demanded not distinction of personnel, but rather, a distinction of function and a system of checks and balances to ensure each institution maintains the ability to regulate and restrain the other elements of government.[4] It can be seen, then, that whilst the separation of powers is undoubtedly important, the precise explanation of the doctrine is open to debate.[5] The Constitutional Reform Act 2005 stated that it aimed to strengthen the separation of powers and did address the need to ensure the independence of the judiciary, primarily by reforming the somewhat anachronistic position of the Lord Chancellor.[6] There remains considerable overlap between the legislative and the executive, as government Ministers are drawn from the Commons and the Lords. There is, too, an argument that there is not a clear functional separation. The executive, in the creation of delegated legislation, exercise some of the functions more properly ascribed to Parliament. The judiciary arguably do not merely interpret law but create it, both through the development of the common law (see, for example, **R v R** [1991] 2 WLR 1065) but, increasingly, through the interpretative functions granted by the European Communities Act and the Human Rights Act.[7]

[7]It is really useful to show that you understand how the role of the judiciary has altered over time.

The principle of Parliamentary sovereignty, as explained by Dicey, is perhaps the clearest of the three doctrines. According to Dicey, Parliament is the supreme law-making body because it is able to legislate on any subject-matter; without question by any other body; and cannot be bound by predecessors or bind successors (thereby ensuring the continuing independence of successive Parliaments).[8] The link with democracy is clear. Parliament, as an elected body, ensures that the will of the people exerts control and influence over the operation of the state. Whilst it may be possible to summarise the doctrine easily, the position in reality has, arguably, never been clear. At the time that Dicey was writing, the franchise did not even extend to women, so Parliament was not representative of the views of the whole population.[9] The party political system has led to concerns that the executive is able to control parliament when governments have a substantial majority; most famously expressed by Lord Hailsham who described an 'elective dictatorship'. In more recent times, a number of factors such as membership of the EU, devolution and the Human Rights Act have arguably diminished the sovereignty of Parliament. Whilst this debate cannot be fully considered here, it should be noted that membership of the EU has at least led to the situation where the judiciary will, on occasion, defer to the European institutions rather than Parliament, as witnessed in the seminal series of cases concerning Factortame.[10]

[8]You should be able to summarise Dicey's theory of supremacy succinctly.

[9]Often, students state that Dicey is 'old fashioned' or 'out of date' without providing evidence. Here, the answer goes further by providing evidence that his theories may always have been questionable. This willingness to interrogate 'traditional' constitutional theory will impress an examiner.

[10]Discursive questions such as this can make it hard to show familiarity with primary sources, so where they can be used to demonstrate a facet of your argument, you should try to incorporate them.

The 'rule of law' is often invoked as central to democracy. However, it cannot be said to be clear, and arguably, the definition adopted depends upon political disposition. Craig argues that those who adopt a formative definition believe the rule of law simply demands a clear mechanism for making laws, and this has no connection with the content of law. Hence, it is theoretically possible to envisage an entirely undemocratic state which nonetheless adheres to

1 SOURCES OF THE CONSTITUTION

[11]The rule of law is probably the hardest doctrine to explain briefly and here, the answer does not try to set out any definition in full. However, reference to substantive/formative conceptions indicates a fairly sophisticated understanding that will reassure the examiner you are comfortable with this doctrine.

the rule of law. More substantive definitions, such as that promulgated by Dicey, imbue the doctrine with notions of morality.[11] It is possible to find examples to support the view that the rule of law is both central to the UK constitution and indicative of democratic values. The case of **M v Home Office** is often cited as evidence that no person is above the law, as even government Ministers are subject to censure by the courts. Equally, however, it is possible to argue that the protection afforded to MPs from civil prosecution for conduct in the Commons demonstrates that there are special protections afforded to particular sections of the establishment.[12]

[12]These contrasting examples are helpful because they show how it is possible to find evidence to support opposing explanations of the relevance of the doctrine.

[13]The answer made the point that the constitution has evolved over time in the introduction; and it is worth reiterating here as it supports the conclusion that there was never a clear ideological basis for the constitution.

Dicey's explanations of the key principles of the constitution reflect his personal values and political ideals. As has been demonstrated, it cannot be said that his definitions of the separation of powers or Parliamentary sovereignty accurately depicted the constitutional arrangements of the time. The same criticism could be levelled at Montesquieu writing of the separation of powers and indeed at many other theorists. How then, can it be said, that the constitution has been based upon these doctrines, when their definitions are so open to criticism and debate? The unwritten constitution has evolved in response to historical events rather than as a result of any coherent doctrinal plan.[13] The principles described are invoked as an attempt to make sense of constitutional arrangements, but cannot be said to form a strong or clear basis for our democratic state.

✓ Make your answer stand out

- By focusing more on how the doctrines relate to a definition of 'democracy'. For example, the public vote for members of Parliament. It could be suggested that the supremacy of Parliament ensures that the views of the public have a central role in how the state is run.

- You could discuss the fact that, even though the doctrines are imprecise, they are clearly considered to be highly relevant by politicians. The Constitutional Reform Act, which is mentioned, is a good example as it specifically promises to uphold the rule of law and reinforce the separation of powers.

- A similar point could be made in respect of the judiciary who often refer to the need to uphold the separation of powers (the clearest example is probably the comments made by Lord Diplock in *Duport Steel Ltd v Sirs [1980] 1 WLR 142*), or the rule of law (which is explicitly discussed in *R v Horseferry Road Magistrates' Court ex parte Bennet* [1994] AC 42).

! **Don't be tempted to...**

- Describe in detail how the constitution has developed, or how power is currently divided between the institutions of state. This is a difficult question, and students often waste time by explaining the personnel and functions of the executive, legislature and judiciary. There is a lot of material to cover here, and therefore the focus must be on the role of constitutional doctrines.

- Set out in detail how Dicey or others have explained the doctrines. There is a temptation to demonstrate that you can remember the three 'rules' underpinning the rule of law, for example. Remember, marks are given for analysis, not description. It is better to focus on one aspect of the doctrine and weigh up the evidence available that suggests it is a strong and clear principle.

- Ignore contradictions. The wording of the question invites you to provide a counter-argument to the statement provided, and consider that the doctrines are, in fact, imprecise.

Parliament and parliamentary supremacy

How this topic may come up in exams

Examiners may require you to demonstrate knowledge about how Parliament is regulated. This necessitates an understanding of Parliamentary privilege, and could be either a problem scenario or an essay question. Here, you will be rewarded for an ability to draw on current examples to support your arguments. Alternatively, you may be asked to discuss the position of Parliament within broader constitutional arrangements and in particular, to discuss the relevance of the doctrine of parliamentary sovereignty. This aspect is commonly tested by essay questions requiring a focus on one or more issues affecting the constitutional position of Parliament.

Attack the question

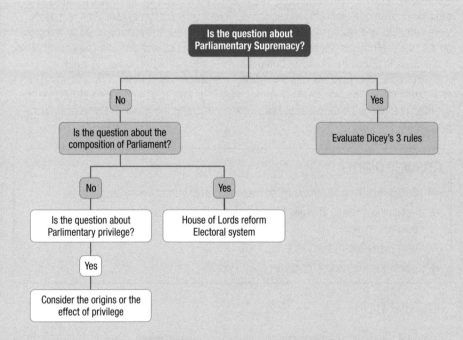

Is the question about
Parliamentary Supremacy?

No

Is the question about the
composition of Parliament?

Yes

Evaluate Dicey's 3 rules

No

Is the question about
Parlimentary privilege?

Yes

House of Lords reform
Electoral system

Yes

Consider the origins or the
effect of privilege

❓ Question 1

Tom, the editor of the student union newspaper, seeks your advice. He recently published an article concerning a local MP, Mr Jones, which reported that the MP had strongly opposed an increase in fuel tax in parliamentary debates. The article paraphrased the questions that were asked and recorded in *Hansard*. The article reported that Mr Jones had referred to a prominent environmental campaigner, Natalie Turner, as a 'blithering idiot'. The proposals were defeated, and two months later, the article alleged, the MP was rewarded with a place on the board. Mr Jones has commenced libel proceedings against Tom, and he has received a summons to attend the House of Commons for 'contempt of the House'. In addition, he has received a letter from Ms Turner's solicitor complaining about the comments about her reported in the article. Tom wants to know if he will be able to defend the court proceedings by using records of the debates, and what the summons to the House of Commons means. Advise Tom.

Answer plan

➡ Identify that the problem concerns the regulation of Parliamentary proceedings.

➡ Explain the privilege awarded to Parliamentary proceedings, and the defence of 'qualified privilege'.

➡ Refer to the Defamation Act 1996, s 13.

➡ Explain the meaning of 'contempt of the House'.

Diagram plan

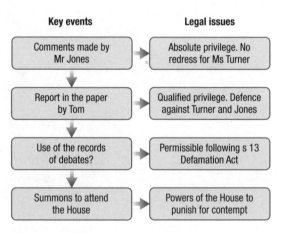

A printable version of this diagram is available from www.pearsoned.co.uk/lawexpressqa

Answer

This scenario raises issues concerning Parliamentary privilege. In considering the comments made regarding Ms Turner, it is necessary to determine the extent of the privilege afforded to Parliamentary proceedings and whether or not this provides protection to Tom. Secondly, in considering the proposed action by Mr Jones, it will be necessary to determine when records of Parliamentary proceedings may be adduced as evidence in court proceedings. Lastly, it will be necessary to address the powers held by Parliament to discipline Members and non-Members alike for contempt.[1]

Parliamentary privilege is a term used to describe rules protecting the House of Commons and the House of Lords from any outside interference. Privilege is enjoyed by both individual Members of Parliament and the collective institutions and, as Erskine May explains, to a certain extent provides exemption from the general law.[2] Relevant to this scenario are the privileges afforded to Parliament to regulate its own affairs, and the protection given to freedom of speech during Parliamentary proceedings.[3]

Article IX of the Bill of Rights states that freedom of speech in Parliament is protected from impeachment or question by any body; this includes the judiciary.[4] Therefore, Parliamentary privilege protects a Member of Parliament from civil actions for defamation in respect of comments made during Parliamentary proceedings. The case of **A v United Kingdom (Application 35373/97)** [2002] All ER (D) 264 (Dec) confirmed the existence of this absolute privilege. In that case, a Member of Parliament made comments about a constituent during a debate which was reported in the press. She claimed that the fact she was unable to challenge the remarks in court breached her Art 6 right to a fair trial, as well as her rights under Art 8 (respect for her private life) and Art 13 (right to a remedy). The European Court found that despite the 'regrettable' nature of the comments, there was no breach of Convention rights as Art IX was necessary to protect the freedom of speech in Parliament. Therefore, it is clear that Ms Turner cannot bring a claim for defamation against the MP Mr Jones.[5] However, the scenario asks us to consider whether or not Tom could be liable for libel in reporting the comments made.[6]

[1]This introduction picks out the important events from the scenario and links them to the legal issue. This is a good way to start an answer to a problem scenario. You should never begin by simply rewriting the facts of the scenario.

[2]It is helpful to learn some explanations of key concepts, so that you can give a succinct definition of the topic area to be addressed.

[3]Rather than listing every example of privilege that you can remember, be specific in identifying those that are relevant.

[4]Article IX of the Bill of Rights is central to a question concerning parliamentary privilege, so it is useful to be able to give a concise explanation.

[5]When using case law, it is vital that you explain how the legal principle identified impacts on the facts of the scenario you are dealing with. Here, it is important to explain that the ruling in *A v UK* means that there is an absolute bar on an action for defamation against the Member of Parliament.

[6]The answer does need to set out the law relating to absolute privilege, but here you remind the examiner that you have not lost focus on the specific questions asked.

Should court proceedings be instigated, Tom would be able to claim the defence of qualified privilege. The report of the debate in *Hansard* attracts absolute privilege due to the Parliamentary Papers Act 1840. It is accepted that there is a public interest in the business of Parliament, and there can be no successful action for defamation against a 'fair and accurate' report of Parliamentary proceedings (**Wason v Walter** (1868) LR 4 QB 73). We are told that Tom has 'paraphrased' the proceedings, but there is no requirement for the report to be verbatim in order for it to attract qualified privilege. This was confirmed in the case of **Cook v Alexander** [1974] QB 279, where a 'Parliamentary sketch' was held not to be defamatory, despite the fact it was a selective account, as it conveyed the general tenor of the debate. In order to succeed against Tom, Ms Turner would have to prove that the report was malicious. On the facts given, this does not appear to be a sustainable claim and Tom should be advised that should an action be brought, he will have a valid defence.[7]

[7]Having set out the relevant law, it is important to then apply this to give advice to Tom, as the question requires.

Tom also includes in the report allegations about the conduct of Mr Jones. This has resulted in an action from the MP as an individual, but also from the House. Dealing first with the action by Mr Jones, these facts appear to recall the events surrounding the libel action brought by the MP Neil Hamilton against the *Guardian* newspapers following the allegation that he took cash for questions in the 1990s.[8] This case demonstrated that in providing protection for MPs from actions in defamation, Art IX also limited the ability of members to sue when libellous statements were made about them. To defend the claim, the *Guardian* wished to adduce evidence of questions asked in the House in order to demonstrate the truth of the allegations. Article IX prevents proceedings in Parliament being questioned in court, and **Prebble v Television New Zealand** (1995) 15 LS 204 confirmed that where a party's defence depended on such inadmissible material, proceedings should be stayed as it would be unjust to deny the defendant the ability to properly present their case. Accordingly, Hamilton was unable to bring his claim. This resulted in the passing of the Defamation

[8]Although you should generally refrain from giving too much factual detail concerning cases, where there are analogous facts, then it is worth highlighting them in order to point out the similarity because this means the ratio is clearly applicable to the scenario.

[9]The information given
regarding the Hamilton affair
is only useful if it is used
to provide a solution
to the problem set out in
the question.

[9]The information given
regarding the Hamilton affair
is only useful if it is used
to provide a solution
to the problem set out in
the question.

[10]In this answer, you don't
need to provide a list of
examples of behaviours that
could be contempt, but this
general definition makes
it clear that you know the
meaning of the term.

[11]This is one of the instances
in which it is helpful to briefly
refer to the facts; you are
using this case to show that
there is a historical precedent
for the House taking action
against journalists for
contempt.

[12]It is easy to highlight
the various methods of
punishment that exist for
contempt, but it is important
to try to assess whether it is
really likely that these would
be invoked.

[13]It is useful to conclude by
providing a summary of the
advice to the client to ensure
that it is clear all points have
been covered.

Act 1996 which, at s 13, amends the Bill of Rights by allowing an individual MP to waive privilege so that an action can proceed. Tom should be advised therefore, that he will be able to adduce evidence of Parliamentary proceedings if the records of his debate will help him argue that the claims made about Mr Jones are correct.[9]

Parliamentary privilege also allows both Houses to discipline Members and non-Members alike for 'contempt' of the House. 'Contempt' is a poorly defined term but would cover any conduct which brings the reputation of the House into disrepute.[10] These matters would be investigated with by the Committee on Standards and Privileges, acting on the advice of, in this case, the Speaker of the Commons. If it is found that the publication of allegations regarding Mr Jones constitute contempt, then Tom could face censure. Junor's Case (HC 38 1956-57) concerned a *Sunday Express* article suggesting that MPs afforded themselves preferential treatment in respect of fuel allowances, and the editor was summoned to appear before the house to be admonished.[11] Theoretically, the House has the power to punish for contempt, including the power to imprison offenders, although this has not been invoked since 1880. The Joint Committee on Privileges has stressed that the power to punish should only be used in extreme circumstances where absolutely necessary for the protection of Parliament. Therefore, it is unlikely that Tom would face any penalty.[12]

It should perhaps be noted that, should the allegations be correct, then Mr Jones would clearly be in contempt, as it is not permitted for any MP to participate in a debate in which he or she has a financial interest.

It can be seen then that the newspaper report may expose Tom to three distinct proceedings. First, Ms Turner could bring an action for libel. However, Tom will be able to claim qualified privilege. Mr Jones could bring libel proceedings and, following the Defamation Act, Tom can adduce records of the debate in his defence. In theory, Tom could be punished for a contempt, but it is doubtful that any penalty would be applied.[13]

Make your answer stand out

- By giving more attention to the legal effect of qualified privilege. You should refer to *Reynolds* v *Times Newspaper Ltd* [2001] 2 AC 127, which remains the key authority.
- By referring to the Convention rights which could be in issue and discussing whether or not Art 10 can assist Tom. This will show the examiner an ability to draw links between different parts of the syllabus.
- When considering whether or not the House might censure Tom for contempt, this could be assessed in the light of the MPs' expenses scandal, which has perhaps made it less likely given the public opprobrium. This would show the examiner an ability to make connections between current affairs, and constitutional issues.

! Don't be tempted to...

- Give generalised information about Parliamentary privilege; the answer needs to focus on solving the problems outlined in the scenario. You do need to outline that the MP enjoys absolute privilege, for example, as this is the background to Tom's potential defence of qualified privilege. However, you should avoid the temptation to spend too long looking at this issue.
- Write a detailed history of the Hamilton affair, or indeed, the other cases you mention. This can be a difficult balance to strike, but, as a rule of thumb, you should only mention the facts to demonstrate that you understand the *ratio*; or to highlight a similarity, or significant difference, from the scenario given.

? Question 2

The Minister for Housing, Mrs Taylor, has recently introduced a Bill to the Commons proposing a simplification to planning procedures which would make it easier for landlords to convert properties into houses for multiple occupation. An MP, Mr Rafiq, receives a letter from his constituent, Alexia Clements, alleging that Mrs Taylor has been bribed by a student housing company who would benefit from the change, and that the company provide Mrs Taylor's daughter with rent-free accommodation whilst she is at university.

Mr Rafiq forwards the letter to the Commissioner for Parliamentary Standards, and to the Shadow Minister for Housing. In a debate on the Bill, Mr Rafiq reads out the letter, including a passage which describes Mrs Taylor as an 'odious, slippery character who cannot be trusted'.

Later on, whilst in the Commons restaurant, Mr Rafiq is asked about the matter by a fellow MP and reads the letter out again. This is overheard by several of Mrs Taylor's colleagues.

Mrs Taylor is informed, and storms into the cafeteria. She pours a jug of water over Mr Rafiq's head.

Advise Mr Rafiq, Ms Clements and Mrs Taylor about the possible consequences of these events.

Answer plan

→ Explain privilege protecting Mr Rafiq from defamation action.

→ Consider definition of 'Parliamentary proceedings'.

→ Discuss different position of Ms Clements – qualified privilege.

→ Consider whether privilege extends to cover criminal activity.

→ Explain the requirements of the Register of Members' Interests and the sanctions for failing to comply.

Diagram plan

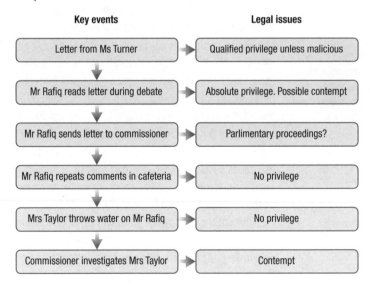

A printable version of this diagram is available from www.pearsoned.co.uk/lawexpressqa

Answer

The scenario raises questions about how far Members of Parliament can claim the protection of privilege to excuse conduct which may breach civil or criminal law, and whether non-Members enjoy any similar protection. In addition, the allegations made about Mrs Taylor require consideration of the mechanisms which exist to ensure Members of Parliament comply with ethical standards.[1]

The allegations made in the letter received by Mr Rafiq may be libellous. Mrs Taylor may be able to bring civil proceedings in respect of some of his actions. When Mr Rafiq reads the contents of the letter during a debate, he enjoys absolute privilege. Article IX of the Bill of Rights enshrined the protection of freedom of speech in Parliament, and no action for defamation can arise in respect of any remarks made during parliamentary proceedings. This would be the position even if Mr Rafiq knew the allegations were false, on the authority of **Wason v Walter** (1868) LR 4 QB 73.[2] However, the protection of absolute privilege only protects Members engaged in Parliamentary proceedings. When Mr Rafiq repeats the comments in the cafeteria, it appears that he is not engaged in the business of Parliament and therefore he would not be able to claim immunity from a civil action in respect of this part of the incident.[3] A question arises as to whether any action can result from the forwarding of the letter to third parties, which is, on the face of it, republication of the libel. It is debatable whether or not this would enjoy the cloak of privilege, as it is not clear that this could be considered to be 'Parliamentary privilege'. The issue was considered in Strauss's case which concerned a letter sent by the MP to the Paymaster General, complaining about methods employed by the London Electricity Board.[4] The Committee of Privileges concluded that the letter was covered by privilege, although a subsequent commons vote rejected this view. The more recent case of **Rost v Edwards** [1990] 2 QB 460 saw the courts refuse to accept evidence of a letter sent to the Speaker as it was accepted this did constitute 'proceedings in Parliament'. In any event, the point is perhaps rather academic as, even if absolute privilege does not apply, Mr Rafiq would almost certainly be able to claim qualified privilege. This protects him from an action unless Mrs Taylor can prove

[2]It is unnecessary to give any details about this case, as the only important issue here is the *ratio*, which means that the advice given to Mr Rafiq about this part of the incident can be given with certainty.

[3]Here, you have shown that you understand that the issue here is whether or not privilege affords a defence, and have done so briefly and with reference to the facts. This shows knowledge, and an ability to apply it.

[4]This is an important case to revise, as the issue of whether or not an event will be considered to be part of 'parliamentary proceedings' is a common area for examination. The additional cases are useful, but this is probably essential.

that he was malicious. The case of **Breech v Freeson** [1972] 1 QB 14 provides support for the suggestion that sending a letter to the Minister on a matter of interest to Parliamentary business would attract qualified privilege, although Bradley and Ewing do suggest that passing a constituents letter on to a Minister without any inquiry as to its truth could be considered malicious.[5] Mr Rafiq should also be advised that irrespective of any civil action, he may also fall to be censured for contempt as a result of his comments during the debate.[6]

The position in respect of Ms Clements is less secure, as non-Members do not enjoy the protection of absolute privilege. She may, however, be able to claim qualified privilege provided the letter is sent without malice, on a matter of public interest.[7]

Mrs Taylor has committed the criminal offence of battery when she throws water over Mr Rafiq.[8] Although parliamentary privilege confers a freedom from arrest within the Commons, it appears this is confined to civil matters. In the case of **Bradlaugh v Gossett** (1884) 12 QBD 271 the courts asserted that there was no authority for the suggestion that criminal jurisdiction was excluded from the House of Commons. Indeed, in the 1970s, a protestor who released a CS gas canister in the Commons was handed over to the police. It is highly unlikely that the fact the incident occurred in the Commons would protect Mrs Taylor from prosecution, as, if privilege were asserted, this would arguably damage the reputation of the House.[9]

Mrs Taylor may also face difficulties if the allegations are investigated by the Commissioner for Parliamentary Standards and found to be correct. The role of the Commissioner was created in response to the report of the Nolan Committee in the wake of the 'cash for questions' scandal during the 1990s. The Commissioner is tasked with maintaining the Register of Members' Interests, and investigating allegations of breaches. The Commissioner reports findings to the Committee on Standards in Public Life, who can impose sanctions. Mrs Taylor should declare, on the Register of Members' Interests, a connection with an organisation providing her with a material benefit. Registration of the connection would not be sufficient in this case, however, as she has initiated proceedings in Parliament by introducing the legislation and should therefore have declared her connection at the introduction of the bill.[10] This would be considered an extremely serious breach of the rules regarding the registration of interests, and a clear contempt. Mrs Taylor should be advised that penalties for contempt can include an order to repay money. Following the 2009 scandal regarding MPs expenses, the Committee ordered a number of MPs to repay large sums of money. In addition, Members can be suspended from Parliament. George Galloway was suspended for 18 days by the Committee in 2006 for concealing matters on the register.[11] In extreme cases, an MP can be required to stand down at the next election. Since the creation of the office of the Commissioner, there has been doubt expressed about the willingness and ability of any Parliamentary body to robustly ensure that Members comply with ethical standards. Loveland referred to the response to the Nolan Committee as 'a damp squib'. This issue arose in the wake of the expenses scandal, and resulted in the Parliamentary Standards Act 2009. This too, has been criticised as during the course of debate clauses which would have resulted in paid advocacy (of the type alleged here) becoming an imprisonable offence were removed. However, given the public concern regarding the conduct of MPs, Mrs Taylor would certainly find herself under considerable pressure to resign irrespective of any action taken by the House.[12]

Mr Rafiq would be covered by absolute or qualified privileges in respect of all actions save for the casual conversation outside of the Commons chamber. Ms Clements would probably be able to rely on qualified privilege. Mrs Taylor may face criminal prosecution for the attack on Mr Rafiq. She may also face sanction from the Committee if the allegations are investigated and validated by the Commissioner on Parliamentary Standards.[13]

[11]You will be rewarded for being able to demonstrate knowledge of examples of the application of law.

[12]Whilst it is important to use the answer to demonstrate a good knowledge of the topic, the information must be utilised to assist in giving an opinion about Mrs Taylor's predicament.

[13]As the answer has dealt with a number of individuals and issues, the conclusion should briefly summarise the advice to each party.

✓ **Make your answer stand out**

■ Conduct of Parliamentary business is extremely topical. You should ensure you keep up to date with developments that occur during your studies, as you may find illustrative examples to use that are not yet in the textbooks. This will demonstrate that you have a clear understanding of the legal principles, and can identify significant issues independently.

■ By demonstrating an understanding of how Parliament operates in more detail, for example by explaining the role that the Speaker would play in each of the possible contempt situations.

❗ **Don't be tempted to...**

■ Spend time explaining the origins of the privileges referred to. Most of the marks in this question will be given for being able to apply the law to the facts given. So, rather than explaining the constitutional justification for absolute privilege, you must instead concentrate on assessing whether Mr Rafiq can claim privilege.

■ Explain the background to the cash for questions scandal in any detail. It is worth mentioning to be able to explain the origins of the office of the Commissioner, but you should avoid writing a long, descriptive, account of what happened.

🖎 Question 3

Membership of the European Union has ensured that parliamentary sovereignty is no longer a significant part of the United Kingdom Constitution.

Discuss.

Answer plan

→ Outline the traditional doctrine of Parliamentary sovereignty.

→ Consider the impact of the EU on the ability to legislate on any subject matter, or to be the supreme law making body.

→ Consider the impact of the doctrine on implied repeal.

→ Discuss whether the 'enrolled bill' rule survives.

Diagram plan

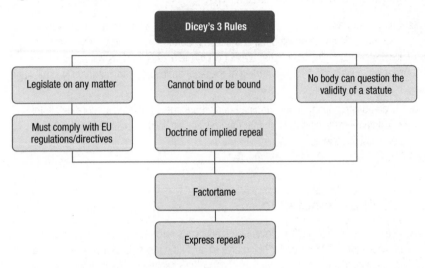

A printable version of this diagram is available from www.pearsoned.co.uk/lawexpressqa

Answer

[1]In order to do well with this question, the focus must be on the impact of membership of the European Union on Parliamentary supremacy. There is a need to explain the key tenents of the doctrine but this should be dealt with as succinctly as possible, so that the answer can move on to address the central issue.

[2]It is important that you can explain s 2 of the Act, as it is this provision that, arguably, impacts on supremacy.

Dicey described the doctrine of parliamentary supremacy as the 'cornerstone' of the UK Constitution. The doctrine consists of three elements. Parliament is the supreme law-making body, able to legislate on any subject-matter of its choosing. No Parliament can bind its successors, or be bound by its predecessors. Once an Act of Parliament has received Royal Assent, no person or body can question the validity of the legislation.[1] It has been argued that membership of the European Union has diluted the principle of Parliamentary supremacy. The United Kingdom became a member of the European Community in 1972, and the European Communities Act 1972, s 2 allows community law to take direct effect in domestic law. Section 2(4) states that domestic legislation should be construed subject to the rule in s 2(1); to give effect to EU rights.[2] It can be argued that these provisions lead to a position where it cannot be said that Parliament remains the supreme law-making body of the United Kingdom, or that Parliament cannot be bound.

The institutions of the European Union can enact legislation which takes direct effect in the United Kingdom without the need for any further action by Parliament. In **Costa v ENEL** (Case 6/64) [1964] ECR 585 the European Court of Justice confirmed that community law prevails over the national law of member states.[3] Therefore, this has led some commentators to suggest that supremacy was ceded to the European institutions. It should be noted, however, that this is limited to matters within the competence of the treaties. Further, although subsequent treaties have extended the scope of the European Union, the United Kingdom has retained the power to opt out of particular provisions.[4] For example, the United Kingdom has opted out of provisions giving the European Union powers in relation to immigration and asylum in the Lisbon Treaty (2009), and retains the power to opt in or out of any policies concerning justice and home affairs.[5]

Although it is clear that Parliament retains the theoretical power to legislate on any matter of its choosing, arguably, membership of the European Union has limited this element of supremacy. Questions arise when domestic legislation conflicts with European Union law.[6] According to Dicey, Parliament cannot be bound by its predecessors; leading to the doctrine of implied repeal, as illustrated by **Vauxhall Estates Ltd v Liverpool Corporation** [1932] 1 KB 733. The case concerned a dispute regarding the compensation scheme applicable in a compulsory purchase of land. The Acquisition of Land (Assessment of Compensation) Act 1919 laid down a scheme, and further stated that any inconsistent provision would be ineffective. The Housing Act of 1925 created a different payment scheme, without expressly repealing the earlier Act. It was held that the later Act impliedly repealed the earlier provisions, and that any suggestion that an Act could prevent a future Parliament from making alterations was inconsistent with the constitution. Accordingly, it would seem clear that any legislation passed after 1972 which conflicts with European Union law should take effect, as s 2(4) could not bind future Parliaments.[7]

In the majority of cases, the courts have been able to resolve any conflict through the process of statutory interpretation, and have determined that, if there is any ambiguity, legislation should be read on the assumption that Parliament's intention would be to comply with EU law.[8] This was the 'purposive' approach adopted in

Pickstone *v* **Freemans [1988] AC 66** and **Lister** *v* **Forth Dry Dock Engineering** [1990] 1 AC 546. In both cases, the courts declined to say that legislation was incompatible with EU law but, in order to reach that position, had to impose an interpretation which ignored the plain meaning of the words of the statute. These cases did not have to determine the correct approach arising if a legislative provision directly contradicted Community law and interpretation was not possible.

[9]Any question considering the effect of EU membership on supremacy will demand that you are able to explain the importance of the *Factortame* litigation, and the fact that it can be said to undermine the doctrine of implied repeal.

The issue fell to be determined in the series of cases concerning the Merchant Shipping Act 1988 (**R** *v* **Secretary of State for Transport ex parte Factortame Ltd** (No. 2) [1991] 1 AC 603).[9] The legislation, which sought to impose a registration requirement on foreign fisherman, contravened community rights concerning discrimination, trade, and the free movements of workers. The company sought an interim injunction suspending the incompatible parts of the legislation pending a ruling from the European Court of Justice (ECJ). This left the House of Lords in a position where they had to determine whether or not to apply an Act of Parliament, or to apply community law. The House of Lords referred the matter to the ECJ for a ruling, and accepted the decision that interim relief should be granted. The matter was ultimately resolved by amending legislation. However, the constitutional effect was an acceptance that Community law took precedence and, therefore, that s 2(4) appeared to be entrenched, and protected from the doctrine of implied repeal.[10]

[10]The issue raised earlier regarding the doctrine of implied repeal and the ECA has now been examined, and a definitive answer can be given.

To this extent then it appears that the 1972 Parliament was able to effectively bind its successors, undermining a key element of the doctrine of Parliamentary supremacy. However, Laws LJ, in the case **Thoburn** *v* **Sunderland City Council** [2002] EWHC 195 (Admin), sought to draw a distinction between 'ordinary' statutes and statutes of 'constitutional significance'. In his view, the latter include all statutes which alter constitutional arrangements. Such Acts, according to this view, are not subject to implied repeal. He argued this is not a position created by, or unique to, the European Communities Act but 'purely from the law of England'. Such statutes can be altered, but only by express repeal. If this is accepted, then the European Communities Act alone has not altered the constitutional position of Parliament.[11] It is clear that, in theory, it would be open to any Parliament to expressly repeal s 2(4) or indeed any other part of

[11]Recognition of the possibility of express repeal is important, as this shows that even though some supremacy can be said to have passed to the European Union, Parliament could reverse that decision.

the Act. In **McCarthys Ltd v Smith** [1979] ICR 785, Lord Denning expressed the clear view that the courts would apply an inconsistent legislative provision if it was made expressly. Such a decision would inevitably lead to conflict between the United Kingdom and the European Union, but this would be a matter for the legislature who can still choose to withdraw from the European Union.

[12]The conclusion should refer directly to the question and provide an answer. No new material is introduced here, but the conclusions refer to matters addressed in the body of the essay.

Membership of the European Union has undoubtedly altered the constitutional landscape and has led to a situation where the domestic courts will not always obey a Parliamentary provision. It should always be remembered, though, that continued membership is a choice, and that any future Parliament could choose to withdraw. Although there may be political, economic and social constraints rendering this proposition purely hypothetical, it would appear that the constitutional position is clear. Any decision to cede supremacy to the European Union has been voluntary, and accordingly, supremacy can theoretically be reclaimed.[12]

 ## Make your answer stand out

- By recognising that Parliamentary supremacy is undermined by numerous factors, not just the EU. The focus needs to be on community law, but you would be rewarded for stating that the growth in the power of the executive, devolution, and the Human Rights Act have also contributed.

- By exploring in more detail the suggestion that express repeal would be possible; arguably this can only be hypothetical as economic and diplomatic concerns would prevent this.

! Don't be tempted to...

- Focus on exploring Dicey's explanation of Parliamentary sovereignty in detail. Students sometimes make the mistake of answering any question on Parliamentary supremacy by explaining each of the rules in detail. You need to be able to recognise that the examiner wants you to focus on the effect of the legislative power of the European institutions.

- Ignore the fact that the United Kingdom is able to negotiate with Europe and opt out of certain provisions. Students sometimes overstate the extent of European powers, which leads to a rather simplistic argument.

Question 4

Since the Human Rights Act 1998, the balance of power has shifted so that it is the judges who are sovereign, rather than Westminster.

Discuss.

Answer plan

→ Outline Dicey's traditional analysis of Parliamentary sovereignty and the role of the courts.

→ Assess the effect of s 3 on the powers of the judiciary.

→ Assess the effect of s 4 on the powers of the judiciary.

→ Consider whether the HRA has significantly altered the relationship between the two institutions of state.

Diagram plan

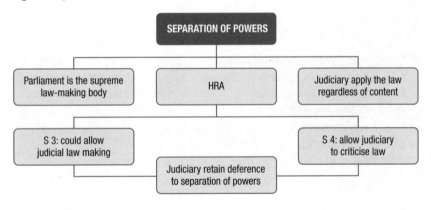

A printable version of this diagram is available from www.pearsoned.co.uk/lawexpressqa

Answer

[1]The respective constitutional roles of the legislature and the judiciary is central to the answer, and so the introduction should briefly set out the traditional position.

It is commonly understood that Parliament occupies a position of supremacy within the United Kingdom. Dicey described Parliamentary supremacy as a 'cornerstone' of the constitution. Under the doctrine of the separation of powers, Parliament has the authority to legislate, and the judiciary apply the law in accordance with Parliament's wishes.[1] The Human Rights Act 1998 imposed new obligations on Parliament when creating legislation, and

²Setting out the central argument about the effect of the HRA in the introduction will give the essay some shape, as the major points can refer back to this statement.

granted the judiciary new powers to interpret and challenge legislation. It is sometimes suggested that this has led to a shift in the constitutional balance; however, it will be argued that the Act has not signalled any significant change.[2]

In considering Parliament's role in the wake of the Human Rights Act, it is helpful to begin by considering the traditional doctrine of parliamentary supremacy. Dicey described three constituent elements. First, Parliament is the supreme law-making body, free to make or unmake legislation on any subject-matter. Secondly, each successive Parliament is sovereign; no Parliament can be bound by its predecessors, or bind its successors. Lastly, no person or body, including the courts, can question the validity of an Act of Parliament.[3] To address the question, it is necessary to consider Parliament's role as the supreme law-making body in the United Kingdom.

[3]This question requires demonstration of an understanding of the doctrine, but it is not the main focus. Therefore, the definition should be set out as succinctly as possible.

[4]It is important to recognise that the Human Rights Act has not granted new rights; citizens were able to enforce article rights prior to 2000, although this would involve the laborious process of taking a claim to the European Court of Human Rights in Strasbourg.

The United Kingdom signed the European Convention on Human Rights in 1950, and it has been possible for an individual to petition the European Court of Human Rights since 1966. It is important to note that it was possible for a citizen to claim that legislation infringed one or more of their rights under the Convention, and to seek redress in Strasbourg. Although the Human Rights Act 1998 incorporated the Convention into domestic law, it did not confer any new rights upon citizens, but rather created a new 'procedural mechanism' for enforcing those rights[4] (**R v Lambert** [2001] UKHL 37). The question is whether the procedures established by the Act have impacted upon the constitutional relationship between Parliament and the judiciary.

In deference to the sovereignty of Parliament, the role of the courts is to interpret and apply legislation regardless of its content. Hence, in **R v IRC ex parte Rossminster** [1980] AC 952, the Lords considered powers conferred by the Taxes Management Act 1970 to be a 'breath-taking' inroad upon rights of privacy and property, but nonetheless felt bound to apply the provisions.[5] The Human Rights Act gives the courts new powers. Section 3 requires the courts to interpret statutes in a manner compatible with Convention rights 'in so far as it is possible to do so'. If this is not possible, then s 4 gives the courts discretion to make a declaration of incompatibility. Amending legislation can then be laid before Parliament although this is not mandatory (s 4).[6]

[5]This case provides a clear illustration of the traditional position, in which the judiciary enforced a law they plainly felt should be changed.

[6]You need to explain s 3 and 4 because these are the critical sections of the HRA here, as they confer power and responsibilities on the judiciary.

[7]It is necessary to display a clear understanding of the mechanics of the Act, and how the particular sections have created powers which could be said to undermine supremacy.

[8]This point refers back to the question by directly addressing the effect of the HRA on Parliamentary supremacy.

[9]Section 4 can be viewed as undermining supremacy by allowing the courts to declare an Act of Parliament incompatible but you should recognise that this is less radical than it may at first appear, as the courts cannot disregard legislation.

It is the operation of these sections of the Human Rights Act which raises questions about the continued supremacy of Parliamentary legislation.[7] Shortly after the Act came into force, the courts had occasion to consider the extent of the power conferred by s 3 in the case of **R v A** [2001] UKHL 25. The courts found that provisions in the Youth Justice and Criminal Evidence Act 1999 conflicted with the rights of defendants under Art 6, and it was held that the statute should be interpreted to give effect to those rights despite the fact that this conflicted with the clear words of the offending legislation. Lord Steyn felt this was acceptable as s 3 of the Human Rights Act allowed for an interpretation that was 'linguistically strained'. In the dissenting judgment, Lord Hope expressed concern that such utilisation of s 3 ran the risk of the judiciary usurping the role of Parliament. If the Human Rights Act allows the courts to effectively rewrite legislation then it is no longer correct to view Parliament as the sole and supreme legislative authority within the constitution.[8]

However, the decisions in cases such as **R v A,** and **Ghaidan v Godin-Mendoza** [2004] UKHL 30 should be viewed in the context of the general development of jurisprudence in the wake of the Human Rights Act. Lord Steyn felt that s 4 should be used as a 'last resort', but the courts have tended to resile from using s 3 to make radical alterations to statute. In **Re S** [2002] UKHL 10, whilst not directly criticising the decision in **R v A**, the judgment cautioned the judiciary against use of interpretative powers being used 'inadvertently' to stray from their constitutional role into making legislation. In **Wilson v First County Trust Ltd** [2003] UKHL 40 the Court of Appeal refused to impose upon the words of statute a 'meaning which they cannot bear', preferring to make a declaration of incompatibility under s 4. Indeed, despite Lord Steyn's view, it seems the courts have tended to defer to Parliament where there is conflict, and to invoke s 4 more frequently than he envisaged.

A declaration of incompatibility does not undermine the legislative authority of Parliament. Section 4 makes it clear that making a declaration has no effect on the parties in the case, as the legislation remains in force unless and until Parliament chooses to amend or revoke it.[9] In **A v Secretary of State for the Home Department** [2004] UKHL 56, a declaration was made in respect

[10]The case of *A* v *UK* is generally used to highlight the increasing power of the judiciary to challenge Parliament; here, you show a detailed knowledge of the authority and should be rewarded for using the case to make a different point.

[11]This is reiterating the point made in the introduction, giving coherence to the answer.

of the provisions in the Anti-Terrorism Crime and Security Act 2001 allowing for the indefinite detention without trial of foreign nationals. Nonetheless, the individuals concerned remained in custody until the Act was repealed by the Prevention of Terrorism Act 2005.[10]

If it is accepted that, where the wording of statute is unambiguous, the courts prefer to use s 4 rather than to attempt an interpretation using s 3, then it is difficult to maintain that the Human Rights Act has resulted in a seismic shift in the Constitutional balance of power.[11] It seems that the judiciary maintain a position of deference to the sovereign power of Parliament.

✓ Make your answer stand out

- By addressing the argument that the Human Rights Act is a 'statute of constitutional significance' which arguably leads to partial entrenchment. This could be used to suggest that the effect has been to entrench the increased powers of the judiciary; therefore undermining the role of Parliament.

- Referring to the number of cases which still fall to be resolved at Strasbourg, which suggests that the domestic judiciary still defer to Parliament to a large extent. A fairly recent example would be *Gillan and Quinton* v *United Kingdom* **[2009] ECHR 28**, in which the European Court of Human Rights held that s 44 of the Terrorism Act 2000 breached Convention rights, overturning the decision of the House of Lords.

! Don't be tempted to...

- Make general points about the Human Rights Act. The question requires you specifically to address the impact of the legislation on the judiciary, so you need to be clear about identifying that s 3 and s 4 are the most relevant.

- Fail to provide evidence of how the courts use their powers. To do well in this question, you will need to be able to use case law effectively to illustrate how the HRA has taken effect.

- Ignore the fact that there are different views that can be taken about the effect of the HRA. You should be able to provide examples of the courts appearing to use the HRA to challenge legislative authority (*R* v *A*) but you will be rewarded if you also provide instances of continuing judicial deference.

Question 5

Parliamentary privilege is 'a cornerstone of parliamentary democracy'. (Joint Committee on Parliamentary Privilege: HL Paper/43/HC 214-1 1999.)

Critically assess the importance of parliamentary privilege in the context of current constitutional arrangements in the United Kingdom.

Answer plan

→ Define Parliamentary privilege.

→ Briefly outline the historical development and importance for democracy.

→ Explain the positive and negative aspects of the privilege of freedom of speech.

→ Explain the meaning of exclusive cognisance and explain the possible impact of the Parliamentary Standards Act 2009.

Diagram plan

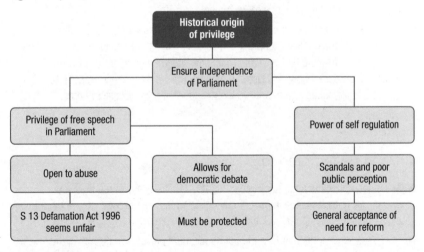

A printable version of this diagram is available from www.pearsoned.co.uk/lawexpressqa

Answer

Parliamentary privileges grant special protections and powers to both Houses of Parliament, both collectively and to individual members.[1] The privileges encompass two main areas: the protection of freedom of speech in the House, and the powers afforded to the Houses to regulate their own affairs. Parliamentary privileges are a product of the historical development of the constitution. The exercise of Parliamentary privilege has been the subject of much debate and some reform, but it could be argued that there is still a need to provide protection for democratic debate.[2]

Parliamentary privilege arose to protect the legislature from undue interference by the monarchy and was enshrined as part of the settlement reached between the legislature and the crown in the Bill of Rights of 1688. Article IX declares that 'proceedings in Parliament' will be free of impeachment or interference from any outside body. Although the Bill of Rights resulted from tension between Parliament and the monarch, as the constitution has developed, it can be seen that the result of a claim of privilege is that the courts may determine whether the privilege indeed exists, but will not intervene further.[3]

A Member of Parliament enjoys the absolute privilege of freedom of speech and cannot be liable for defamation or other legal action in respect of comments made as part of proceedings in Parliament. The respect for freedom of speech is arguably an integral requirement of an effective democracy. It is vital that the legislature is able to debate issues freely and openly without fear of litigation.[4] There are instances where the cloak of privilege has allowed issues to be raised which would otherwise be kept out of the public domain. In 2009, the MP David Davis raised questions in the Commons regarding the government's alleged complicity in subcontracting the torture of terror suspects. Some of the information he referred to was potentially in breach of the Official Secrets Act, and therefore, had it been raised anywhere except for the House, he would have run the risk of prosecution.[5] Privilege can, then, allow Parliament to effectively and robustly hold the executive to account; an important function of the legislature in our constitutional democracy.[6] Similarly, the protections given to Members allowed for the circumvention of the 'super injunction' obtained by Trafigura to prevent details concerning its operations overseas entering the public

[1] Privilege is a fairly complicated concept, and marks will be awarded for the ability to give a brief, and accurate, definition.

[2] A good essay question should always take a stance in relation to the question, as this shows confidence and an ability to more than describe what is meant by the concept of privilege.

[3] You must not succumb to the temptation to write a history essay, but it is useful to highlight why privilege arose, in order to explain the effect on the relationship between the legislature and the courts.

[4] The question refers to the relationship between privilege and democratic values, so it is important to demonstrate an understanding of this argument.

[5] Marks will be given for an ability to illustrate the argument made with examples such as this.

[6] You must ensure that, having outlined the facts, these are then used to help draw conclusions about the central question.

domain. Once a question in Parliament had been tabled, journalists could report the contents. Qualified privilege is given to reports of proceedings in Parliament, provided they are accurate, fair and without malice. Aspects of privilege, then, still have an important role in ensuring open democracy.[7]

[7]Here, the reference to the question ensures that the answer stays focused on the key issues.

The protection of freedom of speech can raise concerns for the citizen. The privilege is absolute and will protect a Member of Parliament with immunity from civil action in defamation, as evidenced in numerous cases including, *inter alia*, **Dillon v Balfour** (1887) 20 LR 600.[8] The scope of the privilege was addressed in **A v UK** [2009] ECHR 3455/05. The European Court of Human Rights held that whilst remarks made in a Commons debate about a woman were 'regrettable', there was no infringement of her rights under Arts 6, 8 and 13, as the privilege fell within the margin of appreciation granted to the state to take steps 'necessary' to ensure democracy. An assertion of democratic freedom will be cold comfort to a citizen whose reputation is impugned. Whilst it may be possible to petition the House seeking retraction, or complain to the speaker, this is arguably no substitute for compensation and proper redress.[9] The Committee on Standards and Privileges acknowledged the fine line between fair comment and abuse, but simply urged members to exercise 'self-restraint'.

[8]The question requires 'critical' analysis, and therefore marks are available for demonstrating an understanding of both sides of the argument. Here, examples demonstrate an awareness of the negative aspects of the privilege of free speech.

[9]Here, you highlight an understanding of the practical effect of a claim of privilege in preventing legal redress.

Further controversy centres on s 13 of the Defamation Act 1996, which was passed in the wake of allegations made in the *Guardian* newspaper about Neil Hamilton. Hamilton instigated libel proceedings against the paper, who sought to adduce evidence from Parliamentary proceedings as part of their defence. Following **Prebble v Television New Zealand Ltd** [1995] 1 AC 321, the evidence was deemed inadmissible, as it was privileged, and accordingly the action was struck out.[10] The Defamation Act allows an individual MP to choose to waive privilege in such circumstances. This has caused concern for two reasons. First, the Joint Committee on Privileges expressed the view that as privilege attaches to the House, a decision to waive privilege should not be in the gift of an individual member. Secondly, it does appear that the result is that Members of Parliament are able to use privilege to speak with impunity about non-Members, but retain the ability to seek redress if they feel their own reputation is called into disrepute. This has the appearance of unfairness, and appears to subvert the notion inherent in the rule of law that, as Dicey asserted, no man is above the law.[11]

[10]It is not necessary to give detail about the Hamilton affair, or its eventual resolution. The information is included simply to explain the change in the law signalled by s 13.

[11]Reference to the rule of law recognises the fact that privilege is linked to a broader debate about democratic values.

Concerns about the special position of Members of Parliament were at the centre of public debate in the wake of the scandal regarding expenses which surfaced in 2009. Details regarding dubious claims were obtained as a result from a request under the Freedom of Information Act 2000. Members of Parliament resisted the release of information on the grounds that it was covered by the privilege protecting proceedings in Parliament. Once in the public domain, questions arose regarding the exclusive cognisance Parliament has over its own affairs. Again, the privilege originated in the time when there was a need to assert the independence of the legislature from interference and oppression, but a succession of scandals in recent decades led many to question whether Parliament should be free from independent audit and control. It is difficult to see that this aspect of privilege still retains force as a protection for democracy.[12] Parliament has many powers to deal with contempt, but no expulsions have occurred in recent times, and suspensions are rare. In the wake of the expenses debacle, the Prime Minister asserted that Parliament would 'no longer operate like a gentleman's club'. The Parliamentary Standards Act 2009 introduced a system of independent audit and control. However, it is notable that during the passage of the Bill, clauses which would have created imprisonable offences to deal with fraudulent claims and paid advocacy were deleted. Crucially, the Act preserves the core of Parliamentary privilege at s 1, which declares that nothing in the statute can be read by the courts as affecting Art IX of the Bill of Rights.

The Parliamentary Standards Act can be seen as an acknowledgement that exclusive cognisance is no longer constitutionally necessary, nor politically possible. However, it can be seen that freedom of speech remains an important privilege that allows the legislature to ensure open and fair governance.[13]

[12]Whilst marks will be given for being able to place the law in context by referencing the expenses scandal, it is important to ensure focus remains on the relationship between privilege and democracy.

[13]The conclusion draws a distinction between the two types of privilege considered in the answer, and attempts to directly address the question.

✓ Make your answer stand out

■ By expanding the explanation of 'democracy' to explore how privilege is connected to the doctrines of separation of powers and the rule of law. You have touched on the fact that privilege allows the Commons to hold the executive to account by asking questions without fear of censure: this could be linked to Bagehot's view of the constitution, in which the ability to operate a system of checks and balances is central to democracy.

■ By ensuring you are abreast of developments in this highly topical area of law. At the time of writing, for example, a number of Members of Parliament have sought to use privilege to protect them from legal action arising from the expenses scandal. If you can use these kind of examples in your answers, you will be rewarded because it will show current awareness.

■ By incorporating reference to earlier calls for reform of privilege. You could consider, for example, Leopold's discussion, in 'Report of the Joint Committee on Parliamentary Privilege' (1999) Public Law 604.

! Don't be tempted to...

■ Concentrate on just one aspect of privilege, as the distinction between freedom of speech and exclusive cognisance is important in this question because the former is far more clearly linked to democracy.

■ Be distracted by discussion of the debate about the extent of privilege: students sometimes spend a long time on this aspect of the topic, using cases such as *Hansard* v *Stockdale*, or Strauss's case. Unfortunately, marks will not be awarded for demonstrating awareness of the issue of the limits of privilege. The question has a specific focus on the benefits or drawbacks of Parliamentary privileges.

■ Read the question as a request to discuss the role of Parliament within the constitution, or the supremacy of Parliament. Students sometimes make the mistake of providing generalised information about the composition of Parliament, or of Dicey's account of supremacy but this will not gather marks. The answer must focus exclusively on the role and utility of privilege.

Question 6

The reform of the House of Lords since 1997 has been ineffective in creating a truly democratic legislature, and proposals falling short of en elected chamber should be rejected. Discuss.

Answer plan

→ Outline the position of the Lords prior to 1997.

→ Describe the key reforms.

→ Outline the role of the Lords in the passage of legislation and scrutiny of the executive.

→ Assess the merits of proposals for further reform.

→ Consider whether 'democracy' could be adversely affected by a fully elected chamber.

Diagram plan

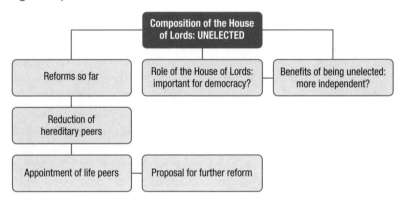

A printable version of this diagram is available from www.pearsoned.co.uk/lawexpressqa

Answer

[1]Use of the correct terminology is not always essential, as you could just as easily state that there are two Houses of Parliament. However, an ability to use terms accurately does show understanding, and makes the answer appear more confident and professional.

[2]You should be able to demonstrate a knowledge of the reforms that have occurred, and further proposals; by so doing you reassure the examiner that you will be using the right source material by setting out the information in the introduction.

[3]It is not necessary to spend too long explaining the detail of the reforms to the Lords, as the question is focused on the relationship between the Upper House and democratic principles.

[4]It is important that the answer focuses on this key issue rather than the effect of reforms to the Law Lords, or the Lord Chancellor.

[5]This paradox is the crux of the question, as most academics acknowledge the fact that the constitutional importance of the Upper Chamber is partially due to the fact it is not subject to election.

In common with the majority of Western democratic states, the United Kingdom has a bicameral legislature.[1] However, the United Kingdom is unique in retaining an entirely unelected second chamber. Reform of the House of Lords was attempted in 1999 and 2005, but the debate regarding the composition and competencies of the Upper House continues. Some proposals for change have been made in the Wakeham report, the report of the Public Administration Committee and the government White Paper of 2008.[2] The role of the Lords in our Parliamentary democracy will be evaluated, and the proposals for reform will be considered.

The House of Lords Act 1999 altered the composition of the House of Lords, reducing the number of elected peers from 750 to 92. The Constitutional Reform Act 2005 made provision for a new Supreme Court, which opened in 2009, moving the Law Lords out of the legislative chamber.[3] Therefore, the majority of the Lords are now life peers, appointed on the basis of previous political office or expertise in their field. However, none of the reforms addresses the fact that the Lords are not elected and, therefore, lack a democratic mandate.[4]

In considering whether the function of the House of Lords is undemocratic, it should be noted that their powers regarding legislation are limited by a number of factors. First, the combined effects of the Parliament Acts 1911 and 1949 are that the Upper Chamber do not debate money bills, have limited powers of delay of other legislation and, in extremis, can be bypassed altogether. Secondly, in recognising the Salisbury convention, which prevents the Lords from voting against legislation which formed part of a governments manifesto commitments, it could be argued that the House acknowledges the lack of a democratic mandate.

Nonetheless, the House of Lords plays a significant role within the constitution, and it could be argued that, paradoxically, their importance derives from the fact that they are not elected.[5] The role of the House is to scrutinise and consider legislation that the Commons has agreed. Often, amendments suggested by the Lords are accepted once a Bill is returned to the Commons. Importantly, the Lords can defeat legislation, and have done so during both Conservative and

[6]It is important to be able to provide evidence to support an assertion that the Lords play a constitutional role in holding the executive to account.

[7]In order to state why the Lords are necessary, criticisms of the Commons have to be acknowledged.

[8]There is no need to go into detail and explain how the whip system works. This is another example of how your use of terminology can demonstrate that you understand the issue without needing to give further explanation.

[9]This is a very important point, as despite the enthusiasm of the Labour government for reform, there does appear to be widespread deference to the role of the Lords.

[10]Although the question does not specifically reference existing proposals for reform, a good student will be aware of the proposals made for further change.

Labour administrations. In recent times, the Lords can be seen as instrumental in maintaining civil liberties, as witnessed in the rejection of proposals to extend the permissible period of detention without charge for terror suspects to 42 days, or the refusal to accept the original proposals of the Anti Terror Crime and Security Bill in 2001.[6] There is a need for a body able to closely scrutinise and check legislation proposed by the executive within our constitution. Arguably, within our Parliamentary system, the Lords are better placed to do so for two reasons. First, the first past the post electoral system for the Commons can lead to a lower House which contains a large majority drawn from the party in power, and in this situation the whip system can ensure that government legislation is agreed, leading to the situation Lord Hailsham famously described as 'an elective dictatorship'.[7] A criticism of the House of Lords was once that the chamber was inherently biased, as the hereditary peers were generally Conservative. There is little doubt that the House of Lords Act aimed, in part, to correct the balance. It is still the case that the majority of peers are Conservative but, importantly, the House now contains a significant proportion of cross party peers who are not influenced in their voting by party whips.[8] Secondly, there is an argument that, as the Lords are not concerned with the need to court either party or public approval for election purposes, they may vote according to conscience.

No government has suggested abolition of the second chamber, and there is deference to the constitutional role of the Lords. The Parliament Acts are rarely invoked, and generally, defeat of a Bill is accepted.[9]

Since the House of Lords Act, further proposals for reform have been mooted.[10] The Wakeham Report suggested a chamber composed mainly of appointed peers, with some proportion being elected. Various figures were suggested up to 20% of the House. In addition, it was suggested that appointment should be made by an independent body. The Public Administration Committee (PAC) provided more radical proposals. Their report argued that it was essential that the second chamber should be composed differently from the Commons, should have substantial powers, and should have legitimacy in the eyes of the public. They proposed that 80% of the House should be elected, and 20% appointed. There was further endorsement for the need for an independent

[11]This, and the last sentence of the previous paragraph, highlight the fact that there is general acceptance of the need for a second chamber with a constitutional role in amending or halting legislation; the issue for debate is really concerned with how members are chosen.

[12]There is no real consensus about how to make the Lords more democratic, and it is helpful to be able to set out some of the differing proposals to demonstrate this fact.

[13]This is a critical part of the conclusion, referring back to the comments of Lord Hailsham, which demonstrate the need for a non-elected chamber.

[14]The question has not specifically asked you to provide a solution, but if you have a clear view, then expressing it in the conclusion makes it clear you are confident enough with the material to make a decision.

appointment commission to remove any suggestion of government effort to influence the views of the house. Views within the legislature remain sharply divided. A vote in both houses on the issue saw the Commons endorsing a wholly or largely elected chamber, whereas the Lords preferred a wholly appointed chamber. Neither Wakeham nor the PAC proposed any alteration to the powers of the second chamber.[11]

In 2008 the government published a White Paper outlining proposals to abolish the remaining hereditary peers and to move towards a system broadly in line with the proposals of the PAC. The paper accepted the need to retain a proportion of appointed peers to ensure independence. Various proposals for an election system which would not compromise independence were suggested including some form of proportional representation, and election for a long term.[12]

However, in 2009, the Constitutional Reform and Governance Bill proposed only the abolition of hereditary peers. Jack Straw explained that this was an acknowledgement that greater reform would not be possible prior to an election. At the time of writing, it remains to be seen whether or not more radical legislation will be introduced. An elected Upper Chamber may appear more democratic, and with the public mandate may be able to take on a more robust stance in criticising the government of the day. A more worrying outcome could be that the political composition of the Commons would be replicated in the Lords, and therefore a vital constitutional mechanism to restrain the executive would be weakened.[13] Even if elections were organised to counter this, arguably, a House constituting professional politicians would be less independently minded. Arguably, then, the most effective safeguard for democracy would be a House appointed by an independent commission.[14]

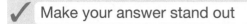

✓ Make your answer stand out

■ Having stated that the Lords will not defeat a Bill which formed part of the governments manifesto, you could address the passage of the Hunting Act 2004. Here, the Parliament Act was invoked following rejection by the Lords. A report prepared for the Lords concluded that the manifesto commitment was to allow a free vote, not to secure a ban, and therefore, there was no breach of the convention. This will be a good point to make because, not only does it give an example of the use of the Parliament Acts, but you have also demonstrated a more detailed understanding of the case and the issues it raised about the role of the Lords.

■ Expanding the comment on the lack of political will to suggest abolition or radical reform. The relatively rare use of the Parliament Acts is worth exploring, as it does seem to suggest that there is an acceptance by the Commons that ignoring the views of the Lords may be seen as unconstitutional, or perhaps, undemocratic.

! Don't be tempted to...

■ Spend time outlining the basic outline of the legislature; you are not required to address the role of the Commons at all in this question.

■ Describing reforms which have taken place in respect of the Lord Chancellor, or the establishment of the Supreme Court. You will not be given marks for knowing these details because they do not relate to the specific point of the question, which concerns the relationship of the legislative function of the Lords and ideas of democracy.

■ Make general statements about the Lords without providing examples to support what you say. It is not enough to say that the Lords reject law that has been approved by the commons: you need to provide an example.

Prerogative powers and constitutional conventions

3

How this topic may come up in exams

Essay questions are more common in this area. Problems may require you to recognise situations in which particular conventions could apply. There is little case law concerning conventions, and therefore you will need to have a number of illustrative examples to draw on. It is important to be able to discuss a range of academic opinions. You should be able to discuss the relationship between prerogative powers and constitutional conventions. This area of the syllabus overlaps with consideration of the separation of powers.

◼ Attack the question

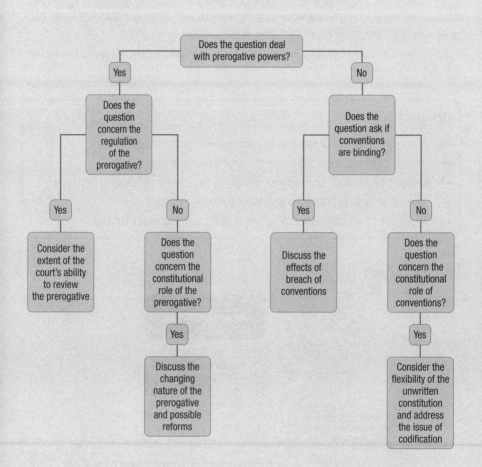

Question 1

'Is it not true that we have found that constitutional conventions that are universally accepted can, arguably, have greater force and staying power than legislation? But surely those conventions, by definition, can apply only if they are universally accepted.' (Viscount Cranbourne: *Hansard* text for February 22 2000: http://www.parliament.the-stationery-office. co.uk/pa/ld199900/ldhansrd/vo000222/text/00222-08.htm.)

To what extent do constitutional conventions remain an important part of the constitution of the United Kingdom?

Answer plan

→ Outline the definitions of conventions given by Dicey and Jennings.

→ Consider particular conventions and the consequences of breach.

→ Analyse how particular conventions could be said to lose their force.

→ Consider whether or not some conventions could be codified.

→ Draw some conclusions about the extent to which conventions are binding.

Diagram plan

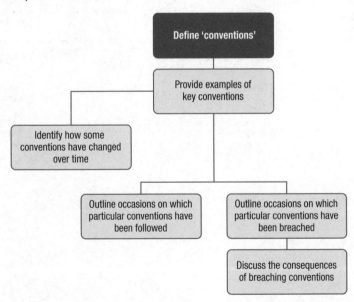

A printable version of this diagram is available from www.pearsoned.co.uk/lawexpressqa

Answer

[1]In order to deal with the issue of conventions, you do need to explain that the constitution is 'unwritten', but you should be as brief as possible.

The constitution of the United Kingdom is generally described as 'unwritten'. Whilst it is true to say that it is not codified within a single document, much of the constitution can be found in formal, written sources. Conventions are an informal, unwritten source of the constitution.[1] The origins and enforceability of conventions are uncertain, and whilst some may appear to have great force, others will fall away over time. Some would argue that the possibility of evolution and change gives the unwritten constitution the benefit of flexibility and responsiveness. Alternatively, it could be suggested that it is inappropriate for rules governing important areas of conduct in public office to be so poorly defined, and without legal sanction.[2]

[2]This question requires an examination of the pros and cons of conventions, so it is helpful to set out the main arguments in the introduction.

[3]Any discussion of conventions must include Dicey's definition as a starting point.

Dicey defined conventions as habits, understanding and practices which are not enforceable by the courts.[3] Constitutional conventions are perhaps more than simply 'habits,' however: as Waldron points out, they are accepted as rules by those who are bound by them despite the lack of legal enforceability (Waldron, J. *The Law* (1990) London: Routledge p. 62). Loveland suggests that the function of a convention is to 'fill in the gaps' in the constitution (Loveland, I. *Constitutional Law, Administrative Law and Human Rights: A Critical Introduction* (5th edn, 2009) Oxford: Oxford University Press, p. 271). It can be hard to determine when a form of conduct is simply an accepted practice, and when it should be considered to be a convention that forms part of the constitution. Jennings argued that a convention requires precedent, acceptance of the precedent by the individuals concerned, and a reason for the rule.[4] (Jennings, I. *The Law and the Constitution* (5th edn, 1959) London: Hodder and Stoughton, p. 134). It is clear, then, that a constitutional convention emerges from tradition and practice, and can indeed carry great weight as a breach may have severe consequences.

[4]It is a good idea to mention Jennings here as, in addition to Dicey, he is one of the most important theorists who have written about this subject.

[5]You need to be able to explain the function of conventions because the question is asking for an evaluation of their place in the constitution.

[6]A good answer will need to be able to examine how a number of conventions have developed over time. There are many conventions that you could focus on but, whichever you choose, make sure you can give some concrete examples to support the argument.

Conventions regulate some of the key relationships between individuals working in the various organs of the state and can therefore be said to be of considerable constitutional importance,[5] and yet a cursory examination highlights how the rules are far from fixed.

By convention, the government of the day should be supported by a majority in the House of Commons, and should resign if it is unable to do so.[6] Whilst for many years it was assumed that this meant defeat on any major policy issue would lead to resignation, as

Loveland points out, this was consistently ignored from the 1970s onwards; so the rule now appears to be that resignation need only follow the loss of an explicit motion of no confidence.

[7]Collective responsibility is a good convention to focus on, as there are so many examples that help illustrate instances where convention is followed, and instances where it appears to have been ignored.

The conduct of ministers in office is largely governed by convention. There are different aspects to this; individual and collective responsibility. The convention of collective responsibility requires all Cabinet Ministers to support government policy once it has been determined, irrespective of their personal views.[7] Numerous examples can be found which demonstrate compliance with the convention, including the resignation of Michael Heseltine over the Westland affair and, more recently, the resignation of Robin Cooke who was unable to support the Iraq war. Collective responsibility can also be used to illustrate the lack of clarity that surrounds the definition and application of conventions. The rule was suspended by the Labour government in the 1970s, allowing Ministers to air their views regarding membership of the European Union, to encourage a public debate. The suspension was temporary, voluntary, and limited to a single issue. This perhaps demonstrates the utility of conventions, which allow flexibility in government. It may be acceptable to envisage a rule that can, with agreement from all parties, be lifted. The convention was flouted, seemingly without agreement, by Clare Short who, like Robin Cooke, was opposed to the Iraq war. She spoke out publicly against the war but remained in Cabinet for another two months, which demonstrates that the operation, or otherwise, of the convention appears to depend upon the discretion and preference of the Prime Minister of the day rather than any legal principle.[8]

[8]This is a good point to make, as it helps develop an argument that conventions are governed by political pressure rather than legal principle.

[9]Here, you acknowledge the argument that flexibility of the unwritten constitution is its greatest strength. As this is one of the key points that is made in favour of conventions, it should certainly be mentioned.

The convention of individual responsibility holds a Minister accountable for conduct whilst in office but the requirements of the rule have shifted over time. It no longer appears to be the case that personal 'scandal' will inevitably result in resignation. In the 1990s, newspaper accounts of an affair led to the resignation of Cecil Parkinson, whereas John Prescott remained in office following similar revelations. Perhaps this is indicative of the constitution responding to reflect the shift in attitude of the public at large.[9] However, as numerous commentators have pointed out, the rule has rarely been fixed, and sexual scandal generally only leads to resignation if there are other implications.[10] Parkinson was a member of a government that stressed moral values, but had fathered an

[10]The answer is referring again to the argument that political issues are the main issue that determines how a convention will operate in any given circumstance. This is going to be a key part of the conclusions, so it is helpful to keep showing how the examples you choose support this opinion.

[11]You do need to be familiar with the facts of the examples that you choose, so that they can be used to support your argument. Remember, though, that you are using the facts to make a point, so keep it as brief as you can.

[12]Rather than simply stating that conventions are important, the answer points to evidence of this by outlining how both government and the judiciary have acknowledged their role.

[13]A good answer will be familiar with a range of academic opinion, and be able to analyse a number of differing academic views.

[14]This is a key point and one which is supported by the examples explored earlier on in the answer.

illegitimate child; it could be argued that it was this hypocrisy that led to the view he was unfit for office.[11]

It appears that a Minister is still accountable for failings within their department, but this convention is also subject to a variety of interpretations. Hence, although the Prime Minister refused to accept it, William Whitelaw felt compelled to offer his resignation following the discovery of an intruder in Buckingham Palace. Thereafter, Ministers appeared to draw a distinction between matters of policy, and matters of administration. James Prior refused to resign following a prison escape, on the grounds it did not result from any decisions he had made.

The precise obligation imposed by a particular convention can be hard to define, and may alter over time and in differing circumstances. The relevance of conventions to the constitution is clear. The Cabinet Office has published guidance on the operation of ministerial responsibility, and the appointment of government. Conventions may not be enforceable in the courts,[12] but they are recognised as an aid to interpretation (see, for example **A-G v Blake (Jonathan Cape, third party)** [1998] 1 All ER 833). Jaconelli suggested that whilst there may be no legal consequence, loss of office occurs so regularly as a result of a breach of convention that it can be considered to be a sanction (Jaconelli , J. (2005) 'Do constitutional conventions bind?' 64(1) CLJ 149). However, Loveland highlights that it is common for a Minister to resign, only to be reinstated a short while later (Parkinson, Blunkett and Mandelson to name but a few). Dewan and Dowding[13] suggest that ministerial resignation is triggered less by convention than political expediency, and occurs when it is required to improve public perceptions of government.[14]

It appears that conventions can fall out of use if public, or political opinion allows. Whilst this demonstrates the ability of the constitution to adapt to changing times, it is perhaps a concern that these 'vital pillars' (Loveland, p. 271) of the constitution have no legal basis.

✓ Make your answer stand out

- By exploring the argument that conventions should be codified in more detail. You could note that the Constitutional Reform and Governance Act 2010 has placed the Ponsonby convention on a statutory footing, and consider whether this signifies a move towards codification. This would be helpful because it shows awareness of recent developments in the law.

- By utilising academic opinion about the possibility of codification. There is a great deal of academic writing on the subject of conventions. An authoritative discussion regarding the benefits and perils of codification can be found in de Smith, S. and Brazier, R. *Constitutional and Administrative Law* (8th edn, 2008), London: Penguin.

- By considering the relationship between conventions and the prerogative and emphasising the role that they play in regulating the use of discretionary power. This would demonstrate an ability to consider constitutional law as a whole, rather than in discrete topic areas.

! Don't be tempted to...

- List all the conventions that you can remember. It is far better to concentrate on two or three examples, and spend time exploring how they operate in some detail. Remember, marks are awarded for the ability to analyse the question, rather than simply remembering the law.

- Ignore the need to be able to provide examples to support your argument. This topic can pose difficulties, because there is a lack of case law authorities (due to the nature of conventions) and therefore, your revision will need to include remembering illustrations from recent political history.

 Question 2

The United Kingdom is typical of states which permit Ministers to use certain powers without parliamentary approval, but it is highly unusual among democracies in having neither a codified constitution nor having made such express grants of power by the legislature.

(Select Committee of Public Administration, 4th Report Session 2003–2004 available at www.publications.parliament.uk/pa/cm200304/cmselect/cmpubadm/422/42202.htm).

Discuss the adequacy of the regulation of the exercise of prerogative powers.

Answer plan

→ Provide a definition of prerogative powers, and identify key powers exercised by Ministers.

→ Explain the role of the court in regulating use of the prerogative.

→ Consider the relationship between Parliament and the prerogative.

→ Highlight some criticisms of the use of the prerogative and proposals for reform.

Diagram plan

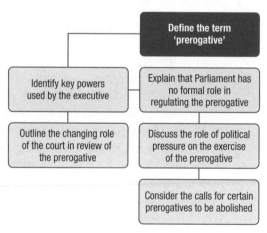

A printable version of this diagram is available from www.pearsoned.co.uk/lawexpressqa

Answer

[1]Although it is not essential to remember quotes, you do need to provide Blackstone's definition of the prerogative. It would be acceptable to paraphrase the definition, but it should be the starting point for an explanation of prerogative power.

[2]The question asks you to consider the regulation of the prerogative, and it is helpful to highlight in the introduction that you recognise that the issue is control of executive power by the other constitutional bodies.

[3]There are many prerogative powers and the answer cannot, and should not, attempt to deal with them all. A more confident approach selects a few for discussion.

[4]*BBC* v *Johns* should be included, as it is demonstrates that prerogative powers are residual, and cannot be expanded.

[5]This is probably the single most important authority regarding the prerogative and must be discussed. It is essential to consider in a question dealing with regulation of the use of the power.

Blackstone described the Royal prerogative as 'that special pre-eminence which the King has, over and above all other persons, and out of the ordinary course of the common law, in right of his royal dignity'.[1] Prerogative powers are those exercisable by the Crown without statutory authority. Although, historically, the prerogative was exercised by the monarch, the majority of powers are now used by ministers of state, and very few remain the personal preserve of the sovereign. The extent to which the judiciary and the legislature are able to regulate the exercise of prerogative powers by the executive has increased;[2] however, there are still some who are concerned by the lack of control that can be exerted by the other constitutional bodies.

The prerogative encompasses a number of important matters of state, including the regulation of the civil service; making treaties; control of the armed forces and the appointment of ministers.[3] The powers that fall within its scope are often of crucial importance to government, and it is perhaps peculiar that the limitations and controls upon the prerogative have not yet been formalised.

Traditionally, the judiciary would not interfere with the exercise of a prerogative power beyond assessing whether or not an action by the executive fell within its scope. The courts refused to countenance any extension of prerogative: Lord Diplock stated in **BBC v Johns** [1965] Ch 32: 'it is 350 years and a civil war too late'[4] for the executive to claim new powers. This position appeared to be contradicted by the controversial judgment in **R v Secretary of State for the Home Department ex parte Northumbria Police Authority** [1989] QB 26, in which it was accepted that a prerogative power to keep the peace existed. Despite the absence of previous authority confirming, it was held that the absence of authority might, in fact, point to 'an unspoken assumption' that it existed.

In more recent times, the courts have adopted a less deferential approach to executive actions following the **'GCHQ' case (Council of Civil Service Unions v Minister for the Civil Service** [1985] AC 374), in which it was held that a decision was not exempt from review simply because it fell within the scope of the prerogative.[5] There remained, however, 'non-justiciable' areas of decision-making, considered matters of policy that were

[6]There are a number of cases that could be used here, and there is no need to include a comprehensive list. It is perfectly acceptable to use one or two, but it is necessary to provide an explanation of the area of the prerogative that your authorities deal with. This shows the examiner that you know how the cases illustrate a change in judicial attitudes.

[7]This point helps to make a balanced argument by acknowledging that in some areas, the judiciary remain deferential.

[8]A good answer will recognise that the question is not limited to the role of the judiciary; you should address the position of Parliament as well.

[9]Reference to the doctrine of Parliamentary supremacy and implied repeal demonstrates an ability to place the topic in context and draw links between different areas of the syllabus.

[10]The prerogative to declare war is an excellent issue to focus on as it has been subject to much recent debate and there are numerous sources of political and academic opinion for you to draw on.

appropriately within the discretion of the executive. These included the disposal of armed forces, matters of national security, the dissolution of Parliament and appointment of ministers, the prerogative of mercy and the making of treaties. Since the **GCHQ case**, it can be seen that the courts are increasingly willing to review a broad range of matters, including some that the judgment sought to exclude. In **R v Secretary of State for the Home Department ex parte Bentley** [1994] QB 349, the prerogative of mercy was subject to review. The treatment of homosexuals in the military was considered in **R v Ministry of Defence ex parte Smith** [1996] QB 517, despite the fact that the matter concerned the disposal of the armed forces.[6] There is, then, an increased degree of regulation of the exercise of the prerogative. Matters which directly concern national security or diplomatic relations, however, appear to remain exempt from judicial interference[7] **R (Abbasi) v Secretary of State for Foreign and Commonwealth Affairs and Secretary of State for the Home Department** [2002] All ER (D) 70, and **R (Al Rawi) v Foreign Secretary** [2007] 2 WLR 1219). Further, in the case of **CND v Prime Minister of the United Kingdom** [2002] All ER 245 the courts refused to interfere with the government's determination of the legal effect of the UN resolution regarding Iraq.

The power to declare war has been the focus of debate about the role of Parliament in regulating the use of the prerogative.[8] Under the doctrine of supremacy, it appears clear that an Act of Parliament can abolish a prerogative power, either expressly or by implied repeal (as confirmed in **Attorney General v De Keysers Royal Hotel** [1920] AC 508).[9] In addition, the exercise of prerogative powers can be put on a statutory footing; see for example the Security Service Act 1989. Many commentators have argued that there should be further legislative action to limit the extent of the prerogative. In 1994, whilst in opposition, the Labour minister Jack Straw referred specifically to the power of ministers to ratify treaties and to declare war as a 'smokescreen' designed to 'obfuscate the use of power for which they are insufficiently accountable'[10] (Straw, J., 'Abolish the Royal Prerogative', in A. Barnett (ed.), *Power and the Throne: The Monarchy Debate* (1994) London: Vintage, p. 129). Following election, the Labour administration made no move to abolish the prerogative to declare war despite the recommendation of the Public Administration Select Committee in 2004, and four private Members Bills on the subject. The Constitutional Reform and Governance Act 2010 has, however, placed the Ponsonby convention of a statutory footing; formalising the requirement for treaties to be laid before Parliament prior to ratification.

[11]This is a key point to make, as you must address the reasons why codification has been called for; this is the central argument.

Those who argue that the legislature should have a greater role in the exercise of key prerogative powers claim that this would ensure greater legitimacy, and increased accountability.[11] A number of witnesses to the House of Lords Constitution Committee made the point that the decision to send troops to war required democratic authorisation (Fifteenth report). It is perhaps for this reason that Tony Blair declared it 'unthinkable' that the decision would occur without consulting Parliament when giving evidence to the liaison committee. It may be politically expedient, but the fact remains that there is no legal requirement to consult the legislature on the matter and, as has been shown, no judicial regulation of such a decision after the fact.[12]

[12]It is useful to be able to draw a distinction between political, and legal, restraints on the exercise of prerogative power.

Since the **GCHQ case** [1985] AC 374, there is no doubt that the use of prerogative powers is subject to greater regulation and control across a range of areas. Successive administrations have, however, resisted pressure to place key decisions in the hands of the legislature. It is undoubtedly true that the exercise of the prerogatives pertaining to issues of defence and diplomatic relations is subject to political scrutiny, and a degree of democratic accountability at the ballot box. Nevertheless, in the absence of judicial sanction or legislative approval, it can be argued that there is still a lack of constitutional control of the prerogative.[13]

[13]You must attempt to address the question directly in your conclusion.

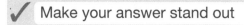

✓ Make your answer stand out

■ When considering the *Northumbria* case, a parallel could be drawn with *Entick* v *Carrington* (1765) 19 St Tr 1029, considered to be a key constitutional case in which it was said that no power existed without a lawful authority. There appears to be a direct contrast between the two decisions, which could be highlighted. This would show the examiner that you are aware of the fact that there are competing interpretations of the constitutional position.

■ By exploring the reasons behind government reluctance to abolish key prerogative powers. This answer has touched on the difference between the views of Jack Straw in opposition, and the actions of the Labour administration. You could consider the utility of discretionary powers to government and argue that these are necessary to enable swift and efficient decision-making.

■ By referring to additional academic and political comment. The reports of the Constitution Committee of the House of Lords regarding the prerogative to declare war are a good starting point: 'Waging War: Parliament's role and responsibility' (2005-06 HL Paper 236-I and II), and the follow-up report (2006-07 HL Paper 51).

! Don't be tempted to...

■ List all the prerogative powers. Focus on a few that have been the subject of judicial or parliamentary consideration.

■ Discuss the personal prerogatives of the monarch. The quote used in the question refers to the power used by Ministers; this is an indication that the examiner is looking for a discussion about the regulation of the executive.

■ Write an answer that concentrates on whether or not there should be codification. Whilst this should be touched upon, it is important not to lose sight of the specific question posed which is whether or not the regulation of existing powers is adequate.

❓ Question 3

The (fictional) government is planning to develop green field sites across the North of England in order to manage a housing crisis and stimulate growth in the economy. The matter is included in the Queen's speech. The Cabinet is torn by a very public row about the plans. In a radio interview the Minister for the Environment, Gulfraz Khan, declares that the plans are 'ludicrous' and states that his colleagues are making a grave mistake.

He is placed under considerable pressure from colleagues to resign, but he refuses to do so.

A few days later, a scandal erupts when an interview is published with a young woman who claims she had an affair with Mr Khan whilst she was a student on a work placement in his constituency office. The media calls for his resignation, but he refuses.

The plans for development go ahead, but within weeks it is clear that the cost will be several million pounds more than originally thought. The plans drawn up by the Department for Housing contain serious anomalies. During question time, the opposition call for the resignation of the Minister for Housing. He refuses.

A political storm follows over the next few weeks, and numerous MPs demand that a vote of confidence is held. The vote takes place and the government loses by three votes. The Prime Minister declares that there will be no election.

Discuss.

Answer plan

→ Outline the role of conventions in the constitution.

→ Discuss the effect of a breach of the convention of collective cabinet responsibility.

→ Consider the differing approaches to ministerial responsibility that may apply in relation to personal, and political scandal.

→ Explore the ramifications of failing to comply with the convention regarding a vote of no confidence.

Diagram plan

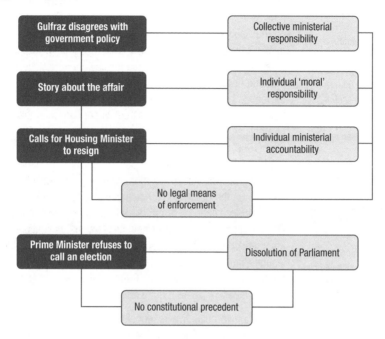

A printable version of this diagram is available from www.pearsoned.co.uk/lawexpressqa

[1]Before addressing the facts of the scenario, the answer should identify conventions as the subject-matter. A brief explanation of constitutional conventions is necessary: Dicey and Jennings are a useful starting point.

[2]You should make reference to the facts of the scenario in your introduction; this reassures the examiner that you are going to be focused on addressing the problem rather than a generalised discussion about conventions. However, don't fall into the trap of writing out all the facts in place of an introduction.

Answer

The United Kingdom is often said to have an unwritten constitution, and there is no single documentary source setting out the roles and responsibilities of the different organs of government. Much of the constitution is now codified, but some of the business of state is regulated by the operation of unwritten conventions. Dicey defined conventions as understandings, habits and practices, which are not enforceable by the courts. Jennings identified that a key characteristic of a convention is that individuals feel themselves to be bound by them.[1] Arguably, the unwritten nature of this element of the constitution leads to difficulty in identifying the precise requirements of a convention. Further, conventions may change over time. The events which occur in relation to the development plans are governed by various constitutional conventions.[2] The requirements of each will be considered, and the ramifications of breaching the conventions will be assessed.

The relationship between Cabinet Ministers is not prescribed by law, but instead is regulated by conventions. These have, to a degree, now been formalised in the Ministerial Code of Conduct published by the Cabinet Office. By convention, the cabinet exercise collective responsibility and present a unified approach to policy. Any differences of opinion can be aired in cabinet discussions, but once agreement has been reached, all Ministers will publicly support the policy, and will not speak or vote against it.[3] Jennings stated that if a Minister cannot express public support, then the convention obliges them to resign (Jennings, I. *Cabinet Government* (3rd edn) (1959) Cambridge: Cambridge University Press). During 2003, Robin Cook resigned from the cabinet as he felt unable to support the Iraq war. According to convention, then, Mr Khan should not criticise the policy, and if he cannot support it, he should resign his position. There is, of course, no legal requirement to do so, which raises the question of how conventional obligations can be enforced.[4] Whilst Mr Cook did resign his position, his Cabinet colleague Clare Short remained in post for two months after publicly denouncing the war in Iraq. The Prime Minister is entitled to dismiss Khan, but cannot legally require resignation.[5]

In addition to collective responsibility, by convention, a Minister takes individual responsibility for the conduct of all those employed by the department. There has been some suggestion that convention requires a Minister to take responsibility for private conduct, and to resign if there is a scandal. Jaconelli argues this is not a 'true' convention, as it does not regulate the business of office. If resignations on such grounds did result from the operation of convention, rather than political expediency then, arguably, the principle has become less rigid as the moral boundaries of wider society have relaxed. Hence, whilst David Mellor resigned in the wake of a sex scandal in 1992, 14 years later John Prescott remained in office despite revelations that he had had an affair. It is, therefore, doubtful that convention requires Mr Khan to resign due to the scandal regarding the student.[6]

It is clear that a convention exists which requires a Minister to be accountable for the actions of the department that they head. A House of Commons research paper lists the options available to a minister who is subject to the convention as: inform and explain; apologise; take remedial steps and, lastly, to resign. There are many examples of ministerial resignation due to failings in their department including, famously, Sir Thomas Dugdale as a result of the 'Crichel Down Affair',[7] despite the fact he had had no personal

[3] It is helpful to adopt a simple structure in which the convention is briefly explained, and then applied to the facts of the scenario.

[4] The answer should identify the conventions that are engaged and recognise that a key issue is the difficulty when they are ignored.

[5] You must make sure that you keep relating the legal points to the facts of this problem scenario.

[6] You should ensure that you can provide contrasting examples of how conventions have operated in practice. This is because the answer will suggest that it is not possible to be certain how conventions will operate in the scenario, as the nature of, and enforcement of conventions depends on many factors.

[7] There are many examples that can be used, and few are essential but the Crichel Down affair is usually cited when discussing ministerial accountability.

[8]Similarly, there are lots of examples to use but including something fairly recent will show that you can relate your studies to events in the current political world.

[9]The answer should recognise that there is no clear precedent that shows how a minister must behave.

[10]This is a key point, as it is often suggested that conventions are enforced by non-legal pressures.

[11]Although it is difficult to predict the outcome of any issue concerning conventions, you will receive credit for attempting to draw some conclusions based on the analysis of examples considered in the answer.

[12]This is such an important point, it is worth setting out explicitly.

[13]Marks will be given for including relevant, current, examples to illustrate the argument as this shows real understanding of the material.

[14]Unlike the conventions considered in relation to ministers, there are no examples to draw on here. The examiner is asking for (informed) speculation.

[15]Bagehot's description of the role of the monarch is important and should be included in this discussion of the constitutional position of the Queen.

involvement in the matter. More recently, Estelle Morris resigned as education secretary following delays in marking A-level exams.[8] It is also possible to find examples where a minister has resisted calls for resignation.[9] The Secretary of State for Northern Ireland, James Prior, refused to resign in 1983 after 38 convicts escaped from the Maze prison on the basis that policy decisions were not the cause of the escape. Michael Howard drew the same distinction between administration and policy when he too declined to resign as Home Secretary in the wake of prison escapes. Analysis of ministerial responses seems to suggest that resignation depends less on the existence of a conventional rule, and more on the political support the individual can command from colleagues and the media.[10] Serious financial anomalies do appear to be issues relating to formulation of policy rather than administration, so the Minister may well face sustained pressure to resign.[11]

In all of the examples concerning the conduct of Ministers, it should be stressed that as conventions are not enforceable by the courts, a refusal to comply carries no legal sanction.[12]

By convention, the Prime Minister should request the dissolution of Parliament and call a general election following a vote of no confidence. This last occurred in 1979 when James Callaghan was defeated by a majority of one. The Coalition government proposed amending the rules to specify that a majority of 55% should be required to force dissolution, but rescinded from that position following considerable opposition.[13] The refusal to request the dissolution of Parliament is a serious breach of convention which has the potential to trigger a constitutional crisis.[14] The power to dissolve Parliament remains within the personal prerogative of the monarch, but conventionally, this is done at the request of the Prime Minister. The monarch has not interfered in political matters for centuries; since the refusal of Queen Anne to assent to a Bill in the eighteenth century. Bagehot described the role of the monarch as the right to be consulted, to encourage, and to warn.[15] There was speculation that, in the event of a hung Parliament, the monarch may be called upon to take a more interventionist approach but in the event, the Queen played no part in the political negotiations that followed the election in May 2010. Should the Prime Minister insist on remaining in office without a democratic mandate, this may demand that the monarch play a greater constitutional role.

[16]The assessment of what could occur in this hypothetical situation should be supported by some academic opinion.

Marshall argued that the Crown should act as a 'genuine instrument of residual constitutional protection' (Marshall, 2002).[16] The breach of convention by the Ministers is not subject to legal sanction but will create considerable political pressure for the individuals concerned. The consequences of refusing to dissolve Parliament are far more serious and may demand unprecedented action by the monarch if political pressure fails.

[17]You must make sure that you do return to the facts of the scenario and summarise your findings.

Whilst convention appears to suggest that Mr Khan should resign, precedents can be found to support his decision to decline to do so. No such precedent exists for the failure to call for the dissolution of parliament.[17]

 Make your answer stand out

- By providing current examples of the operation of conventions that do not yet appear in the textbooks. If you listen to the news, you will certainly be able to find relevant issues. At the time of writing, for example, a Coalition Minister has been criticised for errors in a report presented to Parliament. Convention suggests that he should resign. Inclusion of this kind of material would demonstrate that you really understand the subject-matter.

- You could refer to political research and guidance on the use of conventions. For example, a Commons research paper is available: Research Paper 04/31 'Individual Ministerial Responsibility – Issues and Examples', Powell and Gay, 2004, available at www.parliament.uk/documents/commons/lib/research/rp2004/rp04-082.pdf. The Cabinet Office Manual, published in 2010, included draft guidance on how conventions would operate in the event of a hung Parliament. Use of these kind of sources can show real confidence, provided that they are related to the legal issues.

- By referring to academic commentary. There is a useful article considering the enforcement of conventions: Barber, N. 'Laws and Constitutional Conventions' (2009) LQR 125 at 194.

! Don't be tempted to...

- Explain the relevant conventions without providing examples of how they operate. There is very little case law concerning conventions, but you still need to provide support for any propositions that you make.

- Write a generalised account of the operation of conventions in the constitution. Students who revise the topic assuming it will appear as an essay question can be wrong footed by a problem scenario; ensure that you use the knowledge you have about conventions to draw conclusions about the events described here.

- Ignore the fact that, when dealing with this topic, there are no clear answers. As the answer shows, it is possible to find examples supporting contrasting outcomes here; you will be rewarded for acknowledging this fact.

Question 4

'In a word, the Queen could by prerogative upset all the action of civil government within the government, could disgrace the nation by a bad war or peace, and could, by disbanding our forces, whether land or sea, leave us defenceless against foreign nations.' Walter Bagehot, *The English Constitution* (1963), London: Fontana.

Discuss the relevance of the prerogative powers held by the monarch to the modern constitution.

Answer plan

→ Define the prerogative, and briefly outline the historical development of the power within the constitution.

→ Outline the powers thought to be personal to the monarch.

→ Discuss the limitations upon those powers created by convention.

→ Analyse hypothetical situations in which it is said the monarch may play a decisive role.

Diagram plan

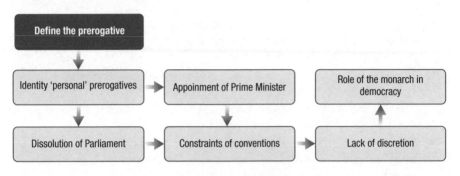

A printable version of this diagram is available from www.pearsoned.co.uk/lawexpressqa

Answer

[1]Blackstone's definition is usually the starting point for a discussion of the prerogative. If you cannot remember the quote, you do need to make sure that you are able to paraphrase the definition. The key point is that the prerogative is a non-legal power.

[2]This is an important point to make, as the relationship between the two 'non-legal' sources of the constitution needs to be explored.

[3]A strong introduction should signal the direction that the argument is going to take.

[4]It is very important to note that the prerogative is exercised without parliamentary approval as this emphasises the special constitutional position of the power.

The Royal prerogative was defined by Blackstone as 'that special pre-eminence which the King has, over and above all other persons, and out of the ordinary course of the common law, in right of his royal dignity'.[1] Prerogative powers are still an important source of constitutional power, although few are considered to be within the personal discretion of the monarch. Powers that are personal to the crown are often constrained by convention to such an extent that it is questionable whether any discretion really exists.[2] Constitutional theorists have hypothesised about situations in which the Queen may be called upon to play a more decisive role in the organisation of the state, but it will be suggested that recent events have demonstrated that the monarch's prerogative is effectively symbolic.[3]

The Bill of Rights of 1689 can be seen as the historical origin of the supremacy of Parliament, and since that point, many of the prerogative powers have been abolished or superseded by statute. Prerogative powers, then, can be described as the residual powers of the state that are not governed by legislation and do not require authorisation by Parliament.[4] They include important matters of governance: the disposition of the armed forces; regulation of the armed forces; the grant of honours; diplomatic relations and making treaties; the appointment of the Prime Minister and the dissolution of Parliament. The majority of powers are now exercisable by the government of the day acting in the name of the Crown. The Queen retains the personal power to grant certain honours, to assent to Bills passed by Parliament, to appoint the Prime Minister, and to dissolve Parliament.

[5]This is an important point to make, as the fact the monarch does not have a democratic mandate supports the argument that the role is necessarily symbolic.

In a modern democratic state, it would be anachronistic if an unelected monarch were to enjoy free reign to choose the government or to determine the duration of Parliament.[5] The discretion of the monarch is constrained by the operation of constitutional conventions which determine how it will be exercised. The dissolution of Parliament results in a general election, but by convention, the power is exercised at the request of the Prime Minister.[6] The Crown has not dissolved Parliament on its own initiative since 1835. Dicey maintained that the power remained and could be exercised in circumstances where the legislature no longer acted in accordance with the 'wishes of the nation' (Dicey, A. *The Law of the Constitution* (1885) London: Macmillan, p. 443). It is, however, almost impossible to imagine a situation in which the monarch could lay greater claim to represent the electorate than the House of Commons. Bagehot asserted that the possibility of a dissolution instigated by the Crown had 'dropped out of the reality of our constitution' (*The English Constitution*, p. 230), and it is submitted this is the more tenable argument.[7]

[6]The relationship between the prerogative and conventions is central to the argument, and the answer should be able to provide illustration of how this operates in practice.

[7]A confident approach will be able to include opposing academic arguments, and to draw some conclusions about the merits of the different views.

Bagehot described the constitutional role as to consult, to encourage, and to warn. It would appear that the monarch plays no significant role in taking a political decision. Bradley and Ewing note that it is recorded that both George V and George VI often insisted on being given the advice of Cabinet in writing if it dealt with contentious issues, suggesting a more active, supervisory, interest in the matters of state (*Constitutional and Administrative Law* (14th edn, 2008) London: Pearson, p. 246). More recently, the Queen's private secretary clarified his view that whilst the monarch may express opinions to the Prime Minister, ultimately, she is bound to act on government advice[8] (*The Times*, 29 July 1986). The monarch has the power to refuse to grant Royal Assent to a Bill, but in practice, this has not taken place since 1704. Jennings maintained that George V believed he had both the legal and constitutional right to refuse assent but recognised that, were this to occur, this would inevitably result in the dissolution of Parliament and an election contested largely on the issue of the extent of royal power.

[8]As there is little case law in this area, the use of examples to illustrate the points made shows a good grasp of the material.

[9]Here, the answer returns to the central argument, that conventions mean the personal prerogative of the monarch has little real effect.

[10]It is important to recognise the range of opinion in this area, and you will need to ensure that you are familiar with the views of at least two academics.

[11]Professor Bognador is one of the leading constitutional lawyers and this is a good point to include, as it demonstrates familiarity with his work.

[12]Reference to these guidelines shows familiarity with the current constitutional position.

[13]It is a fairly commonplace assertion to state that the monarch's constitutional role is symbolic; but can be made more convincing by providing an example.

The monarch is also empowered to appoint a Prime Minister. Again, this should not be misconstrued as conferring freedom of choice upon the Queen. By convention, the monarch will always appoint the person most able to command a majority in the House of Commons.[9] In the first past the post electoral system, this is generally straightforward and requires the appointment of the leader of the political party who obtain the most seats at a general election. There has been considerable academic debate about the appropriate course of action that should occur in circumstances where an election does not produce a clear majority for any party, as, in the absence of a written constitution, it could be suggested that the rules are unclear.[10] Bognador suggested in 1986 that the situation would raise 'major constitutional questions', although by 2008, he had resiled from that view and considered the matter to be a purely political issue[11] (cited in House of Commons paper 'Hung Parliament': www.parliament.uk/documents/commons/lib/research/briefings/snpc-04951.pdf). Brazier felt that the Queen should, in all but the most extreme of circumstances, refrain from involvement in the decision-making process, but did seem prepared to countenance the (albeit remote) possibility that the monarch may need to take action if no political solution could be found. (Brazier, R. *Constitutional Practice* (3rd edn, 1999) Oxford: Oxford University Press). Blackburn argued that any suggestion that the monarch would have a role to play in the event of a hung Parliament was erroneous, and anachronistic.

Prior to the election of 2010, the Cabinet Office published draft guidelines seeking to clarify the position, as the polls suggested that a hung Parliament was likely.[12] It was acknowledged that the monarch would invite the person most likely to be able to command the confidence of the Commons to form a government. It was, however, for the political parties to determine and to clearly communicate to the monarch who that person should be. The guidelines went on to stress that, where a range of possible administrations existed, it would be for the political parties to reach agreement and the monarch would 'not expect' to play a part in deliberations.

In the event, none of the main political parties achieved an overall majority, and negotiations did have to take place to see how a government could be formed. The monarch played no part in negotiations, and appointed the leader of the Coalition government, David Cameron, when asked to do so. This would appear to confirm that, despite academic hypothesising, the exercise of the prerogative power to appoint the Prime Minister is a purely symbolic event.[13]

[14]You will be rewarded for being able to make this kind of assertion as it shows that you are confident enough with the subject-matter to draw your own conclusions.

It could, conceivably, be argued that the extreme position posited by Brazier did not, in fact, arise, as the political parties were able to negotiate to form an administration in a relatively short period of time. It is submitted, however, that the matter is now settled, and the guidelines set out in draft will become constitutional practice.[14]

[15]Here, the answer returns to the suggestion made in the introduction but, having set out the arguments, a clear and certain conclusion can be articulated.

Perhaps Blackburn is correct to criticise continued usage of the term 'personal prerogative', as it appears clear that the monarch does not retain any residual powers involving the exercise of discretion. The constitutional relevance of the monarch is now minimal, as the Queen is simply a figurehead of state.[15]

✓ Make your answer stand out

■ Arguably, the publication of Cabinet Office guidance represents a move towards codification of conventions. You could consider whether or not this can be seen as a signal that the 'flexibility' of the constitution is diminishing and the extent of the personal prerogative will become more certain. This would link your answer into broader issues concerning constitutional reform and demonstrate the ability to draw links between different areas of the syllabus.

■ By considering some constitutional justifications for reserving the personal prerogative in more detail. You could link this to consideration of the rule of law, and the suggestion that, in the final analysis, the monarch may provide protection against arbitrary government. Again, this shows the confidence to place the discussion into a broader context.

! Don't be tempted to...

■ Make unsupported statements of opinion. This question requires you to use academic viewpoints to support the points that are made. There are, as this answer shows, numerous sources that you can refer to. You must make sure that you are able to refer to a number, and it is advisable to try to reference academics with contrasting views (such as Brazier and Blackburn) because this means you can provide support for both sides of the argument.

■ Discuss the prerogative in general terms; it is crucial that the answer focuses exclusively on the issue of the powers that are said to be personal to the monarch. It is more usual to be asked to consider the use of prerogative powers by the executive; you must make sure that you address the question asked here.

Judicial review

4

How this topic may come up in exams

Judicial review is often examined by means of problem scenarios requiring you to provide advice to a hypothetical client, or clients. Most problem questions can be tackled in a similar way, by employing a logically structured approach. Although the amount of case law can be intimidating, answers are improved by demonstrating a solid understanding of the procedures necessary to bring a claim. Essay questions will generally require an evaluation of the effectiveness of judicial review; this often overlaps with the topic of separation of powers and the ability of the judiciary to restrain the arbitrary use of executive power.

Attack the question

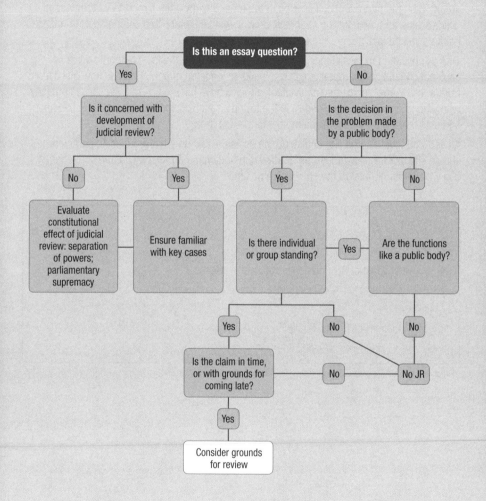

? Question 1

Tina belongs to an environmental pressure group, called Earthwatch. The local authority is empowered by the (Fictitious) Green Act 2010 to award grants to improve the environment in the local area. Tina applies for a grant to purchase equipment to dig irrigation channels around her land to prevent soil erosion in the area. She includes a report by Earthwatch, which states that, without the channels, erosion will take place and some important insect habitats will be lost.

Tina's application for assistance is rejected. The letter from the local authority gives no explanation, and states that she has six weeks to lodge an appeal. Tina has now discovered from a newspaper report that all available monies have been given to a Japanese company who plan to open a recycling centre in the locality. Tina believes that the decision has been taken as there will be increased employment in the area.

Advise Tina whether she can challenge the decision, and on what grounds. In particular, should she ask for assistance from Earthwatch and would it make any difference whether she was within or outside the six-week time limit?

Answer plan

→ Briefly explain the purpose of judicial review.

→ Consider whether the decision is subject to review.

→ Assess the probability of being deemed to have sufficient interest individually, and as a group.

→ Assess the effect of the time limit.

→ Discuss the possible grounds for review.

Diagram plan

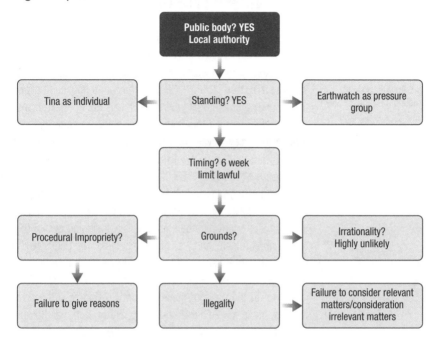

A printable version of this diagram is available from www.pearsoned.co.uk/lawexpressqa

Answer

[1]All problem scenarios concerning judicial review can be introduced by a brief explanation of the purpose of judicial review.

[2]As the decision is made by the local authority, there is no need to discuss how the court approaches decisions made by an organisation that may not be automatically considered to be a public body. This is not an issue in the question, and a confident answer will be able to focus on the aspects of judicial review relevant to the scenario given.

Tina could consider challenging the decision by way of judicial review. Judicial review is a mechanism for scrutinising the decisions made by public bodies to ensure that they have been reached properly, within the limits of the authority granted by statute or the prerogative. Judicial review will not assess the merits of the decision, thereby differing from an appeal; a successful application may result in the decision-maker having to start the process again.[1]

Judicial review is not an automatic right, and Tina will have to obtain leave of the court to make her application.

First, only decisions made by public bodies are reviewable. This is unproblematic as the decision is made by the local authority.[2]

Secondly, Tina must demonstrate that she has sufficient interest in the matter complained of, pursuant to s 31 of the Senior Courts Act 1981. As an individual who directly affected by the decision, this is straightforward. Should she wish to ask Earthwatch to conduct the application for her the situation may be more complex. Earthwatch is classed as a pressure group, and the group would need to be able to show that, despite the fact that many of their members would not be directly affected, they still have standing. In **R v Secretary of State for the Environment ex parte Rose Theatre Trust Co** [1990] 1 QB 504, the courts refused to allow the trust standing stating that where individuals did not have standing, the fact they banded together in large numbers could not confer it upon them collectively. However, in other cases the courts have taken a different view: **R v Inspectorate of Pollution ex parte Greenpeace** [1994] 4 All ER 321.[3] In that case, the courts granted standing to Greenpeace in respect of a decision taking regarding the nuclear power plant at Sellafield, on the basis that the organisation had significant membership (crucially including over 2,000 in the Cumbria region), and was highly reputable. The courts held that the group, with its access to legal and scientific expertise, could mount a better and more focused challenge than any individual member. On the basis of these authorities, Tina could be advised that, as she is a member of the group, Earthwatch may be able to assert that they have standing on similar grounds.

Lastly, application for judicial review must be made promptly, and in any event not more than three months after the decision complained of (Civil Procedure Rules, r 54). The courts have considered whether or not the time limit can be foreshortened in the power given to the authority, as the Act purports to do here. The case of **R v Secretary of State for the Environment ex parte Ostler** [1977] QB 122 remains binding authority for the proposition that such a limitation is valid and lawful. If Tina is outside of the six-week time limit, she would have to ask the court to exercise their inherent discretion to extend the limitation. In determining whether to exercise discretion the courts would consider whether the claimant has a reasonable objective excuse for coming late, the prejudice or hardship to third party rights and good administration in allowing the application, and whether or not the public interest required a review. She could argue that leave should be granted outside of that period on the basis that she was unaware of the crucial and relevant evidence regarding the proposed recycling centre, giving an objective reason for the late application.[4]

[3]As the problem specifically asks the answer to consider the role of the pressure group, it is worth spending some time outlining the contrasting authorities. Given that the issue is highlighted in the question, it seems likely that marks will be given for demonstrating knowledge of this aspect of the subject.

[4]It is not sufficient to state the legal principles, these must be used to draw some conclusions about the likely outcome for Tina.

If Tina is successful in obtaining leave, the courts will go on to consider grounds for judicial review. The grounds were listed in the leading case of **Council of Civil Service Unions v Minister for the Civil Service** [1985] AC 374 as irrationality, procedural impropriety or illegality. Arguably, with the incorporation of the European Convention of Human Rights into domestic law, proportionality should now also be considered as a ground.

⁵Marks will be given for recognising that there are several different grounds that the application could be based on here.

There are several grounds which could be relevant in this case.[5]

⁶Often, students spend too much time explaining matters that are not relevant. Here, the answer is able to demonstrate an understanding of irrationality, but also confidence in quickly dismissing it.

Irrationality is unlikely to be relevant, as the courts apply the test of *Wednesbury* unreasonableness (**Associated Provincial Picture Houses Ltd v Wednesbury Corporation** [1948] 1 KB 223) and must find that the decision is so illogical that no reasonable decision-maker could have arrived at it. This is a high hurdle for any applicant to reach and irrationality is rarely found as a ground.[6]

Tina may wish to argue that there is a procedural impropriety as no reasons have been given for the decision. Where a power specifies that reasons must be given, failure to do so is clearly a procedural impropriety. Even if the Act does not impose that requirement, it could nonetheless be argued the absence of reasons is a procedural impropriety as it is a breach of natural justice. The courts have accepted that there is no common law duty to disclose reasons, but where none are disclosed, it may lead the court to feel no adequate reasons exist (**Padfield v Minister of Agriculture, Food and Fisheries** [1968] AC 997).

⁷This is a useful case, as it can be used to explain several different heads of illegality. Here, the case can be used as authority for two grounds; failure to take into account relevant considerations, and taking into account irrelevant matters.

Tina could also seek to argue that the decision is reviewable under one of the heads of illegality. She may seek to argue that local authority has failed to take into account relevant considerations (the environmental impact as outlined in Earthwatch's report). In the case of **R v Secretary of State for the Home Department ex parte Venables** [1988] AC 407,[7] the Home Secretary's decision to extend the sentence tariff for two juvenile offenders was bad, as he had failed to take into account the progress made in custody – a mandatory requirement in the power given to him. In this instance, the Act does specify grants must be made to benefit the environment. If Tina can show that the key motivation for the decision was to increase employment in the area, she could argue this is an irrelevant consideration; where the power specifies the relevant considerations, the decision-maker is not permitted to consider other matters. In the

Venables case, the Home Secretary allowed his decision to be influenced by public opinion, which was deemed irrelevant.

Tina may feel that the discretion has been exercised for an improper purpose; to obtain an economic benefit. If this can be demonstrated, the decision will be rendered illegal, as in the case of **Porter v Magill** [2001] UKHL 67, where the decision to sell council property was not for a proper purpose under the Housing Act, but to gain electoral advantage. The local authority must exercise discretion to improve the environment, not for economic gain.

[8]As the question has specifically asked for a focus on matters to do with obtaining leave, and the grounds for review, there is no need to expand on the available remedies.

If Tina is successful in proving there are grounds for review, the court will then consider what, if any remedies are applicable. It seems likely that the court would grant a quashing order to revoke the original decision, and an order for mandamus to force the local authority to take the decision again.[8]

 Make your answer stand out

- By acknowledging the fact that it is difficult to predict accurately whether the courts will grant an application on particular grounds. The authorities appear to show that decisions are taken on a case-by-case basis and you could advise Tina of this. This approach could show the examiner that you understand how legal principles operate in practice.

- By incorporating additional case law when dealing with relevant and irrelevant considerations. There are numerous cases that could be addressed here and you could seek to make the point that the authority only need to demonstrate that they have considered the environmental impact report. Cases such as *Tesco Stores* v *Secretary of State for the Environment* [1995] 2 All ER 636 make it clear that the decision-maker is entitled to determine how much importance should be given to any one factor. This would show the examiner, first, that you are aware of a broad range of case law authorities, but also, secondly, that you understand some of the practical difficulties Tina faces in establishing grounds for review.

! **Don't be tempted to...**

- List all the grounds for review that you can remember. You will get more marks for being able to pick out a few that are applicable. It is always important to remember that marks are given for application of relevant law, but judicial review seems to be an area where students are particularly likely to tell the examiner everything they know. It can be daunting, because you don't want to miss a relevant ground. An answer that includes a discussion of two grounds that could be relevant but omits a third will get higher marks than an answer listing every possible ground without explaining how they are relevant.

- Examine the merits of the decision made by the authority. Students sometimes do make statements about whether or not Tina should have received the grant, but remember, you are only concerned with the procedure used to make the decision.

? Question 2

Manpreet lives in a village on the outskirts of Leeds, and her back garden looks over a nature reserve (Sleepyglade). It is very quiet and secluded.

In the summer of 2010, Manpreet goes away on holiday for two months. On her return, she finds a letter from her local authority which states:

'Planning permission has been granted for a bypass to be constructed between Leeds and Bradford. Permission has been granted by the Planning Committee pursuant to the powers contained in s 37 of the (fictitious) Local Town Planning Act:

> Local authorities are empowered to authorize planning permission for road building programmes in their area and must take account of the environmental impact of their plans. An outline of the proposals must be circulated as widely as possible in the local area for at least three months. If no objections are lodged, plans must be published and circulated to all those living within one mile on either side of the planned route, and any objections must be lodged within six weeks.'

Manpreet also finds a letter containing the plans which appears to have been posted one day after she left for her holiday. Finally, she finds a letter posted a week ago from the Nature Reservists, a campaign group, offering to assist any person wishing to challenge the plans. The plans show that the bypass will go past the end of Manpreet's garden and Sleepyglade will be destroyed; she wishes to challenge the decision.

Manpreet does not recall seeing the proposal outline anywhere before she went away. In fact, the council posted a notice in the office windows, and placed a half-page advert in the local newspaper.

Advise Manpreet of any action she can take.

Answer plan

→ Consider the issues relevant to leave; the timing and the role of the Nature Reservists.

→ Discuss the possible ground of procedural impropriety.

→ Discuss the possible ground of illegality.

→ Assess the strength of the claim.

Diagram plan

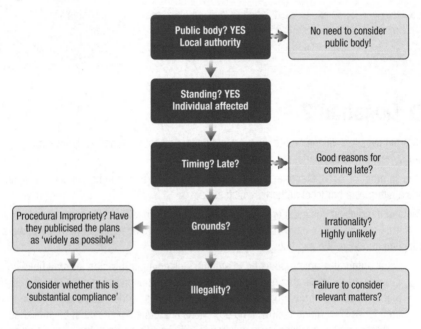

A printable version of this diagram is available from www.pearsoned.co.uk/lawexpressqa

Answer

[1]When revising, it is worth learning a definition of judicial review, as it will always be necessary to give a brief explanation.

Manpreet may consider seeking judicial review of the decision to build the road. Judicial review is the process by which the courts can scrutinise the decisions made by public bodies in the exercise of discretionary powers. Judicial review is not an appeal on the merits, but a means of ensuring that decisions are reached in a proper and fair manner.[1]

Judicial review is not an automatic right; Manpreet will need to obtain leave of the court. Only decisions made by a public body are subject to judicial review. The leave procedure is governed by the Senior Courts Act 1981, which requires that claims should be made promptly, and by a person with sufficient interest in the matter complained of (s 31). 'Promptly' is further defined by r 54 of the Civil Procedure Rules as within three months.

The local authority, as a branch of the executive, is a public body; making the decision capable of review. Although Manpreet is seeking advice within three months of the decision, s 37 states that appeals must be lodged within six weeks. **R v Secretary of State for the Environment ex parte Ostler** [1977] QB 122 is authority for the fact that partial ouster clauses of this nature are lawful, and therefore it is permissible for the council to set a shorter time limit.[2] Although Manpreet is late in lodging her claim, the court does have the discretion to allow a claim to be brought out of time provided there is a good reason (CPR 54(5)). In this instance, Manpreet may wish to argue that she was unaware of the application due to the failure to properly publicise the proposals and the fact she was away when the letter was sent. However, Manpreet should be advised that even where there is good reason, the courts may refuse a late application if this would cause administrative difficulties or prejudice to third party interest (**R v Dairy Produce Quota Tribunal for England and Wales ex parte Caswell** [1990] 2 AC 738).[3]

The next issue to consider would be whether or not Manpreet will be deemed to have sufficient interest in the matter complained of (*locus standi*). This would appear straightforward, as she will be able to argue that she is an individual directly affected by the decision. It would be open to Manpreet to consider asking the Nature Reservists to bring the claim instead. There are cases in which 'pressure groups' have been awarded standing. In **R v Inspectorate of Pollution ex parte Greenpeace** [1994] 4 All ER 321,[4] factors to consider were held to include the expertise and resources of the group, the absence of other challengers, and the public importance of the issue. A factor that appeared to be of relevance in that case was the fact that members of the organisation did have individual standing. It would seem arguable that the Nature Reservists could claim standing as they do represent the interests

[2]As the excerpt from the statute is set out for you, your examiner clearly expects that you will notice and explain the partial ouster clause.

[3]It is hard to give Manpreet clear advice, as there are a number of variables. Marks will be given for acknowledging this.

[4]There are a number of cases that could be used to give examples of standing being given to a group, but this is the leading authority and should definitely be mentioned.

of individuals affected by the council's actions and may be better placed to bring the claim than any single resident of the area.

If permission to bring the claim is granted, it will be necessary to assess whether or not there are grounds upon which the decision can be challenged. Lord Diplock reiterated the main grounds in **Council of Civil Service Unions v Minister for Civil Service** [1985] AC 374 as illegality, irrationality and procedural impropriety. The most likely grounds would seem to be procedural impropriety and illegality.[5]

[5]Stating the appropriate grounds shows an ability to focus on the important issues and to reach appropriate conclusions.

Where a power conferred by statute imposes a requirement to follow a procedure, failure to comply may invalidate the decision. In this case, Manpreet may seek to argue that the notice in the council windows, and the newspaper advert, do not meet the need to publicise the proposals 'as widely as possible'.[6] Following **R v Immigration Appeal Tribunal ex parte Jeyeanthan** it seems that the key concern for the court will be whether or not there has been substantial compliance, and if so, whether or not strict compliance can be waived. This will require the court to consider the consequence of non-compliance in the particular case. Although failure to consult as directed can render a decision unlawful, it is not clear whether or not there were representations made to, and considered by, the council from individuals who did see the notice.[7]

[6]The question contained the relevant wording of the statute, and this is for a reason; your examiner is expecting you to consider the precise meaning of the words used.

[7]This part of the answer does use the authorities to assess the merits of Manpreet's case, and does not make the mistake of stating that a particular outcome is certain when additional information would be needed before firm conclusions could be reached.

The second potential ground for judicial review would be one of the heads of illegality. Here, the power granted to the council confers an obligation to take into account the relevant consideration of impact upon the environment. It will, therefore, be mandatory for the council to demonstrate that consideration has been given to the impact of the destruction of the nature reserve. A failure to take into account relevant matters can render a decision unlawful. However, Manpreet should be advised that provided the council can show that the issue was raised; it is for the body exercising the discretion to determine what weight to give to the particular consideration specified in the power.[8] (**Tesco Stores Ltd v Secretary of State for the Environment** [1995] 2 All ER 636.)

[8]It is important not to speculate too much here. There is no information available about how the decision was reached. It is better to advise Manpreet of possible difficulties.

[9]More marks will be given for noting that not many grounds are applicable than for listing lots of grounds that are not, realistically, going to be used. This shows more confidence with the material.

Assuming that the council can show evidence that an assessment was made of the environmental impact, then there are few other grounds which would appear to be readily available.[9] Manpreet may wish to argue that the decision is irrational, although further evidence would be needed to support this ground. Irrationality is assessed using the principle of '*Wednesbury* unreasonableness'(**Associated Provincial Picture Houses Ltd v Wednesbury Corporation** [1948] I KB 223); a decision will be irrational if it is one that no reasonable decision-maker could have reached. This has been confirmed in later case law including by Lord Scarman in **Nottinghamshire County Council v Secretary of State for the Environment** [1986] AC 240, in which he stated that the action complained of would need to be 'verging on absurdity'. This is an extremely difficult ground to argue, and rarely succeeds.

[10]It can be daunting to conclude by stating that the advice cannot be definite. However, as the essay has demonstrated an awareness of the legal complexities, this is a more confident approach.

Manpreet may be able to bring a claim for judicial review despite the fact that, on the face of it, she is out of time, if the court is minded to exercise the discretion to allow a late claim. Standing is not problematic, and she may be able to ask the Nature Reservists to bring the claim. It is not possible to give clear advice on the likely outcome, as further information would be needed to determine the strength of the available grounds.[10] Manpreet should be mindful of the fact that, if successful, this may not prevent the eventual construction of the road as the effect of any remedy in judicial review is to require the decision-maker to follow the correct procedure. The eventual decision arrived at may be the same.

✓ Make your answer stand out

- By considering some additional cases regarding relevant and irrelevant considerations. You could discuss the case of *R v Somerset County Council ex parte Fewings* [1995] 3 All ER 20. This is a useful authority to quote because the judgment addresses the difficulty in distinguishing between the grounds of relevant/irrelevant considerations and acting for an improper purpose. This would show the examiner that you are able to address the 'grey' areas of the law.

- By including some more detailed discussion of the requirement to publicise the plans. You might wish to argue that this imposes a mandatory duty of consultation on the local authority. A good authority to use here would be *R v Secretary of State for Social Security ex parte Association of Metropolitan Authorities* (1992) 25 HLR 131, in which a decision was invalidated for lack of consultation. This would show an ability to draw parallels between cases even where they are not directly analogous.

! Don't be tempted to...

■ Give detailed information about the facts of the cases mentioned. Marks are given for showing an understanding of the *ratio*, and an ability to apply this to the scenario given. For example, there is no need to tell your examiner anything about the facts of *Jeyeanthan*. In order to explain the facts, you would need to be able to remember a lot of detail about immigration law, and it would take up quite a lot of space in your answer. There is a lot of case law in this area, and you need to be able to refer to a substantial amount of cases in order to do well, so make sure your revision concentrates on the ratios rather than the facts.

■ Incorporate advice regarding the classification of a public body. There is no need to discuss the distinction between *R* v *Panel on Takeovers and Mergers ex parte Datafin plc* [1987] 2 WLR 69 and *R* v *Disciplinary Committee of the Jockey Club ex parte Aga Khan* [1993] 1 WLR 909 in this kind of question, where the decision-making authority is clearly a public body. A good answer will see what areas of discussion are highlighted by the question, rather than trying to provide an exhaustive account of the topic.

❓ Question 3

The (fictitious) Regulation of Independent Traders Act 2006 introduces a requirement for all window cleaners to be licensed by local authorities.

When the act comes into force, Tommy, who has had a window cleaning round in Pretshire for four years, applies for a licence. His application is turned down.

He checks the Act. Section 33 states that applicants have eight weeks to appeal against the refusal of a licence. It further specifies that appeals should be dealt with at an oral hearing in front of the council's committee for licensing.

Tommy submits his appeal, and receives a date for his hearing. He attends, and takes with him a bundle of references from satisfied customers. The local authority is overwhelmed with appeals, so appoint a number of subcommittees to deal with the hearings.

Tommy's hearing is chaired by Mr Jones. Mr Jones informs Tommy that he is unsuitable for a licence, as there have been a number of complaints made about him by customers. Mr Jones refuses to give Tommy details of the complaints, claiming this would breach data protection, and refuses to look at the references he has provided.

Two days later, Tommy receives a letter stating that the decision to refuse a licence has been upheld. No further details are given in the letter.

Two weeks later, he discovers that his old round is now being operated by Mrs Jones, the wife of the chairman of the subcommittee who dealt with his appeal.

Advise Tommy of any action he can take.

Answer plan

→ Confirm that the decision is subject to review.

→ Note the partial ouster clause and consider the effect.

→ Identify the possible grounds.

→ Discuss the difficulty in establishing bias and bad faith.

→ Discuss the court's approach to a failure to give reasons.

→ Draw some conclusions about the likelihood of success.

Diagram plan

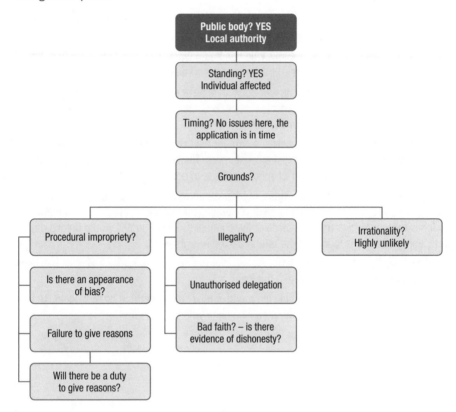

A printable version of this diagram is available from www.pearsoned.co.uk/lawexpressqa

Answer

Tommy should be advised to consider bringing an action for judicial review. Judicial review is the process by which the courts can scrutinise the decision-making process of public bodies. Judicial review differs from an appeal on the merits: a successful application will result in the public body having to undertake the decision-making procedure again.

Judicial review is not an automatic right and requires the permission of the court. The leave procedure is governed by s 31 of the Senior Courts Act 1981, which stipulates that claims must be lodged promptly, by a person with sufficient interest in the matter complained of.

[1]There is no need to waste space on elements of the judicial review procedure that are unproblematic in the given scenario, but you have worked through each stage.

A claim can only lie against a public body exercising discretionary decision-making powers. This is unproblematic as the decision is made by a local authority in pursuance of powers conferred by statute.[1]

[2]As the problem refers to a partial ouster clause is mentioned, it should be dealt with but a confident answer will be able to give clear advice about this.

The Civil Procedure Rules state that all claims must be brought within three months (r 54). Section 33 of the Act in this problem limits the time for bringing an appeal to eight weeks. This is lawful, on the authority of **R v Secretary of State for the Environment ex parte Ostler** [1977] QB 122, which confirms that partial ouster clauses are acceptable. In any event, it does seem that Tommy lodges the initial appeal within time. There is nothing in the scenario to indicate how long ago the letter refusing the appeal was received, but it would seem that, as that is the decision complained of, he would have three months from that date in which to lodge his claim.[2]

[3]Marks are given for explaining that standing is needed, but there is no need to spend time on this issue, as it is clear Tommy satisfies the requirement.

The requirement that the claimant demonstrate sufficient interest (*locus standi*) also seems straightforward. A person who is directly affected by the decision is eligible and Tommy satisfies this requirement.[3]

[4]Judicial review problems can focus on different aspects of the topic. This scenario does not raise any contentious issues about the leave procedure, so this can be dealt with quickly to allow time to focus on detailed discussion of the possible grounds.

It would seem likely that Tommy will be granted permission to bring a claim for judicial review and consideration can be given to whether or not there are good grounds.[4] The grounds for judicial review were listed by Lord Diplock in **Council of Civil Service Unions v Minister for the Civil Service** [1985] AC 374 as illegality, irrationality and procedural impropriety. There would seem to be a number of potential grounds in this instance.

First, it may be possible to argue that the decision is illegal. There are a number of circumstances in which a public body may act illegally in reaching a decision. The decision must be taken by the person or body authorised to do so. We are told that the authority creates subcommittees to deal with the volume of applications. There does not appear to be anything in the act which allows for this delegation. As in **Barnard v National Dock Labour Board** [1953] 2 QB 18, it appears this decision may be invalid, as it results from an unauthorised delegation.[5]

[5]It is not necessary to give any details about this case. Reference is only required to demonstrate that there is an authority to support the conclusion that unauthorised delegation is unlawful.

The most worrying aspect of this scenario may be the indication that Mr Jones has refused Tommy's application for no other reason than to grant the licence to his wife, as it may have been made in 'bad faith'. This is a serious charge to level at a public authority. The authorities are clear that 'bad faith' means dishonesty (**Cannock Chase District Council v Kelly** [1978] 1 All ER 152) and there is a high evidential burden on the claimant. Later case law makes it clear that dishonesty does not necessarily require proof that the decision-maker acted for financial gain; it will suffice if they are aware that their behaviour is unlawful (**Watkins v Secretary of State for the Home Department** [2006] UKHL 17). Here, it seems that there may be an arguable case.[6]

[6]It is important that you don't make the mistake of assuming that bad faith is an easy ground to argue – you do need to spell out what the cases show will need to be proved.

It certainly would appear that the hearing itself was flawed, and Tommy may therefore be able to argue that the decision was reached following procedural impropriety. This head of judicial review incorporates the requirements of natural justice at common law which include the need for a fair hearing and the absence of bias.[7] This is a long-established ground for judicial review. For example, **Ridge v Baldwin** [1964] AC 40 found against the Police Authority who dismissed a Chief Constable at a private hearing without giving him the opportunity to answer the charges levelled against him. This bears analogy with the situation here, where Mr Jones refuses to disclose the substance of the complaints against Tommy; thereby rendering it impossible for him to rebut them.[8]

[7]Sometimes students make the mistake of ignoring the issue of natural justice, concentrating instead on types of illegality such as bad faith or improper purpose. This problem does require a detailed discussion of bias, and the need for a fair hearing.

[8]This is an example of an instance in which it is helpful to briefly summarise the facts of a case, because they are similar to the facts given. This makes it more likely that the authority would be followed.

Tommy may also be aggrieved that no reasons were given to him for the refusal. A failure to give reasons will not automatically create procedural impropriety (unless mandatory because specified in statute). The courts have shown an increasing willingness to infer

[9]It is important to have some case law authorities to illustrate how this ground is applied, as this enables a conclusion to be reached about this aspect of Tommy's claim.

a requirement to give reasons in cases where a person's liberty is at stake (**R v Secretary of State ex parte Doody** [1994] 1 AC 531), or where the body is exercising a judicial function (**R v Civil Service Appeal Board ex parte Cunningham** [1991] 4 All ER 310). It does not appear that this would be such a case.[9]

Natural justice also demands that the decision-maker is free from any suggestion of bias. Tommy may seek to argue that there has been procedural impropriety here as a result of Mrs Jones's application for a licence and the conflict of interests this creates. It is not necessary to demonstrate that actual bias existed. Although there has been some judicial uncertainty about the precise requirements, the decision in **Porter v Magill** [2001] 1 WLR 700 confirmed that the correct question would be to ask whether a fair minded observer would conclude there was a 'real possibility' of bias. Further, any person who sits in a judicial capacity should be automatically disqualified from making any decision in which they have a pecuniary interest. There is no need to prove that the decision-maker did in fact profit, the mere appearance of bias is sufficient for 'justice must not only be done, it must be seen to be done' (**R v Sussex Justices ex parte McCarthy** [1923] All ER 233).[10] There would appear to be the possibility of bias here.

[10]Whilst it may be unrealistic to learn a large number of quotations, this is a famous maxim and worth remembering.

[11]In some scenarios it is hard to give clear advice. Here, there are clearly some good grounds, and this can be confidently stated.

It appears that Tommy should be advised that he can make an application for judicial review of the local authority's decision and that there would appear to be good grounds for the claim. The clearest argument appears to be that the decision was reached following an unauthorised delegation and in circumstances that appear to be biased.[11]

If successful, Tommy will be granted a remedy. This may include damages but this is not automatic. The most likely remedy would be a quashing order, rendering the initial decision null and void and therefore requiring a new decision-making process to commence.

Make your answer stand out

■ By broadening the discussion regarding the issue of bias. The *Sussex* case is concerned with bias in a judicial context. Authority could be cited to show that a financial interest on the part of a decision-maker has been held to be biased (*R* v *Hendon RDC ex parte Chorley* [1933] 2 KB 696).

■ By incorporating some academic comment on the legal issues raised. You could consider Goudkamp, J., 'Facing up to actual bias' (2008) CJQ 32, which suggests that litigants should be bolder in asserting actual, rather than the appearance of, bias in appropriate cases (albeit in the context of judicial bias). You could use this to argue that Tommy should consider drafting his claim in those terms given the facts of this scenario. This would show the examiner that you are able to reflect on academic opinion, and use this to assist you in formulating advice.

! **Don't be tempted to...**

■ Speculate about facts not given in the scenario. A weak answer might state as a matter of fact that Mr Jones is profiting from the operation of the window round. The problem does not make this clear and a good lawyer never makes assumptions!

■ Fail to use the authorities cited to reach conclusions. This answer has been clear about gathering evidence from the authorities in order to make some specific points about Tommy's case. For example, it is useful to state that, following *Doody* and *Cunningham,* the court may infer a duty to give reasons in cases involving liberty or the exercise of a judicial function. However, the information is only useful if it informs your conclusions about the likely outcome here.

Question 4

In the last 25 years, judicial review has developed as a formidable means of controlling the use of executive power and providing the citizen with redress.

Discuss.

Answer plan

→ Explain the process of judicial review.

→ Explain the relationship between judicial review and the separation of powers.

→ Identify significant changes in the specified time period including the *GCHQ case*, and the introduction of the Human Rights Act 1998.

→ Consider arguments for and against the suggestion that judicial review is an effective method of controlling the executive.

→ Analyse any problems for the citizen in obtaining review.

Diagram plan

A printable version of this diagram is available from www.pearsoned.co.uk/lawexpressqa

Answer

[1]This question is not about the mechanics of judicial review, but rather, its constitutional role. Therefore, the introduction should make clear that the focus of the question has been understood.

Judicial review is the means by which the decision-making processes of the executive can be scrutinised and declared to be incorrect. Therefore, judicial review can be seen as a powerful tool allowing the judiciary to hold the executive to account. It could be argued that this is part of the system of checks and balances that exist between the organs of state to ensure a functional separation of powers, strengthening the constitutional arrangements of the United Kingdom and ensuring that the citizen is protected from the risk of the abuse of discretionary powers.[1] However, this must be balanced against the limitations that the judiciary accept upon their powers of review, and the difficulties which face the individual wishing to bring a claim.

The right of the court to review the actions of the executive is one that the judiciary robustly defend. The decision in **Ansiminic Ltd v Foreign Compensation Commission** [1969] 2 AC 147 confirmed that any discretionary power which purports to deny the right of judicial review will be declared unlawful. More recently, in *obiter* comments, the Lords suggested that if Parliament passed an Act abolishing judicial review, the judiciary may countenance the constitutionally unprecedented step of refusing to apply an Act of Parliament (**R (Jackson) v Attorney General** [2005] UKHL 56).[2] The constitutional importance of the procedure, then, is clear.

The mid-1980s can be selected as a starting point for an analysis of the function and scope of judicial review in modern times, as the seminal case **Council of Civil Service Unions v Minister for the Civil Service** [1985] AC 374 (GCHQ case) signalled a shift in the attitude of the judiciary towards the crown.[3] Previously, there had been an acceptance that the courts had no power to examine the exercise of a prerogative power, and the role of the judiciary would be limited to determining whether a claimed prerogative did indeed exist. This had the effect of ensuring that the exercise of all discretionary power by the executive can be examined and held to account, whether it derives from the prerogative or is delegated by statute. It is important to recognise, however, that the courts continued to accept that not every action of the government could be scrutinised, as 'excluded categories' remained. These included matters pertaining to the signing of treaties, foreign affairs, the prerogative of mercy, and issues affecting national security. The rationale for the existence of excluded categories is that certain matters of 'high policy' are for determination by the Crown and therefore judicial interference threatens the separation of powers.[4]

Since the decision in the **GCHQ case**, it is possible to argue that the courts have grown more willing to review the exercise of powers in a broader range of areas. For example, in **R v Secretary of State for Foreign Affairs ex parte Everett** [1989] QB 811, it was held that the issue of passports (previously considered to fall within the area of foreign affairs) is reviewable. The exercise of the prerogative of mercy has been reviewed on more than

[2]This is an important authority to cite, but you must make sure that you note the comments are obiter to avoid giving the examiner the impression that you believe that this is a reality, rather than a hypothesis.

[3]By asking for consideration of developments in the last 25 years, the question is inviting you to recognise the seminal *GCHQ case* as the starting point for discussion. It would be difficult to get good marks here without outlining the reasons why the case was so important.

[4]Here, the answer refers back to the constitutional considerations outlined in the introduction, ensuring that the focus on the developing argument is maintained.

[5]There are a variety of different cases that could be referenced, but one or two examples are required to support the suggestion that judicial review can be said to be used more effectively to control the executive.

one occasion, including the case of **R v Secretary of State for the Home Department ex parte Bentley** [1994] QB 349. In **R v Ministry of Defence ex parte Smith** [1996] QB 517, the courts rejected the government assertion that a decision to exclude homosexuals from the armed services was non-justiciable, despite the fact it concerned disposition of the armed forces.[5] It can be argued, therefore, that in recent decades judicial review has taken on increased importance in ensuring that the executive utilises its powers correctly.

[6]Marks will be given for recognising that the *GCHQ case* has not resulted in review of all areas of executive action.

Nonetheless, it should be noted that the judiciary are unwilling to review the exercise of any government power which concern matters that are clearly concerned with national security or diplomatic relations.[6] Therefore, in the cases of **R (Abbasi) v Secretary of State for Foreign and Commonwealth Affairs and Secretary of State for the Home Department** [2002] All ER (D) 70 and **R (Al Rawi) v Foreign Secretary** [2007] 2 WLR 1219 the court refused to interfere with the decision by government not to make representations on behalf of detainees at Guantanamo Bay, and in the case brought by **CND v Prime Minister of the United Kingdom** [2002] All ER 245 the courts refused to interfere with the government's determination of the legal effect of the UN resolution.

[7]At this stage of the argument, having looked at some evidence, it is possible to refer back to the question and draw some preliminary conclusions.

Accordingly, the view that judicial review is able to control the use of executive power can only be given partial endorsement. The judiciary may not accept the existence of any non-justiciable categories, but deference to the executive remains to the extent that significant areas are still deemed to be the province of government.[7]

[8]The question raises two issues; the role of the courts in controlling the executive, and access to review for the citizen. The answer needs to ensure both matters are dealt with.

It is right to say that relatively few claims of judicial review will now be excluded on the basis that the subject-matter cannot be reviewed. The vast majority of cases do not touch on matters of government policy or the use of prerogative powers. However, it is not the case that every citizen seeking review of the exercise of a statutory discretion will be able to avail themselves of the assistance of the courts.[8] Judicial review is not a right, and permission of the court is required. It is not possible to consider every aspect of the leave procedure here, but some of the potentially problematic areas can be considered.[9]

[9]As it is not possible to discuss every aspect of review in the time allowed, it is helpful to set out the parameters of the discussion.

Only the actions of a public body are open to review, and further, only matters concerning public, rather than private law. This is not always a straightforward determination as the boundaries between public and private bodies, and indeed, public and private law, can be indistinct. This can be seen by looking at the distinctions between **R v Disciplinary Committee of the Jockey Club ex parte Aga Khan** [1993] 1 WLR 909 and **R v Panel on Takeovers and Mergers ex parte Datafin plc** [1987] 2 WLR 699. The Jockey Club was declared to be a private body even though it had broad powers to regulate an important activity. The Panel was held to be a public body despite the fact the organisation was not acting on behalf of the state. The claimant will need to satisfy the court that the body is exercising powers analogous to those available to the state, which may mean redress is unavailable in some cases.[10]

[10]You must keep returning to the question at the end of every point you make.

A claim will be excluded if it is brought out of time. It is fair to say that the three-month limit imposed by CPR (r 54) is not overly restrictive, and is indeed more generous than equivalent EU provisions, which allow for two months. However, partial ouster clauses are lawful (**R v Secretary of State for the Environment ex parte Ostler** [1977] QB 122), and these can make it difficult for an aggrieved citizen to lodge a claim. It will also be necessary to demonstrate 'sufficient interest' which can be viewed as a tool to exclude frivolous claims. However, the courts considered the meaning of sufficient interest in the case IRC, and concluded it was designed only to exclude 'mischief makers, busybodies and cranks', and therefore, the majority of individuals who can claim to be affected by a decision will be granted standing.

[11]When answering an essay question, you must ensure that you conclude by addressing the issues that you were specifically asked to discuss. You must be prepared to offer an opinion on the material you have outlined.

Judicial review is not capable of challenging every executive action, nor can it protect every citizen. As has been shown, despite an increasing willingness by the judiciary to examine the actions of the state, limitations remain. Nonetheless, it is right to say that the scope of judicial review has increased significantly since the **GCHQ case**, and there is a greater willingness by the courts to scrutinise the use of government powers.[11]

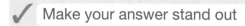

✓ Make your answer stand out

- By expanding the discussion about the sufficient interest test and suggesting it is less onerous than it once was. You could cite the case of *R (Edwards)* v *Environment Agency* [2004] EWHC 736 (Admin), in which it was held the applicant had sufficient interest in a decision despite evidence that suggested he had displayed little interest in the issue during a long consultation process. This could be used to support the argument that the test does not prevent interested parties from lodging a claim.

- By considering the effect of the Human Rights Act on the constitutional role of judicial review. Jowell, J., 'Beyond the rule of law: towards constitutional judicial review' [2000] PL 671–83 is a good starting point for additional reading. You could suggest that the HRA has resulted in a situation where judicial review is able to offer better protection for the citizen. This would show your examiner that you can see the connections between different areas of the syllabus.

- By outlining some of the contrasting academic argument about the role of judicial review in challenging legislation. Waldron has suggested that this poses a challenge to notions of democracy. Lever has rejected this argument. (Waldron, J., 'The core of the case against judicial review' (2006) 115 Yale Law Journal 1346, and Lever, A., 'Is judicial review undemocratic' [2007] PL 280–98). You must remember that it will not be enough to cite the views of academics, however, unless you use the arguments to answer the question your examiner has asked.

! Don't be tempted to...

- Provide statements about the role or effect of judicial review that you cannot support with authority, or examples. Marks cannot be given for unsupported opinion. A weaker answer might make the (valid) point that the judiciary will still defer to the executive when matters of foreign policy are in issue. More credit will be given to the student who can state that this can be ascertained from the decisions in *Abbasi*, or *Al Rawi*.

- Give a descriptive account of the process of judicial review. Students often expect this topic to appear as a problem scenario, and are therefore unprepared to engage in the kind of analysis needed here. Weak answers, then, tend to explain the various stages of the review process and outline the various grounds of a claim without using knowledge of the subject to offer an answer to the question. If you do not feel able to put together an argument about the role of judicial review, it would be better to avoid answering this question altogether.

❓ Question 5

Taylor wishes to open a bar in the Meanwood area of Leeds. He makes an application to Leeds City Council Licensing Committee for permission to sell alcohol for consumption on the premises. The Committee meets each month to consider applications, using the power delegated by the Licensing Act 2003, which provides, at s 4, that an application may be refused to comply with one of the following objectives:

(a) the prevention of crime and disorder;

(b) public safety;

(c) the prevention of public nuisance; and

(d) the protection of children from harm.

The Act further provides that any appeal against refusal of a licence must be made within four weeks.

Taylor is asked to address his application to Mr Greaves, the chair of the committee. Before posting the form, he decides to telephone Mr Greaves to make sure he has included everything relevant. During the course of the call, Mr Greaves tells Taylor not to worry, and that there are no reasons why the application should not be granted.

Two days after the committee meets Taylor recieves a letter which simply states that the application has been refused. He telephones the council to ask why, but is told that the minutes will be made publicly available online in two weeks. Five weeks later, the minutes are finally posted online with a note explaining they are late due to staff shortages. The minutes regarding Taylor's application state:

> The committee feels that there are too many bars in the area at present, and the commercial viability of existing licensed premises will be undermined if further applications are agreed.

Taylor seeks your advice about any action he can take.

Answer plan

- Explain the process of judicial review.
- Consider the problems raised by the timing of the application.
- Identify and assess the merits of the potential grounds.
- Draw some conclusions about the merits of Taylor's case.

Diagram plan

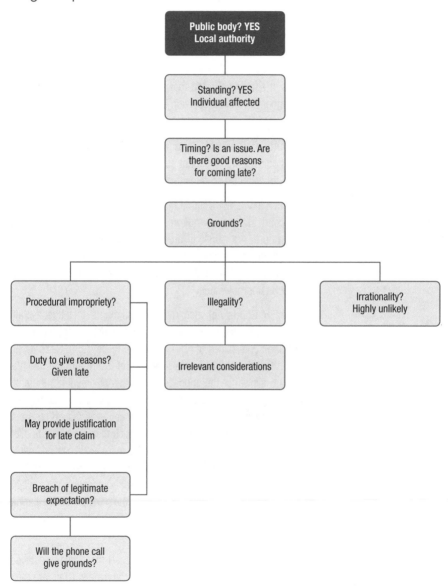

A printable version of this diagram is available from www.pearsoned.co.uk/lawexpressqa

Answer

Taylor should be advised to consider bringing a claim for judicial review of the decision not to grant a licence. Judicial review is the mechanism which allows the courts to scutinise the decision-making process of executive bodies exercising discretionary powers. It should be noted that a judicial review is concerned with the manner in which a decision is reached, and is not an appeal on the merits.

The courts are only able to judicially review decisions reached by public bodies. Here, the local authority is clearly acting as a public body in the exercise of delegated power.

[1] It is useful to show that all the requirements of the leave procedure are understood, but as standing is not problematic in this scenario, it should be dealt with swiftly.

Judicial review is not a right, and Taylor will need to seek the leave of the court. The leave requirements are now set out at s 31 of the Senior Courts Act 1981. In order to obtain leave, he will need to demonstrate that he has sufficient interest in the matter complained of (*locus standi*). Here, as he is directly affected by the decision then this will be unproblematic.[1]

The Senior Courts Act also requires claimants to lodge a claim 'promptly', and certainly no later than three months from the date of the decision complained of (Civil Procedure Rules, r 54). Here, we are told that the statute imposes a time limit of less than three months. Rule 54.5 allows for the imposition of a shorter time limit; therefore Taylor is out of time. However, the court can exercise discretion and take the decision to allow the claim to proceed even though he is outside of the time limit. The court may exercise their discretion to allow late application if there are good, objective reasons for coming later (**R v Secretary of State for Trade and Industry ex parte Greenpeace** [1998] ELR 415). Here, it seems that as the minutes were not available at the correct time, Taylor was unaware of the grounds for the application until the deadline had passed, and it is arguable that this is a case in which the court should exercise it's discretion.[2]

[2] The authority cited here allows the answer to draw conclusions about the likely outcome of this case.

Assuming that leave is granted, the court will then have to consider whether or not there are grounds for judicial review. There are three categories of grounds for judicial review, outlined in the **Council of Civil Service Unions v Minister for the Civil Service** [1985] AC 374 as illegality, procedural impropriety and irrationality. Taylor may have grounds falling under the headings of procedural impropriety and illegality.

[3]You should attempt some explanation of 'natural justice', even though it is a vague concept. This reassures your examiner that you do understand this key concept.

[4]It is helpful to provide this brief definition. Not only have you shown the examiner that you know what it means, you have also shown you understand something about the legal status of an expectation.

[5]This is a really useful authority to cite, as the facts are similar to those in the problem. It can give a clear indication of the approach a court is likely to take when assessing the merits of Taylor's claim.

[6]You must remember to keep returning to the facts of the scenario, and using the law you have outlined to draw conclusions about the facts of the problem.

[7]It is a good idea to note the fact that the question has not specified that there is a requirement to give reasons. Some students will assume that there is because reasons have been provided. A better answer will make the point that there is a need to check the legislation carefully, as this is what a lawyer would do in practice.

Procedural impropriety can occur either through the failing to comply with statutory requirements, or through a general failure to comply with what are sometimes referred to as 'the rules of natural justice'. This somewhat ill-defined concept deals with the standards of fairness that the courts have seemed to consider demand protection in all proceedings.[3] There have been a number of cases in which a prior indication of the outcome of a decision has been held to create a 'legitimate expectation'. A legitimate expectation is not a 'legal right' but the courts can find circumstances where equity demands that it is given protection, as it would be unfair to thwart the expectation.[4] For example, in **R v Inland Revenue Comissioners ex parte Preston** [1985] AC 835 it was held it would amount to an abuse to allow the IRC to renege on an assurance given to taxpayers that their affairs would not be investigated provided certain conditions were complied with. Although it is clear then, that a legitimate expectation can be created by an assurance, it is not certain that Taylor would be successful. A distinction can be drawn between the situation in the **Preston** case and the authority from **R v Liverpool Corporation ex parte Liverpool Taxi Fleet Operators** [1972] 2 QB 299 concerning an indication given regarding the probable grant of a licence, in which it was held that an undertaking given by a chair of the committee was *prima facie* unlawful as this would fetter the discretion of the decision-making body itself.[5] The expectation created in the minds of the taxpayers is, arguably, more worthy of protection as, if not honoured, the effect is punitive and potentially a threat to liberty. Here, the facts seem to be more analogous with the **Liverpool** case and it appears that the assurance given to Taylor will not give rise to an expectation that the courts will protect.[6]

There is no general duty to give reasons, so Taylor will be unable to argue that the failure to provide reasons automatically amounts to a procedural impropriety. However, as the council appears to accept that reasons should be given and provide a timescale, the issue requires some consideration and certainly, further investigation of the provisions of the enabling Act. If the legislation stipulates that reasons must be provided, and gives a timescale, then the failure to comply may be a procedural impropriety.[7] If that is the case, the court would need to determine whether or not the non-compliance should be considered to be 'substantial' following **R v Immigration**

[8]Marks will be given here for noting that the late reasons may provide procedural assistance, even if not part of the substantive claim.

Appeal Tribunal ex parte Jeyeanthan [1999] 3 All ER 231. In this case, it is difficult to see how the late provision of reasons impacts on the decision-making process. This aspect of the case is more helpful in assisting Taylor to persuade the course to allow the late claim.[8]

[9]It is necessary to show that there are authorities to support this ground, but here, as there is little controversy about the applicability of the ground, it isn't necessary to explain the *ratios* or facts in any detail.

Taylor may wish to argue that the decision should be considered to be illegal. Illegality can arise in a variety of ways. Where the statute provides that certain factors need to be considered in the decision-making process, it is not permissible to take account of other matters. The courts have been willing to hold a decision to be illegal where it has been taken on the basis of irrelevant matters in numerous cases including **Wheeler v Leicester City Council** [1985] AC 1054 and **R v Secretary of State for the Home Department ex parte Venables** [1997] 3 WLR 23.[9] Here, the statute sets out the matters that need to be considered, and the commercial effect on other businesses will therefore be deemed irrelevant. This would seem to be the ground that is most likely to succeed.[10]

[10]Although it will be concluded that this ground is the most appropriate on which to base a claim, little space is given to it in the answer. This is because it is very straightforward, and more marks are available for exploring the more contentious issues in more detail.

If the application is successful, the court has the discretion to provide a remedy, and all remedies will have the effect of ensuring that the decision is taken again. Here, it is probable that a quashing order will be made to void the original decision.

 ## Make your answer stand out

- By spending more time discussing the issue of legitimate expectations which has attracted considerable academic comment. There is an excellent overview of the topic in Craig, P.,'Legitimate expectations: a conceptual analysis' (1992) 108 LQR 79–98, which clearly explains the different circumstances in which an expectation could be said to arise.

- By incorporating some more recent case law that has addressed the issue of legitimate expectations. You may wish to start by considering the journal article; Knight, C.J.S., 'Expectations in transition: recent developments in legitimate expectations' [2009] PL 15–24, which discusses a number of important authorities. You will be rewarded if you can incorporate relevant academic comment.

- By giving more detail regarding the late provision of reasons. A clear explanation of this area can be found by Schaeffer, A., 'Reasons and rationalisations: late reasons in judicial review' [2004] JR 151. This would show the examiner that you have a detailed understanding of the topic.

! Don't be tempted to...

■ Speculate about the merits of the decision. It may seem self-evident that the licence should have been granted, given the wording of the statute. Students sometimes suggest that as a result of a review, the decision will be reversed. You must remember, however, that the purpose of judicial review is to assess the manner in which the decision was made, and the effect of any remedy given is to ensure that the decision is made again, using the correct procedure.

? Question 6

Marie Chadwick seeks your advice. She has a degenerative illness, and is cared for by her husband. Twice a week, the local authority arranges transport to take her to a daycare facility two miles from her home, so that Mr Chadwick can have some respite. The Chadwicks do not have a car and Marie's disabilities make it impossible for her to use public transport.

Last week, she received a letter from the local authority, informing her that the facility has been selected for closure. A place has been provided for her at an alternative facility 25 miles from her home. Mr Chadwick telephoned the local authority to ask what time the transport would collect Marie and was told that the policy was not to provide transport for journeys over 20 miles long.

The (fictitious) Local Authority (Patient Care) Act 1987 states, at s 12:

> The authority has a duty to provide adequate support for patients with long-term health needs, and their carers. Facilities should be available that are appropriate and accessible for patients and their carers. In determining the appropriate provision, the authority may consider such factors as appear relevant.

Marie tells you that she feels the decision to close the daycare facility is absurd and she wants to know if she can go to court to change the decision. She would like compensation for the price of the taxi fares to and from the new centre, as well as damages for her distress.

Advise Marie.

Answer plan

→ Explain the process of judicial review.

→ Analyse the possible available grounds against the local authority.

→ Discuss the availability of compensation or damages.

→ Mention other remedies that may be available.

→ Outline the effect of a remedy.

Diagram plan

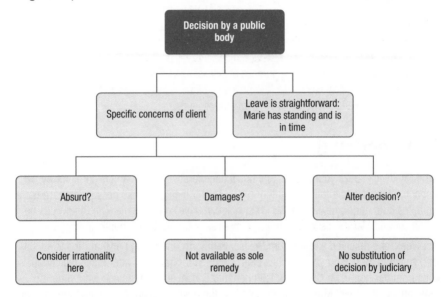

A printable version of this diagram is available from www.pearsoned.co.uk/lawexpressqa

Answer

Marie may be able to apply for a judicial review of the local authority's decision to close the respite facility and cease to provide transport. A judicial review is a mechanism which allows the courts to consider the process by which a public body exercising delegated powers has reached a decision. Marie should note that judicial review is a procedure concerned with ensuring that discretionary powers are exercised lawfully and fairly; it is not an appeal regarding the merits of the decision. Marie will need to be advised of the available remedies, as it may not be possible to claim compensation or damages.

The courts may review any decision made by a public body exercising delegated powers. This is not problematic, as the local authority is clearly a public body and therefore amenable to review. It should be noted that leave is required to bring an application. Dealing first with the application to review the local authority's decision: it appears that leave should be granted. Marie is an individual who has sufficient interest in the matter complained of (s 31, Senior Courts Act 1981) so this is unproblematic. An application must be brought promptly and in any event, no later than three months after the decision complained of (Civil Procedure Rules 1998, r 54). As the letter was received last week, then it seems the application will be in time.[1]

Provided leave is granted, the courts will need to consider the grounds for the application. There are a number of potential grounds for review, listed in **Council of Civil Service Unions v Minister for the Civil Service** [1985] AC 374 as irrationality, illegality and procedural unfairness. Arguably, the Human Rights Act 1998 has allowed for the development of a fourth substantive ground of review: proportionality. Marie has stated that she believes the decision is absurd. She may wish, then, to consider whether it would be possible to argue that the decision was irrational.[2] The test to be applied is drawn from the case of **Associated Provincial Picture Houses Ltd v Wednesbury Corporation** [1948] 1 KB 223, in which it was held a decision would be irrational only if no reasonable decision-maker could have reached the same conclusion. Successive cases reinforce the point that the test for irrationality is stringently applied and demonstrate that the judiciary are wary of stepping outside of constitutional boundaries by interfering with executive autonomy,[3] a point stressed in **R v Secretary of State for the Home Department ex parte Brind** [1991] 1 AC 696. Marie should note that an extremely high threshold has been set in respect of claims for irrationality. Judicial support for a claim in similar circumstances can be found in **R (B) v Worcestershire County Council** [2009] EWHC 2915. In that case, the failure to carry out proper assessment meant that the authority had been unable to arrive at a rational decision.[4] Further information would be required regarding the decision-making process, but this could be an arguable ground if it can be shown that the authority has not obtained the information needed to determine whether or not the closure was necessary. The lack of transport may suggest that the authority did not obtain all the material required. Whilst it is for the authority to determine 'relevant' factors, they should be mindful of the statutory duty to consider accessibility.[5]

It is probably worth challenging the decision not to provide transport for Marie as a separate ground of claim to ensure that, if the centre does close, the authority have to reconsider the issue. Where an authority has discretion, any policy which is a binding rule preventing proper consideration may be considered to be 'fettering discretion' and this will be illegal (see, for example, **British Oxygen Co v Board of Trade** [1971] AC 610).[6] As the authority stated the refusal was on policy grounds this may well be a point worth exploring.

Marie has instructed that she wishes to obtain damages. Damages may be awarded, and accordingly may be included in a claim (CPR 54.3(2)), but cannot be the sole remedy claimed.[7] Damages will only be payable if they would have been recoverable in a civil claim (s 31(4), Senior Courts Act). **R (Kurdistan Workers Party) v Secretary of State for the Home Department** [2002] EWHC 644 confirmed that damages can be awarded but cannot be 'a good reason for permitting judicial review'.[8] The appropriate remedy to be claimed may be determined in part by the speed at which a claim can be lodged and whether or not the centre is still open at that time. If it is, then Marie should seek a prohibiting order, to prevent the closure, and a quashing order to void the decision.[9] Together, this would have the effect of ensuring the centre remained open whilst the authority reconsiders the decision.

Marie has indicated that she hopes the court will change the decision and must be advised that this is highly unlikely.[10] The effect and intention of judicial review remedies is, in the main, to make sure that those empowered to exercise discretion do so fairly and lawfully. It would be usurpation of the power conferred on the relevant body for the judiciary to substitute their discretion for that of the decision-maker.[11] A successful judicial review, then, will result in the matter being remitted to the local authority for reconsideration. The CPR and the Senior Courts Act do both state that the court may take the decision itself but only in circumstances where there is 'no purpose to be served in remitting the matter'[12] (CPR 54.19(3)). This will only be appropriate where the initial decision was taken by a court or tribunal and resulted from an error of law where, without the error, only one result would be possible. In other words, it is only appropriate as a time saving device as confirmed in **R (Dhadly) v London Borough of Greenwich** [2001] EWCA Civ 8122.

It seems that Marie has good grounds to seek judicial review of the local authorities actions. She may be awarded damages, but the primary remedy will result in reconsideration of the decision.

✓ Make your answer stand out

- By spending more time considering the grounds that could be relevant to both parts of the decision. You do need to focus on irrationality because the question demands this but, if space permits, you could open up the discussion to consider whether or not a decision made solely for financial reasons could be classified as for an improper purpose. This would be impressive, as this is quite a narrow point and beyond the scope of generalist text books. It would show real confidence in analysing the law.

- By referring to the Law Commission report (No. 322) on the issue of damages published in May 2010, *Administrative Redress: Public Bodies and the Citizen* (available at: www.lawcom.gov.uk/docs/lc322.pdf). The Law Commission propose that damages should be available as a sole remedy in review proceedings. Although you must limit your advice to the current law, you could suggest that there is a perceptible shift in favour of the award of damages which could assist Marie. This would show the examiner that you have read around the subject.

- By explaining the available remedies in more detail. There are a number of useful texts you could consider including: Sunkin, M., 'Remedies available in judicial review proceedings,' in D. Feldman (ed.), *English Public Law* (2nd edn, 2010) Oxford: Oxford University Press.

! Don't be tempted to...

- Ignore the wording of the question. Your examiner will provide clues that should help you find the issues that they really want you to talk about. Here, use of the word 'absurdity' should trigger you to consider irrationality. Students who fail to pay close attention to the wording can miss this kind of hint and lose out on valuable marks.

- Similarly, you must spend more time discussing the effect of successful review here because the client has raised it. You need to show the examiner that you can point out the issues that matter to the client, and advise accordingly.

The European Convention on Human Rights and the Human Rights Act 1998

How this topic may come up in exams

This topic lends itself to essay questions which ask you to consider the impact of the Human Rights Act 1998. This issue is pervasive, and could overlap with any area of the syllabus. You could be asked to discuss the effect of Convention rights on the constitutional doctrines considered in Chapters 1 and 2, or to assess any number of the substantive rights in connection with laws concerning terrorism, police powers, or freedom of assembly. Problem questions could ask you to address the use of the Human Rights Act in challenging or creating domestic legislation.

Attack the question

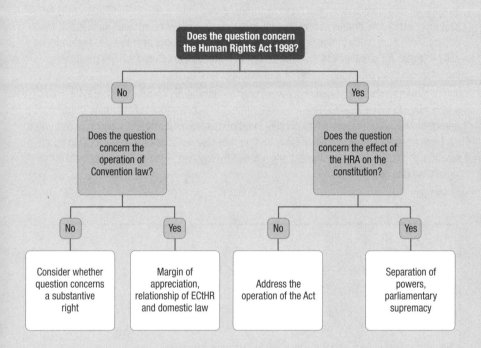

❓ Question 1

The (fictional) University Attendance Act 2010 aims to raise educational standards by ensuring that students take their studies seriously and get enough sleep. Section 10 makes it mandatory for all students to reside in university managed accommodation during their studies. All universities are required to fit computerised entry systems to residences. The system must record details of any student who returns to their room after midnight. If this occurs more than twice in a seven-day period, all bank accounts belonging to that student will be frozen for one week (s 13). If the student continues to return late, the penalties increase, and can result in the loss of a university place (s 15).

Jim is a mature student at university who, prior to starting his course, lived with his wife and family. No university residence could be found to accommodate his family. Therefore, he returns home every weekend from Friday to Monday to see them. He is very disturbed when his bank accounts are frozen, and he is told he may lose his place. He seeks advice about whether or not the Act of Parliament was made lawfully and whether or not Human Rights legislation can assist him.

Advise Jim.

Answer plan

→ Identify the Convention rights infringed by the legislation.

→ Discuss the legality of the Act of Parliament.

→ Explain the possibility of a claim following the Human Rights Act 1998.

→ Assess the likely approach of the court to the legislation using s 3 and s 4 of the Act.

→ Draw conclusions about the likelihood of obtaining redress.

Diagram plan

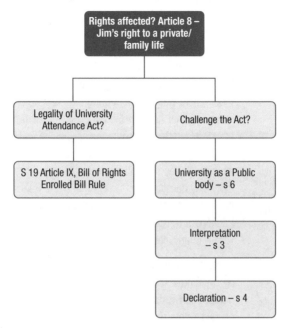

A printable version of this diagram is available from www.pearsoned.co.uk/lawexpressqa

Answer

[1]This succinct introduction shows an understanding of the issues that need to be discussed, and also suggests that a particular conclusion will be reached. This shows confidence with the material.

[2]Before launching into a discussion about how the Human Rights Act works, it is necessary to be able to demonstrate why the legislation should be challenged, by reference to Convention rights. This can be done swiftly, to ensure more weight is given to discussion of how the matters will be dealt with in the domestic courts.

It seems clear that the (fictitious) University Attendance Act (the Act) is in breach of Art 8 of the European Convention on Human Rights. The Human Rights Act 1998 (HRA) provides a mechanism for the citizen to enforce Convention rights in the domestic courts; however, it is not clear that this will provide Jim with effective redress.[1]

Article 8 enshrines the right to a private and family life, and any interference must be justified for one of the reasons specified in Art 8(2). It is not possible to construe the interference with Jim's family arrangements as 'necessary' for the purpose of protecting national security, public safety, health and morals, the rights of others, or to prevent disorder. Therefore, implementation of the Act leads to an unjustifiable interference with Jim's human rights.[2]

[3]This gives a clear answer, but more explanation is needed because the question specifically asks for consideration of this issue.

[4]When dealing with the HRA, the answer should refrain from making general statements about the effect of the legislation, and should ensure that specific sections are referenced.

[5]Marks will be awarded for noticing that the type of organisation may pose a problem, as it shows familiarity with the procedural issues.

[6]Evidence needs to be provided to support the conclusion that the university is a public body; there are a number of cases that could be cited here.

[7]This is an important point to be aware of, and one that is often overlooked. Reference to horizontal effect shows an understanding of the operation of convention law. There is no need to provide a detailed explanation as correct use of the term shows that the issue is understood.

Jim queries whether the Act of Parliament is lawful. Regardless of whether or not legislative provisions conflict with convention rights, any Act of Parliament is lawful and will be enforced in the courts.[3] Section 19 of the Human Rights Act imposes a requirement that a Minister introducing a Bill to Parliament must make a declaration of compatibility with the Convention or, if this is not possible, explain that the government wishes the legislation to be passed. Even if this requirement was not met during the passage of the legislation, then it appears that Art IX of the Bill of Rights will preclude the possibility of judicial interference with 'proceedings' in Parliament. The constitution rests upon the notion of the legislative supremacy of Parliament, which includes the notion (articulated by Dicey) that no person or body may question the validity of an Act of Parliament. The HRA does not alter this state of affairs, and explicitly protects the authority of Parliament by stating that its provisions do not affect the continued validity of any incompatible legislation (s 3(2)(b), s 4(6)).[4]

However, Jim may be able to seek a remedy in the domestic courts by bringing a claim against the university for breaching his Art 8 rights. The HRA states that any person who is a victim of a breach of their rights may bring proceedings (s 7). This will not be problematic for Jim as he is clearly directly affected. An action can only lie against a public authority (s 6); this issue requires some consideration. Universities are independent organisations, although they may receive a degree of subsidy from the state.[5] The courts have, in a number of cases, found that if the function of a body can be construed as governmental, then a claim can be actionable. In particular, any body permitted to exercise coercive powers against the individual will almost certainly be considered to be a public body (**R (Munjaz) v Mersey Care NHS Trust** [2005] UKHL 58). Considering the punitive powers given to the university, it seems highly probable that it will be dealt with as a public body.[6] In any event, s 6 makes it clear that courts and tribunals are public bodies, creating an indirect horizontal effect.[7] As a result, even if the university is a private body, when dealing with a dispute over the Act, the courts are required to uphold Jim's Convention rights.

The HRA imposes a duty on the courts to interpret existing legislation as compatible with convention rights 'in so far as it is possible to do so' (s 3). The extent of the interpretative duty has been questioned in numerous cases since the Act came into effect. It is clear that the provision confers considerable powers on the court to interpret statutes as compliant even when the literal meaning of the words are unambiguous. On occasion, the judiciary have utilised the power to impose a meaning that 'linguistically may appear strained' (**R v A** [2001] UKHL 25, per Lord Steyn). This does not, however, extend so far as to allow the judiciary to engage in a process of interpretation tantamount to drafting legislation.[8] This point was stressed in **Re S** [2002] UKHL 10, in which the Lords confirmed that the HRA maintains the 'constitutional boundary', and preserves parliamentary sovereignty. The scenario above does not include the precise wording of the statute. However, the effect of these sections are to authorise substantial interference with the domestic and financial affairs of students and it is hard to see how the courts could read down or read into[9] such provisions to force compliance. Therefore, it would appear unlikely that the courts would be able to utilise s 3 to assist Jim.[10]

Where legislation conflicts with a convention right, the superior courts have the discretion to make a declaration of incompatibility (s 4, HRA). Referred to in **R v A** (above) as a 'last resort' a declaration will generally only be made where s 3 has been considered and it is deemed impossible to impose a convention compliant meaning on the wording. Once made, the government can determine whether any action is necessary. If it is felt appropriate to alter the legislation this can be done either by introducing a new statute or, under s 10, taking remedial action and amending the offending provisions by ministerial order. Any order should be limited to removing the incompatible portions of the legislation, and is subject to retrospective parliamentary approval.[11] Jim should be advised that a declaration of incompatibility is likely to be made in this case.

As highlighted above, s 4(6) makes it clear that a declaration does not affect the validity of the Act. Therefore, as expressly stated at s 4(6)(b), it is not binding on the parties to the case. The courts will enforce the law as it exists when dealing with the case. A declaration of incompatibility will not assist Jim in obtaining redress in the domestic courts.[12]

[8]The possibilities afforded by s 3 should not be overstated; marks will be given for recognising that it does not authorise rewriting legislation.

[9]This shows considerable confidence by referring to the judicial terminology.

[10]It is crucial to keep returning to the facts of the scenario and answering the question, which asks you to advise Jim.

[11]This section demonstrates awareness of the effect of a declaration.

[12]This is an important point, because the answer needs to focus not just on whether or not the courts will approve of the legislation, but on the impact of any decisions on Jim's situation.

[13]Because the question requires you to focus on advising Jim, you do need to acknowledge the fact that he has the option to take a claim to Strasbourg.

If a declaration of incompatibility is made by the superior court, then Jim could consider taking his case to the European Court of Human Rights to seek a remedy.[13] Where a declaration has been made, then the government is likely to wish to settle the matter as the outcome of the case would appear to be almost inevitable.

[14]The conclusion needs to refer back to the issues that the question raised, and summarise the advice given.

The Act includes provisions which infringe Jim's right to a private and family life. However, this does not render the statute unlawful, and it will be upheld by the court unless and until the government repeals or amends the law. Therefore, the HRA does not provide Jim with assistance in the short term, and he may still need to appeal to the European Court of Human Rights in order to obtain redress.[14]

✓ Make your answer stand out

- By providing more detail about the redress available in Strasbourg, and explaining the concept of a 'friendly settlement'. This will show the examiner you have a detailed understanding of the operation of Convention law. You must, of course, ensure that you relate this to Jim's situation.

- By explaining what is meant by indirect horizontal effect, and providing some authority to illustrate this point. A good example might be *Goodwin* v *UK* (1996) 22 EHRR 123, in which (as Loveland points out) the European Court concludes a state may be in breach if citizens can rely on legal provisions that restrict the access to convention rights of others. (Loveland, I., *Constitutional Law, Administrative Law and Human Rights: A Critical Introduction* (4th edn, 2009) Oxford: Oxford University Press.)

! Don't be tempted to...

- Spend time discussing the limits of Art 8. The focus of the question is not on the extent of Convention rights. It is not necessary, then, to enter into a detailed discussion about the margin of appreciation afforded to states in cases like *Handyside* v *UK*. You must make sure you focus on what action Jim may be able to take in this case.

- Refer to the HRA in general terms. It is very important that you do know which sections are relevant, and why. The more detail you can give, the better. For example, it is clearly right to say that the courts may make a declaration of incompatibility (s 4). It is more impressive if you can also reference s 4(6) and explain that this has no effect on the case being determined. It is even better if you can highlight that this section serves to preserve the principle of parliamentary supremacy as this would show you are making links between the different areas of the syllabus.

 Question 2

The Human Rights Act has strengthened the constitutional position of the Judiciary, and weakened the position of the executive.

Discuss.

Answer plan

→ Outline briefly, the functions of the judiciary and the executive.

→ Explain the powers given to the judiciary by the HRA (s 3, and s 4).

→ Provide examples to demonstrate judicial 'strength'.

→ Consider the role of the European Court of Human Rights.

Diagram plan

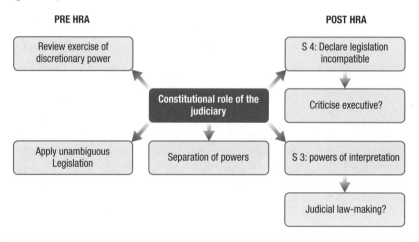

A printable version of this diagram is available from www.pearsoned.co.uk/lawexpressqa

Answer

The Labour government introduced the Human Rights Act (HRA) shortly after coming to power, proclaiming that it was 'bringing rights home'. A decade later, senior government figures are highly critical of the Act; Jack Straw as Justice Minister stated he was 'frustrated' by the Act in late 2008. The Conservative party have

[1]The question refers to the clash between the executive and the judiciary, but you will need to recognise that this arises through challenges made in the courts to legislative provisions.

[2]Many answers to this question will be too descriptive. Marks will be available for asserting a clear point of view.

[3]You will be rewarded for noting that this question is focused on the impact of the HRA on the separation of powers. You should not spend too long explaining the doctrine, but a brief explanation is needed,

[4]This question does pose some difficulty by requiring the focus to be on the relationship between the executive and the judiciary. The Human Rights Act is primarily concerned with approaches to legislation. This section explains why a discussion of the judicial approach to legislation is permissible, as most statute originates from government.

stated that they will seek to abolish the Act and replace it with a British Bill of Rights. It is clear, then, that the Act is a source of concern to the major political parties. Since 2000, there have been several cases in which the superior courts have utilised powers granted by the Human Rights Act to challenge legislation.[1] This may lead to the conclusion that the Human Rights Act has increased the ability of the judiciary to hold the other organs of state to account. It will be argued, however, that whilst there are instances in which the judiciary has appeared to challenge legislation supported by the executive; these can be best characterised as political, rather than constitutional issues.[2]

Although the United Kingdom does not have a written document which enshrines the authorities and functions of the organs of state, the doctrine of the separation of powers can be considered to be an integral part of the constitution.[3] According to the doctrine, the roles of the organs of state are distinct: Parliament is the supreme law-making body, the executive is responsible for introducing policy and administration, and the judiciary interprets and applies the law. The Human Rights Act granted new discretionary powers to the judiciary when considering statute. It would seem that, if there is a shift in the constitutional balance of power, the relationship between the legislature and the judiciary would be the one affected. The question presupposes an acceptance of the view famously promulgated by Lord Hailsham that there is the potential for an 'elected dictatorship' if a party of government enjoys a large majority in the Commons. Challenges made to legislation introduced by government could be viewed as, to some extent, undermining the ability of the executive to administer policy.[4]

It is perhaps appropriate to emphasise that the HRA did not increase or alter the rights of the citizen. The right of petition to the Court of Human Rights has existed since 1966. The HRA aimed to ensure that Convention rights are incorporated into domestic law and accordingly are enforceable in domestic courts.

The HRA gives the judiciary powers to uphold convention rights. Prior to the HRA, where an unambiguous legislative provision conflicted with a Convention right, the constitutional principle of parliamentary supremacy required the court to apply the statute in accordance with the clear meaning. Section 3 of the HRA grants the courts powers to interpret statutes as Convention compliant 'in so

[5]The answer needs to ensure that it does have a clear focus on identifiable legal issues. The discussion must be centred on the provisions of the Human Rights Act rather than a broad, political, debate.

[6]There are numerous cases dealing with s 3. *R* v *A* is useful because it represents an example of a very broad use of the interpretative power. The phrase 'linguistically strained' is worth remembering, as it is a useful way of briefly explaining that the power can be used to alter the obvious meaning of a statutory provision.

[7]You should do more than explain the powers given to the courts by the HRA; this needs to be related to the issue of power within the constitution.

[8]Here, the developing argument refers back to the issue in the question, to maintain focus.

[9]A preliminary conclusion can be reached here, before moving on to the next part of the argument.

[10]The answer reminds the marker that the key issue is the relationship between the judiciary, and the executive.

far as it is possible to do so'. It is clear that this allows the courts to read down, or read into, provisions even where there is no ambiguity present.[5] The scope of this power is evident in cases such as **Ghaidan v Mendoza** [2004] UKHL 30, where the court was prepared to read additional words into the statute, or **R v A** [2001] UKHL 25, where the judiciary were prepared to infer a meaning that was 'linguistically strained'.[6]

Critics of the HRA could argue that s 3 has the potential to fundamentally alter the constitutional landscape, by granting a degree of legislative power to the judiciary, allowing them to subvert the intention of Parliament.[7] Consider the case of **R v A** (above), which concerned safeguards against the cross-examination of rape victims contained within s 41 of the Youth Justice and Criminal Evidence Act 1999. The clear aim of Parliament was to ensure that the trial process did not allow questions to be asked regarding sexual history, and yet the judiciary interpreted the provision as meaning that questions were permissible if necessary for a fair trial within the meaning of Art 6. Decisions such as this lend weight to suggestions that the HRA gives power to unelected members of the judiciary in formulating policy.[8] However, this must be balanced against numerous instances where the courts have declared themselves unwilling to impose a meaning that goes 'against the grain' of the statute, as was said in **Ghaidan v Mendoza** (above). Therefore, it would seem that despite the additional powers contained at s 3, the judiciary remain largely respectful of constitutional boundaries and do not seek to stray beyond the 'outer limit' (**Re W (Care Plan)** [2001] EWCA Civ 757) by embarking on a process of drafting legislation.[9]

Where it is not possible for a statutory provision to be interpreted as compliant with conventions using s 3, then s 4 of the HRA gives the superior courts the discretion to issue a declaration of incompatibility. This has no effect on the parties in the case, but allows the judiciary to give a clear signal to the executive that the statute requires consideration.[10] The HRA contains a provision for the executive to take remedial action to amend the offending part of the legislation (s 10). During the passage of the Human Rights Act through Parliament, the government envisaged that s 4 would rarely be invoked and this has proved to be the case. In the period 2000–2006 the government amended existing law or introduced new legislation in nine cases following a declaration of incompatibility. (Joint Committee on Human Rights, 23rd Report of 2006). The significance of s 4 should not be overstated, however, as the HRA is careful to preserve the supremacy of domestic law. A s 4 declaration cannot compel the executive to review the legislation, and unless government determines that change is necessary, the courts will continue to enforce the law. It can be argued then, that the constitutional balance is unchanged. Legislative change occurs not because of coercive pressure from the court, but as a result of political necessity.[11] A series of decisions concerning asylum and terrorism have indeed resulted in the judiciary making strong criticism of particular statutes and this has resulted in legislative change. In **A v Secretary of State for the Home Department**, the House of Lords declared that Part IV of the ATCSA was unlawful; this resulted in repeal and a shift in policy as regards foreign terror suspects. It should be remembered that the courts are guided by Convention principles, and judgments of the Court in Strasbourg. If s 4 did not provide a means of resolving the issue domestically, then a negative judgment from Strasbourg would inevitably follow. Therefore, the pressure for change is extrinsic rather than domestic.[12]

[11]This is the crux of the argument suggested at the outset, and at this stage, evidence has been shown to support this assertion.

[12]This is a point worth making, as the courts are not creating new rights, but simply enforcing those protected by the Convention.

Political leaders may express concerns about the HRA, but on closer examination, it seems that the Act does not in fact make radical alteration to the constitutional position of the judiciary. Arguably, pressure on the executive regarding particular policy choices stems not from the judiciary, but from Strasbourg.

✓ Make your answer stand out

- By giving more consideration to the issue raised regarding extrinsic pressure on the executive. Some academics suggest that the domestic courts are beginning to adopt a more radical approach than that taken by Strasbourg (see, for example, Fenwick, H., *Civil Liberties and Human Rights* (4th edn, 2007) London: Routledge Cavendish, ch 4).

- By keeping up to date with current developments. It will be interesting to see how the Coalition government balances the conflict between the pre-election commitment to the HRA expressed by the Liberal Democrats, and Conservative promises of radical reform. If you can comment on developments as they arise and set these in the context of the constitutional balance of power, this will impress upon your examiner that you are confident with the topic and able to form an opinion.

Question 3

The wide margin afforded to signatory states undermines the concept of 'fundamental freedoms' in the United Kingdom.

Discuss.

Answer plan

→ Explain the terms 'qualified rights' and 'margin of appreciation'.

→ Outline the supervisory role of the European Court of Human Rights.

→ Consider the justification for differing margins for different rights.

→ Assess the role of the domestic courts in applying margins of appreciation.

Diagram plan

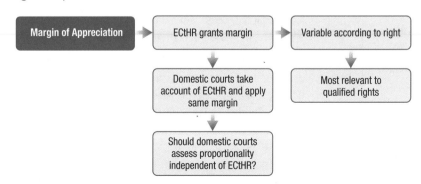

A printable version of this diagram is available from www.pearsoned.co.uk/lawexpressqa

Answer

The European Convention on Human Rights and Fundamental Freedoms was drafted in the aftermath of the Second World War, as the atrocities that occurred during the Nazi regime became apparent. Signatories to the Convention agree to secure the rights contained within the treaty, and the European Court of Human Rights (ECtHR) is empowered to determine whether an action by a state is compatible with that duty. In so doing, the ECtHR may afford the state a 'margin of appreciation'; it is the effect of this judicial concept that must be examined. It can be argued that the margin of appreciation has, on occasion, allowed the UK government to enact legislation that runs contrary to the spirit of the Convention.[1]

The Convention seeks to set a common standard of rights and freedoms for the signatory states. Article 1 of the Convention places the primary responsibility for securing those rights upon the states. The role of the ECtHR can be seen as supervisory; to review the decisions made by states about how to achieve the objectives of the Treaty.[2] The notion of 'margin of appreciation' has emerged over time, as a result of the fact that the language of the Treaty permits restrictions on many of the Article rights. Few rights are 'absolute'; the majority are subject to qualification. For example, Art 8 sets out the right to a private and family life, but Art 8(2) recognises that a state may interfere with that right if it is 'necessary' for one of the following purposes: national security, public safety or economic well being; to prevent crime and disorder; to protect health or morals, or to protect the freedoms of others. In determining whether the action of a state falls within one of the permitted qualifications, the ECtHR acknowledges that the domestic authorities may be better placed to judge what is necessary in the context of their own cultural values and norms; this degree of deference is the 'margin' of appreciation.[3]

Decisions of the ECtHR show that the 'margin' is not fixed, and the degree of flexibility granted to the state may vary according to the nature of the right itself, and also to the reason claimed for qualification.[4] In **Sunday Times v UK** (1979) 2 EHRR 245, the court drew a distinction between issues such as health and morals, and more 'objective' issues such as judicial autonomy (the qualification being claimed in that case). When dealing with an objective issue, the court were not prepared to allow a wide margin, whereas in **Handyside v UK** (1976) 1 EHRR 737[5] the court refused to interfere with the

---

[1] The introduction signals that the key issue is going to be addressed, and that a view will be taken about the question.

[2] This is a key point to make here as it makes clear that you understand the respective roles of the signatory states and the ECtHR.

[3] It is essential to be able to give an explanation of the term 'margin of appreciation', and to do so, reference to the existence of qualifications on Convention rights is required.

[4] The imprecise boundaries of the margin of appreciation needs to be noted, as this forms part of the argument that will be developed about the need for domestic courts to be rigorous in assessing the validity of a particular qualification.

[5] Handyside is a useful authority, as it is a clear illustration of application of a margin of appreciation.

domestic government's determination of the moral need for obscenity legislation. A broad margin is also evident when dealing with social policy issues, considered to be matters where there can be legitimate political difference and debate. Therefore, in **Hatton v UK** (2003) 37 EHRR 28 the court refused to hold that in allowing night flights from Heathrow the state interfered with the Art 8 rights of the claimant. Here, the state was permitted to reach a determination that the interference was necessary for the economic well being of the nation and the ECtHR deferred to that determination.

It is important to note that the existence of a margin of appreciation does not mean that the court will not review the exercise of discretion. However, as Fenwick notes, if the margin permitted is wide, then the ECtHR will engage in minimal supervision; limited largely to ensuring any discretion was exercised in good faith. If the margin is narrow, then there will be a more rigorous examination of the restriction to ensure it is proportionate to the aim. The notion of a margin of appreciation is controversial. As Loveland points out, viewed in a positive light, the concept shows an appropriate respect for the autonomy of democratically elected national governments. Alternatively, it could be argued that the ECtHR has on occasion abdicated responsibility for ensuring that the rights of minority groups are protected.[6]

[6]A willingness to acknowledge the academic debate ensures that the answer is not overly descriptive; analysis of the issue will be rewarded by the marker.

Matters of national security are conceded to be sensitive, and historically, the ECtHR has been reluctant to interfere with a domestic determination of necessity. The case of **Brannigan and McBride v UK** (17 EHRR 539) caused considerable concern when the court upheld the legality of a derogation from Art 5 applied by the government. The derogation arose following the judgment in **Brogan v UK** (1988) 11 EHRR 117, in which the ECtHR held that periods of detention authorised under terrorism legislation were an unjustified interference with the right to liberty. It is difficult to reconcile the decision in **Brannigan** with the ECtHR's role in ensuring robust protection for fundamental freedoms, as there appears to be a tacit endorsement of actions previously considered to be in breach of the convention.[7]

[7]This is a useful case to cite, as it provides support for the suggestion in the question that fundamental freedoms are undermined by the application of a margin of appreciation.

It is possible to endorse the notion of the margin of appreciation, as it properly emphasises the role of the state in determining how best to balance the freedoms of the individual against the broader public interest. However, the approach of the domestic courts to

[8]The central argument, that the margin of appreciation has a detrimental effect on the protection of rights in the domestic courts, is being developed here. It would not be sufficient to refer to Fenwick's argument; the answer must also incorporate some illustrative authority to support this view.

the margin of appreciation could be viewed as leading to a 'watering down' of the convention, as Fenwick suggests.[8] Section 2 of the Human Rights Act requires the courts to give weight to the ECtHR judgments. There are a number of cases in which decisions appear to suggest that where Strasbourg has afforded a considerable margin to the state, the domestic courts should also give judicial deference to the decision-maker. For example, in the case of **Gillan and Quinton v UK** [2009] ECHR 28, the House of Lords had to determine whether the exercise of stop and search powers authorised by the Terrorism Act 2000 breached (*inter alia*) Art 8. The state claimed that any interference was necessary in the interests of national security. The judgment suggests that, once deference is given on that issue, there can be no interference with the exercise of the power and no circumstance in which the use of the provision would be disproportionate. Fenwick refers to this as 'double deference'. As noted above, acknowledgement of a margin of appreciation does not mean the ECtHR will not address the restriction. In the case of **Gillan**, when the matter reached Strasbourg the court was unanimous in finding a breach of Art 8.

There will always be a need to balance individual and majority freedoms, and there is unlikely to ever be a homogenous culture across Europe. The concept of a margin of appreciation, therefore, is helpful in acknowledging these facts whilst nevertheless seeking to maintain a common standard of rights and freedoms. It can be argued, however, that if deference to national autonomy is not followed by rigorous examination of executive power in the domestic courts, some of the protection for individual freedoms envisaged in the Treaty will be lost.[9]

[9]The conclusion is justified, as the argument has been developed throughout the answer.

✓ Make your answer stand out

- By exploring some of the the academic views referred to regarding deference in more detail. Fenwick is an excellent text (*Civil Liberties and Human Rights* (4th edn, 2007) London: Routledge).

- By acknowledging that the decisions of Strasbourg do not always lead to a clear conclusion about the existence of the margin of appreciation in respect of a particular convention right. Although you have alluded to different justifications for restrictions on a right resulting in a differential approach (through *Sunday Times* and *Handyside*) you could make the point that this somewhat undermines the notion of a 'fundamental' right.

- By exploring the notion of 'double deference' in more detail. Good use has been made of the recent litigation concerning *Gillan*. You could question whether or not the Strasbourg decision marks a shift towards more stringent supervision from the ECtHR. This would show the ability to draw conclusions about the developing law.

! Don't be tempted to...

- Assume that the marker will know you understand the term 'margin of appreciation'. You do need to be able to give a definition.

- Use terminology incorrectly. A surprisingly large number of students refer to the permitted restrictions on Convention rights as 'derogations' and lose marks. Ensure you know the difference between qualifications upon a right for a permitted purpose, and the process of derogation which allows a state to withdraw from the obligation to protect a convention right in certain limited circumstances.

- Fail to explain how the cases you cite support the argument. Too many students make statements along the lines of '*Handyside* v *UK* is an example of the margin of appreciation'. You need to explain that the judgment demonstrates that the ECtHR allowed the state the margin to determine the most appropriate standard of morality for its own population.

❓ Question 4

The government publishes a consultation paper proposing a new Bill provisionally entitled 'the Criminal Trial Bill'. The aim of the legislation is to ensure that more criminal convictions are obtained, by reversing the burden of proof so that defendants will need to prove their innocence in all cases.

Discuss the legality of these proposals, and the difficulties in passing and enforcing the legislation in light of the Human Rights Act 1998.

Answer plan

→ Explain the presumption of innocence in domestic law, and under Art 6.

→ Explain the difference between a legal and evidential burden of proof, with examples.

→ Consider whether the proposals are in breach of Art 6(2).

→ Outline the effect of s 19.

→ Analyse the likely approach of the courts in enforcing the legislation, in light of ss 3 and 4 of the HRA.

Diagram plan

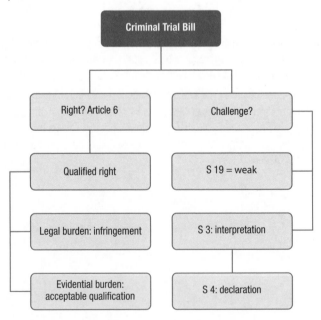

A printable version of this diagram is available from www.pearsoned.co.uk/lawexpressqa

Answer

The proposals contained in the Bill would, if enacted, remove the presumption of innocence in criminal trials, described as the 'golden thread' running through the English legal system (**Woolmington v DPP** [1935] AC 462). The presumption of innocence in criminal trials is expressly protected by Art 6(2) of the European Convention on Human Rights.[1] It is probable that these proposals could violate the Convention. The Human Rights Act (HRA) would enable the domestic courts to seek to circumvent the effects of the proposals.

[2]Some knowledge of criminal law is needed, to be able to explain the different burdens of proof. This question cannot really be attempted without a specific appreciation of the rights conferred by Art 6, and an understanding of the operation of the burden of proof.

As a general principle, defendants in criminal trials are innocent until all elements of the crime are proved beyond reasonable doubt. However, the concept of a reversal of the burden of proof is not novel, particularly in relation to defences. A distinction should be drawn between an evidential and a legal burden. The imposition of an evidential burden upon the defendant can be understood as a partial reversal of the burden of proof: the defendant needs to raise some evidence of the existence of the defence, thereafter, the task reverts to the crown to disprove the claim.[2] Often, all that is required is for the defendant to make the claim. For example, a person accused of an offence against the person can state they acted in self-defence. It is then for the crown to provide evidence that their actions were not a legitimate use of reasonable force. An evidential burden does not equate to a presumption of guilt, and would not therefore, be considered a breach of Art 6(2).[3]

[3]The focus is returned to human rights; it is important to return to the central issue even when referring to other areas of law to make sure that all material is utilised to answer the question.

The imposition of a legal burden is more onerous, and requires the defendant to prove a particular matter. A legal burden upon the defendant is rare at common law (the defence of insanity is a rare example), but may be imposed by statute (generally in relation to defences). A legal burden has the clear potential to violate Art 6.

[4]Discussion of the European approach was necessary, but the answer needs to move to consideration of the domestic application of Convention law.

The European Court of Human Rights (ECtHR) makes it clear that Art 6(2) is not absolute, confirming in **Salabiaku v France** (1988) 13 EHRR 379 that presumptions may be justified, provided that they remain within reasonable limits. When determining whether or not a particular presumption is justified, consideration will be given to what is at stake. The domestic courts have adopted a similar approach and stressed the importance of proportionality.[4] Therefore, whether or not the imposition of a legal burden

[5]This is probably the most crucial case to include in the answer, as the judgment clearly sets out the matters that will be considered when assessing if placing a burden on the defendant is justifiable.

[6]Having outlined the authority, this must be used to answer the question posed about the suggested legislation.

[7]The question requires an explanation of the impact of the HRA on the passage of legislation, so s 19 must be explained. A confident answer can deal with this quickly as it is not controversial. This allows space to explore the effect of s 3 in more detail.

[8]This is a really useful detail to include, as it shows you are aware of the practical impact of particular statutory provisions.

is justifiable will depend on issues including the seriousness of the allegation, and whether or not the matter is one the defendant can reasonably be expected to prove. In the conjoined appeals **Sheldrake v DPP; Attorney General's Reference (No. 4 of 2002)** [2004] UKHL 43[5] the House of Lords reached differing conclusions in each case. Sheldrake was charged with being in charge of a motor vehicle whilst under the influence. Statute provided a defence if he could prove that he was not intending to drive the vehicle. The legal burden in this instance was justified, as it was for a legitimate purpose (the protection of road users) and was a matter the defendant could reasonably be expected to adduce evidence about. This was distinct from the situation in the second case which concerned the offence of belonging to a proscribed organisation. Section 11(2) of the Terrorism Act 2000 provides for a defence where the defendant can show that they joined prior to the date of proscription and have had no involvement since that time. Here, the House held that this required the defendant to prove a negative which would be difficult to do, placing the provision in conflict with Art 6. The suggested legislation, applicable to all offences, would certainly be in violation of Art 6(2), as it is too broad and would encompass a requirement on the defendant to produce evidence about matters that it would be difficult, or impossible, to obtain.[6]

If the Bill was to be placed before Parliament, the HRA requires that the minister make a 'statement of compatibility' prior to the second reading (s 19). This cannot be viewed as creating a particularly onerous obligation.[7] Since the HRA came into force, there has been a declaration of compatibility made in almost every case, barring the Communications Act 2003.[8] It should be noted that, where a declaration cannot be made, the Minister is only required to state that the government wishes to proceed with the Bill. In any event, no reasons are required to justify either the confirmation of compatibility, or why a non-compatible Bill is still desirable. Section 19 has no relevance once a Bill is enacted, as the principle of Parliamentary sovereignty means that the court will not question the legality of proceedings in Parliament and cannot declare an enrolled Act to be unlawful.

The question of enforcement is more complex. Should the Bill become law, it is likely that there would be numerous appeals against conviction on the basis that the provisions breach Art 6(2). The HRA provides a mechanism for the citizen to enforce Convention rights in the domestic courts. Section 3 confers a power on the court to interpret legislation 'in so far as is possible' to make it compliant with convention rights. In **Sheldrake** (above), the courts were prepared to read down into the Terrorism Act that the burden imposed was merely evidential. This was despite the unambiguous wording of the statute, and the fact that elsewhere in the Terrorism Act the legislation listed the provisions that conferred an evidential burden and did not include s 11(2) in that list.[9] Therefore, despite the apparently clear intention of the statute, the courts were prepared to declare that the legislation must have been intended to comply with Art 6(2). It seems possible, then, that the aim of government in enacting the Bill will be thwarted if the judiciary feel able to utilise their powers under s 3.[10]

Given the extremely broad scope of the proposals, it is possible that no interpretation by the courts will be able to make the legislation compliant. In that circumstance, the HRA enables the court to make a declaration of incompatibility (s 4).[11] Whilst this does not impose any obligation on the executive to rectify the incompatibility, there could be political pressure to do so. It would seem certain that any claim to the ECtHR would have a good chance of success as such sweeping alterations to the trial process would be unlikely to satisfy the requirement of proportionality outlined in **Salabiaku** (above).

It can therefore be seen that although the Bill would be 'lawful' if enacted, it would be difficult for it to be enforced as the HRA would allow the courts to seek to mitigate the effect of the proposals using s 3, or to declare it incompatible with the Convention using s 4.[12]

[9]Even though you have already discussed *Sheldrake*, you need to give relevant detail from the judgment here, as you are making a different point, which is to do with the procedural approach of the court, rather than the decision that the statute breached Convention rights.

[10]The answer keeps focus, by referring back to the question; you were asked to consider the difficulties that might arise in enforcing the legislation, and your conclusion is that the courts would not enforce the provisions.

[11]You should not spend too much time on considering possible government responses to a declaration of incompatibility because that would be beyond the scope of the question, which focuses on enforcement.

[12]All the evidence has been presented, and a clear conclusion can be succinctly set out.

Make your answer stand out

■ Consideration could be given to the suggestions raised in the case of *Jackson* v *Attorney General* [2005] All ER (D) 285 that there may be circumstances in which the courts would declare an Act to be unlawful. It could be argued that this Bill, if enacted, would be unconscionable and could spark constitutional rebellion by the judiciary!

■ By referring to some academic arguments on the role of the judiciary in upholding human rights. The journal *Public Law* is a good source of relevant material, including Hickman, T., 'The courts and politics after the Human Rights Act: a comment (2008) PL 84. You should make a habit of checking the journal for up-to-date sources of opinion.

 Don't be tempted to...

■ Be diverted into a general discussion about the morality, or otherwise, of the aims of the Bill. Be sure to focus on the legal issues raised in relation to the Human Rights Act.

■ Be diverted into a discussion about the criminal law. This is a fairly tricky question because you do need to be able to cross-reference your knowledge of the criminal law to explain the issue of burden of proof, but make sure you do bring the discussion back to the HRA.

🖾 Question 5

The Human Rights Act 1998 has had little impact in increasing the protection of rights and freedoms of citizens of the United Kingdom.

Discuss.

Answer plan

→ Briefly outline the position prior to the HRA.

→ Explain that the HRA has not introduced new rights.

→ Outline the ways in which the HRA allows the citizen to enforce human rights.

→ Analyse the effectiveness of the Act, with reference to authorities.

Diagram plan

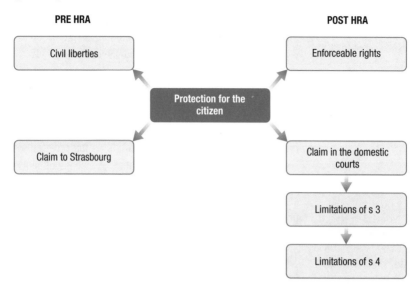

A printable version of this diagram is available from www.pearsoned.co.uk/lawexpressqa

Answer

[1]It is worth making sure that you have a concise summary of the purpose of the HRA at your fingertips, as many questions, like this one, ask you to assess how successful it has been in achieving its aims.

[2]A confident introduction sets out the approach that will be taken in the body of the answer.

[3]In order to determine the impact of the HRA, the answer needs to briefly explain the 'traditional' approach to rights in the United Kingdom.

The Human Rights Act 1998 (HRA) incorporated the European Convention on Human Rights into domestic law and provides a mechanism for the individual to seek protection of their rights in the domestic courts.[1] The HRA has been the focus of considerable media and political attention as a result of a number of high profile cases involving contentious issues such as prisoner rights, but it is not clear that it has been consistently applied to increase the protection afforded to citizens.[2]

Traditionally, the British subject enjoyed civil liberties rather than 'rights'.[3] Using this approach, an individual enjoys freedom to do any thing unless a law exists to prevent it. In Dicey's view of the constitution, the role of the judiciary is to ensure that civil liberties are maintained by preventing the arbitrary use of power. This traditional approach is perhaps best exemplified by the ruling in **Entick *v* Carrington** (1765) 19 State Tr 1029, in which the court held that, without legal authorisation, there was no power to enter an individual's home. Parliament is free to enact law on any subject, and accordingly, is able to remove or restrict the liberty of the

[4]Whilst there will be credit for being able to explain the Diceyean position, the strength of the answer is improved by being able to identify examples that explain the traditional approach.

[5]If you have a clear opinion, then do not be afraid to say so; you must be prepared to provide evidence to support what you say.

[6]The cases referred to are used to make a specific point about the issue raised in the question. The facts are not important here; only the fact they show the broad scope of s 3, therefore you don't need to waste the word count explaining the background.

[7]Most students will note the power to make a declaration of incompatibility; more marks will be given here for being able to comment on how little it has been used in practice. This shows you have done more than simply learn the sections of the HRA, and have understood how it operates.

[8]Again, the marker is reassured that each point made is relevant to the question.

citizen at will. Prior to the HRA, the courts would have no option but to enforce a statute, even when, as was the case in **IRC v Rossminster** [1980] AC 952, it was held that the interference with the privacy of the individual was 'breath-taking'. The Public Order Acts between the 1930s and the mid-1990s can be viewed as an incremental reduction in freedom to protest, and a corresponding increase in the powers of the police to regulate and control association.[4]

The European Convention on Human Rights provided some measure of protection in the domestic courts as the provisions of the Treaty were an aid to the interpretation of ambiguous legislation, and the judgments of the European Court of Human Rights (ECtHR) carried some persuasive force. In cases where there was no ambiguity, however, the citizen had no legal option but to seek redress by petition to the ECtHR, a costly and time-consuming process.

The HRA undoubtedly gives the judiciary greater scope to uphold the rights protected under the Convention.[5] The courts now have a duty to interpret legislation as compatible with the Convention 'so far as it is possible' (s 3). The courts have been clear that the duty applies even where there is no ambiguity, and can allow an interpretation that is 'linguistically strained' (**R v A** [2001] UKHL 25), and even the reading in of additional phrases (**Ghaidan v Godin Mendoza** [2004] UKHL 30). This can be viewed as a significant increase in protection for the rights of the citizen where the courts are willing to accept that the exercise of a statutory power infringes a Convention right.[6]

Where the court is unable to utilise interpretative powers to uphold a right, a declaration of incompatibility may be made (s 4). This can result in remedial action by the executive to amend the offending legislation, or introduce new legislation (s 10). However, it should be noted that the use of s 4 remains relatively rare, and a declaration of incompatibility cannot compel the executive to take action.[7] In addition, the HRA makes it clear that a declaration has no effect on the continued validity of the legislation and no impact on the parties to the case (s 4(6)). Therefore, the citizen who has been affected by the provision in question will still have little option but to look to Strasbourg for redress.[8]

The HRA has created mechanisms to assist the courts in protecting the rights of the citizen where they find that there has, in fact, been a violation. The judiciary has often accepted that deference to the decisions made by the executive or legislature should be granted. This was the position set out in the leading case of **R v DPP ex parte Kebiline** [2000] 2 AC 326, in which the court explained the need for deference on democratic grounds. This does respect the principle of the separation of powers, but arguably, has greatly reduced the impact of the HRA in protecting the rights of the individual,[9] in particular, when dealing with matters of some political sensitivity such as issues pertaining to national security. In the case of **R (Gillan) v Commissioner of Police for the Metropolis** [2006] UKHL 12, having indicated that deference should be given to the executive regarding the need for legislation, the judgment went on to state that it was hard to conceive of a situation where the use of powers of stop and search authorised by the statute would be disproportionate. This case can be seen as an example of the courts failing to protect the Convention rights of the citizen, a point supported by the subsequent judgment of the ECtHR, which unanimously found the powers to be unlawful. This can be contrasted, however, with instances in which the courts have been proactive and vocal in their support for Convention rights, such as the case of **A v Secretary of State for the Home Department** [2004] UKHL 56, in which a declaration of incompatibility in respect of the Anti-Terrorism Crime and Security Act was accompanied by stringent criticism.[10]

The HRA gives the citizen the right to bring a claim in respect of a violation of a Convention right by a 'public authority' (s 6). Therefore, all public authorities are required to seek to uphold individual rights. There has been some judicial difficulty in determining precisely how to determine whether or not a body is public. The case of **Anston Cantlow Parochial Church Council v Wallbank** [2003] UKHL 37 held that the authority should be 'governmental' and the test is primarily functional.[11] This may mean that there are instances where the individual has no claim against the body responsible for infringing their rights, but it should be remembered that s 6 specifies that courts and tribunals are public bodies which creates indirect horizontal effect.[12]

[9]Reference to the separation of powers is useful here, as it shows that you understand the constitutional context.

[10]This paragraph, and the cases cited, are important as this material forms the basis of the conclusion that the judiciary are inconsistent in upholding individual rights.

[11]In this instance, there is no need to give the facts of *Anston*; only the fact that it is authority for the fact that the function of the body in question must be considered.

[12]The final point made, again, refers back to the question by focusing on the effect of the HRA for individuals.

[13]The conclusion is quite brief, but the argument has been developed throughout the answer so can be summarised succinctly here.

The HRA has significantly increased the protection that can be afforded to convention rights in the domestic courts, by providing a route for redress against public bodies. However, the efficacy of the act depends in large part on the attitude of the judiciary to assessing the proportionality of executive action and this, as has been suggested, has not been consistent.[13]

 ## Make your answer stand out

- By considering, the effect of s 6(2), which affords a defence to a public authority that it is acting in accordance with primary legislation. This leaves the citizen in the unsatisfactory position of seeking a declaration under s 4 which, as the answer shows, has no bearing on the parties to a case. By making this point, you reinforce the argument that the HRA does not provide the individual with adequate redress.
- By expanding the argument that the ECtHR still has an important role in providing protection for UK citizens. You could do so by referencing cases in which the ECtHR has overturned domestic decisions and ruled that UK legislation is unlawful. *Gillan* v *UK* is a good, recent, example to cite here.

! Don't be tempted to...

- Simply describe the provisions of the HRA. It is important to show an understanding of how the Act works, but the answer must use the material to offer analysis of how effective it is in protecting individual rights.
- Spend too long outlining the position prior to the HRA. The focus of your answer must be on how effective the changes have been.

Question 6

The Human Rights Act is a significant factor in the loss of Parliamentary Sovereignty.
Discuss.

Answer plan

→ Briefly outline the key components of the doctrine of Parliamentary sovereignty.

→ Describe the major effects of the HRA.

→ Assess the impact of the HRA on the passage of legislation.

→ Analyse the impact of the HRA on existing legislation and consider whether or not this
undermines the supremacy of Parliament.

Diagram plan

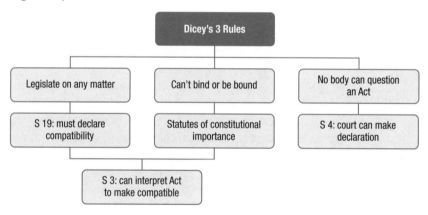

A printable version of this diagram is available from www.pearsoned.co.uk/lawexpressqa

Answer

[1]Any question that requires an explanation of parliamentary sovereignty requires the answer to show familiarity with the views of Dicey.

Dicey, writing in the nineteenth century, argued that Parliamentary supremacy was the cornerstone of the British constitution. His exposition of the doctrine acts as a starting point to assess whether or not the Human Rights Act (HRA) has had any significant effect on the position of the legislature.[1] It will be argued that there has been little real alteration to the constitutional arrangement of the United Kingdom.

According to Dicey, the doctrine of Parliamentary supremacy encompasses three aspects. First, Parliament is free to legislate on any subject-matter. Secondly, Parliament cannot be bound by a predecessor or bind a successor. Lastly, no person or body can question the validity of an act of Parliament. The effect of the HRA can be evaluated against these precepts in turn.[2]

[2]This is helpful, as it shows the marker that there will be a clear, logical structure.

In the case of **Madzimbamuto v Lardner-Burke** [1969] AC 645, Lord Reid observed that there were no constitutional or legal mechanisms to prevent Parliament acting, even if morally or politically 'highly improper'.[3] The HRA requires Parliament to be mindful of the European Convention of Human Rights in respect of all legislation. Section 19 stipulates that a Minister introducing legislation must make a statement of compatibility prior to the second reading of the Bill. If it is not possible, then the Minister must confirm that government still wishes to proceed. It is not necessary to give reasons to support either position. It is submitted that the effect of s 19 is limited.[4] Since the HRA came into force in 2000, there has only been one instance of a Bill being laid before Parliament without a statement of compatibility (enacted as the Communications Act 2003). A statement can be made even where there has been a derogation from an articled right in order to achieve compatibility (in respect of the Art 5 and the Anti-Terrorism Crime and Security Act 2001). Even if a statement is not made, or if an unsupportable statement is made, it is difficult to see how any challenge could be made, as deference to the legislative autonomy of Parliament would prevent this.[5] Article IX of the Bill of Rights protects proceedings in Parliament from judicial scrutiny, even where there have been allegations that Parliament has been defrauded (**British Railways Board v Pickin** [1974] AC 765). Although s 19 may require Parliament to follow a particular process, the lack of sanction for non-compliance undermines the claim that this can be viewed as constitutionally significant.[6]

[3]Whilst the answer could simply state that Parliament was entitled to legislate as it chose, the case is a useful illustration. The facts aren't required; the key point is the comment in the judgment that the moral content of a statute was constitutionally irrelevant.

[4]Credit will be given for giving a view, but this must be followed with some illustrative examples to support the assertion.

[5]This is a useful point to make, as it shows that the HRA does not infringe the principle of legislative supremacy.

[6]This kind of 'mini conclusion,' when you reach the end of each point, is a useful habit to get into. You can then be certain that you make sure you are focused on the question posed throughout your answer.

According to the Diceyean view, each successive Parliament is supreme, and cannot be bound by legislation enacted by a predecessor. Therefore, no statute can become entrenched. This aspect of the doctrine is illustrated by **Vauxhall Estates Ltd v Liverpool Corporation** [1932] 1 KB 733.[7] The case concerned a dispute regarding the compensation scheme applicable in a compulsory purchase of land. The Acquisition of Land (Assessment of

[7]It is not necessary to provide the facts of cases but here, a brief explanation of this key authority will demonstrate that the doctrine of implied repeal has been understood.

<table>
</table>

[8]It is not enough to state that the HRA may be a statute of constitutional significance; you must state this suggests the doctrine of implied repeal does not apply because it is this fact that impacts upon the principle of parliamentary supremacy.

[9]The operation of s 3 is almost always crucial to a discussion about the HRA, so it is worth making sure you know the critical wording from the section.

[10]It is important to use the authorities properly to help you build your answer to the question. Here, *Ghaidan* v *Mendoza* is used to show that there you can provide an example of words being read into a statute; but there is no need to give the facts.

[11]These are important cases that generally serve inter-changeable purposes as they both give examples of the use of s 3. Here, the use of these two short phrases from the judgment allows you to make a point about the limits of the interpretative power.

[12]Simply explaining the effect of s 4 will not be sufficient, if this isn't related back to consideration of the sovereignty of Parliament.

Compensation) Act 1919 laid down a scheme, and further stated that any inconsistent provision would be ineffective. The Housing Act of 1925 created a different payment scheme, without expressly repealing the earlier act. It was held that the later Act impliedly repealed the earlier provisions. More recently, it has been suggested that some statutes are entrenched. Case law has tended to centre on the European Communities Act 1972 (in particular, the series of cases concerning Factortame) but the arguments are equally applicable to the HRA. Indeed, Laws LJ included the Act in a list of statutes he suggested were 'of constitutional significance' and, therefore, not subject to the doctrine of implied repeal.[8]

The HRA imposes a duty on the judiciary to interpret legislation as compatible with convention rights 'so far as is possible to do so' (s 3).[9] The courts have, in a number of cases, indicated that this obligation extends to cover unambiguous statutory provisions, and even authorises the judiciary to read words into statute (see, for example, **Ghaidan v Mendoza** [2004] UKHL 30). It could be argued that this veers close to judicial legislation and therefore, an erosion of the legislative supremacy of Parliament.[10] Although there have been cases where it could be argued that the intention of Parliament has been subverted by the imposition of an interpretation that is 'linguistically strained' (**R v A** [2001] UKHL 25), the courts have been clear that a meaning cannot be imposed that goes 'against the grain' of the legislation (**Ghaidan v Mendoza**[11]).

If the courts are faced with a piece of legislation that cannot be read as compliant using s 3, then s 4 allows a declaration of incompatibility to be made. Hence, the judiciary make a clear statement to the executive that legislation is unsatisfactory. This could be viewed as permitting the judiciary to question the validity of an Act of Parliament, thereby undermining the last of the Diceyean precepts.[12] It should be noted that the judiciary view s 4 as a last resort, and declarations of incompatibility are relatively rare. Even when a declaration is made the supremacy of Parliament is preserved, as the section provides that the making of a declaration has no effect on the validity of the legislation, or on the parties to the case in which it is made. It may be the case that, where a declaration is made, the executive feels pressed to react, but this could be seen as a political choice rather than a constitutional requirement.

[13]The conclusion can draw together the material and focus directly on the constitutional impact of the Act.

It may appear that, in passing the Human Rights Act, Parliament has voluntarily ceded some constitutional authority to the judiciary. The impact should not be overstated, however, as the language of the Act is careful to maintain the supremacy of Parliament.[13] The effect of s 19 is, in reality, minimal, and has little effect on the ability of the House to legislate as it sees fit. The power to make a declaration of incompatibility is rarely used, and certainly does not empower the judiciary to ignore or overturn a legislative provision. The greatest threat to the autonomy of Parliament, then, is the interpretative duty imposed by s 3, but it is possible to argue that in utilising their powers, the judiciary are mindful of the intention of Parliament and respectful of the constitutional boundary between interpretation and legislation. Although it may be the case that the doctrine of implied repeal does not apply, the Act is not entrenched as express repeal is a possibility; indeed, the Conservative party have pledged to make this a reality.[14] The Human Rights Act has undoubtedly had significant impact as it allows the courts to evaluate the compatibility of legislation with the Convention, but the constitutional supremacy of Parliament is preserved.

[14]Reference to the Conservative party plans demonstrates an ability to place the subject in context.

 Make your answer stand out

- By expanding the discussion regarding 'statutes of constitutional significance', as the issue has been the subject of considerable academic debate. A good article commenting on the implications of Thoburn is Campbell, D. and Young, J., 'The metric martyrs and the entrenchment jurisprudence of Lord Justice Laws' [2002] PL 399. It is possible to argue that this is not a new argument; Bradley and Ewing outline statutes that could be said to be, practically, at least, entrenched (*Constitutional and Administrative Law* (14th edn) London: Pearson, pp. 62–70).

- By discussing the voluntary nature of any cessation of supremacy in more detail. Although linked to the issue of entrenchment, you could consider the political criticism of the HRA (including calls for it to be repealed and replaced by the Conservative party during the 2010 election campaign) and ask whether this is feasible. This would show an ability to comment on new developments.

! Don't be tempted to...

■ Provide an answer that concentrates on a general discussion regarding the doctrine of Parliamentary supremacy. Although it is crucial to set out the Diceyean criteria, these must be used as a springboard to consider the constitutional effect of the HRA.

■ Simply describe the different provisions of s 3 and s 4. You must be prepared, when dealing with a question like this, to reach some conclusions and state an opinion about the impact of the Act on parliamentary supremacy. Remember, marks are given for analysis of the law, not for simply restating it.

Freedom of association and assembly

How this topic may come up in exams

This topic is commonly examined by problem scenarios, which often require an evaluation of the provisions of the Public Order Act 1986. These questions are generally fairly straightforward, provided you have a good understanding of the statutory provisions. Essay questions often concern the compatibility of statutory and common law powers with rights under Arts 10 and 11 of the Convention. Students should be aware of provisions contained in other legislation that impact on freedom of assembly. An understanding of the common law powers available to the police to prevent a breach of the peace is crucial.

Attack the question

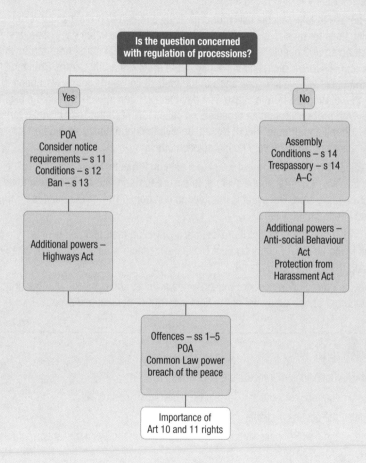

Is the question concerned with regulation of processions?

Yes

No

POA
Consider notice
requirements – s 11
Conditions – s 12
Ban – s 13

Assembly
Conditions – s 14
Trespassory – s 14
A–C

Additional powers –
Highways Act

Additional powers –
Anti-social Behaviour
Act
Protection from
Harassment Act

Offences – ss 1–5
POA
Common Law power
breach of the peace

Importance of
Art 10 and 11 rights

❓ Question 1

Brendan and Simon are the organisers of a group called 'Citizen Beats', who believe that the public should have greater access to more free music events. At the annual general meeting, a campaign strategy for the months ahead is agreed.

Brendan agrees to take responsibility for organising a march to protest about recent changes to licensing laws for music venues. The march is to take place in ten days' time, and he hopes that about 200 people will attend. A route is planned that starts from the Town Hall in Leeds, and will follow a circular, mile long, route around the City Centre. Brendan intends that the marchers will walk in the centre of the road, to cause maximum disruption to the city and create attention for the cause. The day that Brendan intends to hold the event also coincides with procession that an organisation called 'Silent Nights' has planned for the same day, on the same route. 'Silent Nights' believe that loud music should be banned. The two groups are known to be very hostile to each other.

Simon decides to hold a free music event in a field on the outskirts of Headingley. He arranges the hire of a large sound system, to ensure that the music will be able to be heard in the surrounding area. The event is intended to last from 11pm to 6am and is arranged to take place in one month's time.

Brendan and Simon begin to distribute leaflets advertising their planned events. One of the leaflets is found by Chief Superintendent Didson, who seeks your advice about whether he is able to stop the events going ahead.

Please advise Chief Superintendent Didson of his powers, and consider whether or not it matters whether or not the owner of the field is aware of the planned event.

Answer plan

→ Provide definitions of 'procession' and 'assembly'.

→ Explain the requirements of s 11 that Brendan should comply with.

→ Outline the powers available under s 12 and s 13.

→ Outline the powers available under s 14, and s 14A in the event the landowner has not given permission.

→ Consider powers of arrest at common law and under the Public Order Act.

Diagram plan

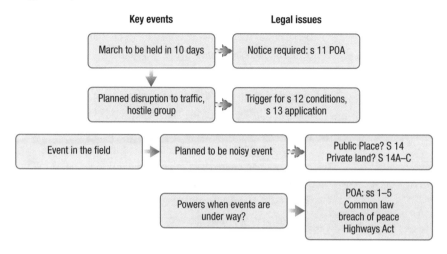

Key events   **Legal issues**

Key events	Legal issues
March to be held in 10 days	Notice required: s 11 POA
Planned disruption to traffic, hostile group	Trigger for s 12 conditions, s 13 application
Event in the field → Planned to be noisy event	Public Place? S 14 Private land? S 14A–C
Powers when events are under way?	POA: ss 1–5 Common law breach of peace Highways Act

A printable version of this diagram is available from www.pearsoned.co.uk/lawexpressqa

Answer

Brendan and Simon are planning two events to raise public awareness of their campaign. The freedom to protest is seen as central to political democracy and therefore the freedom of assembly is protected by Art 10 of the European Convention of Human Rights. The Convention recognises legitimate reasons to interfere with the right, such as the prevention of disorder or crime; permitted qualifications are listed at Art 10(2).[1] The main restrictions on the freedom to assembly are contained within the Public Order Act 1986, which imposes obligations on the organisers of protests, and gives the police powers to control public gatherings. Chief Superintendent Didson will need to be advised about these provisions, and some additional statutory and common law powers.

[1] It is useful to demonstrate an awareness of the Convention rights engaged by the issues raised in the question.

A procession is defined at common law as 'a body of persons moving along a route' (**Flockhart v Robinson** [1950] 2 KB 498[2]). Section 11 of the Public Order Act 1986 (POA) requires the organisers of processions to give written notice of their intentions, provided the procession is for one of the specified purposes. These include events designed to show support for, or to publicise, a campaign. Brendan should have provided written notice six days in advance of the planned event, including details of the route, expected numbers,

[2] This area of the syllabus can feel a little short on case law authority, so where there is a relevant case it will always be helpful to cite it.

[3]The question states that advice should be given to Superintendent Didson. A good answer needs to remember this and use the information to set out the powers available to the police.

the duration, and his details, unless it is not reasonably practicable to provide notice (s 11(1)). Chief Inspector Didson should be aware that, if the notice does not arrive in the next four days, Brendan will be liable for a summary offence unless he can claim he was not aware of the notice requirements (s 11(8)).[3]

Section 12 gives the police powers to impose conditions on a procession if there is a risk of serious damage to property, serious disruption to the life of the community, or serious public disorder (s 12(1)(a)), or if it is felt the purpose of the march is to intimidate others (s 12(1)(b)).[4] If these conditions are met, any necessary conditions can be imposed to address the risk, including the route. The route is intended to cause disruption, and to ensure confrontation with the rival group. It would seem there are reasonable grounds to impose conditions on the route, time, or duration.[5] Chief Superintendent Didson should notify Brendan of these in writing (s 12(3)). Failure to comply will be an arrestable offence.

[4]The majority of students know that s 12 allows conditions to be imposed, but many fail to note that this is not an absolute power and is dependent on identifying one of the specified risk factors.

[5]It is not sufficient to set out the powers given by s 12; these must be used to analyse the information provided.

In addition, the most senior officer present at the procession is authorised to impose new or additional conditions that appear necessary, thereby allowing the police to react to any unforeseen risks that may arise on the day.

[6]Students often make the mistake of stating that the option to apply for a ban is available, without qualifying this by pointing out that it is a draconian power that is rarely justified.

[7]The fact that notice is not needed for an assembly is a very simple point that is often overlooked, but marks will be given for noting the differences between the two kinds of public order events.

If there are no conditions that could be imposed that would be sufficient to mitigate the risks outlined above, an application can be made to the local authority to ban the procession (s 13). The Chief Inspector should note that a ban cannot be imposed on a particular organisation or event, but will apply to all (or a class of) processions within a specified area for a period of time not exceeding three months. Therefore, a ban will only be granted if the risks posed by the event are extremely serious.[6] The limitations on this section perhaps highlight the general importance of the Art 10 right and the unwillingness of the legislature to contemplate a situation where legitimate public protest is curtailed without good reason.[7] In this scenario it should be noted that both planned processions would be unable to go ahead if a ban is granted.

⁸Awareness of this distinction from processing will be rewarded by the examiner.

⁹The question requires the answer to consider the provisions pertaining to trespassory assemblies. It is important to make the point that unless this applies, the Public Order Act does not confer any power on the Chief Superintendent; that is why this point is crucial.

¹⁰You do not need to give a lot of detail about the offences in the Public Order Act here, there is certainly no need to describe the constituent elements of the crimes.

¹¹Questions concerning public order tend to invite statute-based answers; where possible and appropriate, case law should be used to demonstrate how the courts interpret statutory provisions.

The planned assembly is not subject to notice requirements.[8] The POA gives powers to impose conditions on an assembly in a public place (defined at s 16), mirroring the provisions at s 12. Although the noisy event is likely to cause 'serious disruption', it is not clear that POA will assist, as it appears it will be on private land. It will, therefore, be critical to ascertain whether or not the landowner has given permission, and whether there are any limits on that permission. If the landowner has not given permission, or if the event is likely to go beyond the limits, it will be considered a trespassory assembly as defined at s 14(a) of the POA. Sections 14(a)–(c) of the POA were inserted by the Criminal Justice and Public Order Act 1994, specifically to allow for the control of 'raves', which were prevalent at the time.[9] Chief Inspector Didson can make an application to ban trespassory assemblies in a designated area for a period of time no longer than four days. Unlike the powers contained at s 13, there is no need to demonstrate that conditions have been considered and exhausted prior to making an application. Once a ban is in place, Simon should be informed of the order. Once aware, continuing with the event is an offence (s 14(b)). In addition, the police are empowered to stop vehicles or persons on route to the event and direct them to turn away (s 14(c)).

If the procession is allowed to go ahead, with or without conditions, criminal offences are created by ss 1–5 of the POA in the event of disorder. These range from riot (s 1) to disorderly conduct (s 5).[10] Section 137 of the Highways Act makes obstruction of the highway an arrestable offence. Obstruction can be construed as any behaviour other than passing along the highway, or activities reasonably incidental to the activity. Chief Superintendent Didson should note that the courts have, on occasion, taken a liberal view of permissible 'incidental' activities in order to protect the right to protest (**Hirst and Agu v Chief Constable of West Yorkshire** (1987) 85 Cr App R 143).[11] The police have the common law power of arrest for breach of the peace, or to prevent an imminent breach of the peace. This power is potentially extremely broad, as the officers present have considerable discretion to determine what constitutes a threat to the peace. The House of Lords, in **R (Laporte) v Chief Constable of Yorkshire** [2006] UKHL 55 have, however, confirmed that an arrest will not be justified unless it can be demonstrated that there is an immediate threat. The decision pointed out that the Public Order Act created carefully defined powers and offences to deal with protest, whilst allowing for democratic demonstrations, and that therefore, co-existing common law powers could not be used disproportionately and indiscriminately. The Chief Superintendent should note this decision, and be aware that, since the Human Rights Act, the courts have been less willing to automatically endorse the discretionary decisions of the police.[12]

[12]This case allows the answer to be a little more discursive and demonstrate a broader knowledge of the relationship between the Public Order Act and human rights law.

Chief Superintendent Didson can try to impose prior controls on the procession, and his officers are empowered to deal with any disorder that occurs. His powers in relation to the assembly will depend on whether or not it is a trespassory event.[13]

[13]As with all problem scenarios, a summary of the advice given is a useful way to conclude the answer.

✓ Make your answer stand out

- By expanding the discussion regarding the imposition of conditions. The officer could be advised about the types of conditions that have been endorsed by the courts in cases such as *Police* v *Reid* [1987] Crim LR 702, or more recently, *Austin and Saxby* v *Commissioner of Police of the Metropolis* [2005] HRLR 20. This would allow you to demonstrate your ability to consider the effect of a variety of judgments on the facts you are dealing with.

- By discussing the implications of the broad sweep of discretionary powers available to the police, and considering whether or not judicial review can be an adequate protection for Convention rights in this context. You could suggest that any review of decisions taken during a demonstration will occur after the opportunity to rectify the decision has passed.

! Don't be tempted to...

- Simply outline the relevant sections of the Public Order Act. Answers on this topic have a tendency to be rather descriptive. There is a danger that students will just set out the statutory provisions, and fail to apply these to provide advice as required.

- Make the mistake of outlining the law without being specific about tailoring the advice for the police officer. This is a popular topic in exams, and most students will be able to state the powers given in the Public Order Act. In order to get higher marks, you will need to make sure that your answer concentrates on assessing the powers given to the police (rather than the responsibilities of organisers).

❓ Question 2

You are approached by the leader of the Student Union on Monday morning, seeking your advice. Westchester City Council has recently begun to publicise their intention to ban 'student nights' in all city centre pubs, bars and clubs. The Student Union intends to invite students to gather in Central Square outside the City Council offices at 2pm on Friday afternoon to protest. This has been chosen as a suitable time because the licensing committee meets at 2.15pm and the protestors will be able to protest at members of the committee as they enter for the meeting.

It is then intended that the students march to Westchester Park, past the University campus, before holding a rally in the Park.

The Student Union anticipates that a large number of students will attend.

Please advise the Student Union of the following matters:

As organizers, are there any steps that should be taken before the protest?

What powers, if any will the police have prior to, and during the protest?

Answer plan

→ Define 'procession' and 'assembly'.

→ Outline the powers available to the police during the first assembly.

→ Explain the obligations on the organisers of the procession.

→ Discuss the powers of arrest available to the police.

Diagram plan

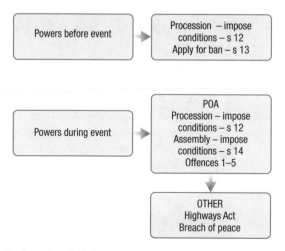

A printable version of this diagram is available from www.pearsoned.co.uk/lawexpressqa

Answer

[1]The introduction identifies the key legal provisions that need to be addressed. This is a good way to begin an answer to a problem question, and certainly better than simply rewriting the facts.

[2]It is not necessary to reproduce the sections of the statute that apply in their entirety. It is clear from the reference to s 16 here that there is an understanding of its effect.

[3]It is a good idea to keep reminding the examiner that you are using the law to advise the parties as required, by applying the points made about the law to the facts.

[4]Most students will state that 'the police' can impose conditions; so inclusion of this additional detail will show that you have read the statute thoroughly.

[5]By making this point, you show the examiner firstly that you are familiar with a broader range of cases, and secondly, that you can evaluate the effect of the judgment.

[6]Knowledge of the case law allows for a more analytical approach to the problem. Rather than simply listing the powers available to the police, a view can be given about the legality of any conditions imposed.

The right to protest is considered to be central to fair and open democracy, and as such is protected by Art 10 of the European Convention of Human Rights. The Convention acknowledges that protest could lead to disorder, and disruption to society, hence, qualifications are permitted at Art 10(2). The Public Order Act 1986 contains the main statutory controls that are likely to affect the planned activities of the student union, although they will also need to be advised of additional powers in the Highways Act, and at common law.[1]

The gathering outside the Council offices will be an assembly in a public place (defined at s 16),[2] within the scope of the POA. Since the Anti-Social Behaviour Act 2003 amended s 16, only two persons need attend for the powers of restraint to arise. It is not necessary for the organisers to take any particular steps prior to the assembly, but they should be advised of the powers that can be utilised to control the protest once it is in progress.[3] Section 14 of the Public Order Act enables the most senior officer on the scene[4] to impose such conditions as he or she believes are necessary to prevent serious damage, disorder or disruption to the life of the community; or if it is felt that the purpose of the protest is to intimidate others. The case of **Police v Reid** [1987] Crim LR 702 concerned a protest outside an embassy in which participants shouted at persons entering the building. It was held that conditions imposed to prevent this were unlawful, as intimidation is more than mere discomfort. This is one of the few cases concerning the use of s 14 in which the domestic courts have been prepared to interfere with the discretion of the police.[5] In **R (Brehony) v Chief Constable of Greater Manchester** [2005] EWHC 640, it was held that s 6 of the HRA imposes a requirement for any condition to be proportionate to the risk involved, but the court decided that inconvenience to Christmas shoppers could be construed as 'serious disruption' to the life of the community. The House of Lords have agreed that the controversial technique of detaining protestors in a location for a period of time (kettling) can be a lawful condition and compliant with Arts 5, 10 and 11, provided it is used sparingly and when necessary (**Austin and Saxby v Commissioner of Police of the Metropolis** [2005] HRLR 20; it should be noted this case is now due for consideration by the European Court of Human Rights).[6] Once a condition has been made, failure to comply will

[7]There will be no additional marks given for repeating the same information that you have already provided.

[8]You must distinguish between the two types of protest which occur in this scenario.

[9]It is important to offer some solutions to the union, rather than just setting out the law which applies.

[10]There is no need to reiterate the grounds here, as they have been explained above, it would be a waste of your word count, but you should make it clear you know that the grounds are set out at s 12 in respect of the procession.

[11]Very often, students state that s 13 gives the police the power to ban processions; you will be rewarded for noting that the power is only to make the application.

be an offence. The planned rally in the park will also be an assembly, and all the same considerations apply.[7] The organisers need to note that there is no means available to appeal the conditions at the time, and any subsequent review is unlikely to be successful, given the existing authorities.

Once the students begin the march to the park, the protest becomes a procession,[8] defined at common law as 'a body of persons moving along a route' (**Flockhart v Robinson** [1950] 2 KB 498). As the intention is to express support for, and publicise, a campaign, it is governed by s 11 of the POA, which imposes an obligation on the organisers to give advance notice of the event. The notice must be in writing, and must contain details of the date, time, route and duration of the march, together with details of those organising the event. Failure to provide the notice (unless it is not reasonably practicable to do so) is an offence (s 11(7)). The notice must be given six clear days before the planned event. Therefore, the Student Union will be unable to comply with this requirement and may wish to consider putting the event back.[9] Section 11 requires notice to be given, but there is no need to seek authorisation for the event.

Once notice has been received by the police, conditions can be imposed on the conduct of the march on the same grounds which justify the imposition of conditions on an assembly (s 12).[10] If imposed in advance, the conditions must be authorised by the Chief of Police and notified to the organisers in writing. Failure to comply with a condition will be a criminal offence. In addition, the most senior police officer on the scene will be able to react to changing circumstances on the date of the event and can impose additional conditions as necessary. The organisers will be liable for a failure to comply with a condition, unless they can argue in defence that the failure arose from circumstances beyond their control (s 12(4)).

If the Chief of Police does not feel that any conditions are sufficient to prevent disorder, then s 13 allows for an application to be made to ban the procession.[11] The local authority can issue a banning order if it is felt that the march will lead to serious public disorder, but the ban will be applicable to any procession in a specified area for a period of up to three months. This power has rarely been used since the POA came into force, perhaps because the powers contained in s 12 are broad enough to allow the police to contain and control disorder. There is no power to ban an assembly in a public place (although a ban could be sought if either assembly was due to take place on private land (s 14(a)).

Once the protest is underway, the police have considerable powers to control any disorder which may arise. The POA creates arrestable offences ranging in seriousness from riot (s 1) to the minor offence of disorderly conduct (s 5).[12] Arguably, these offences give the police sufficient powers to contain any disorder, but there are additional powers available. The march along the public highway could lead to obstruction of the highway which is an offence contrary to s 137 of the Highways Act. It should be noted that the courts have been willing to protect the right to protest by holding that an otherwise lawful protest march can be considered a legitimate use of the highway (**Hirst and Agu v Chief Constable of West Yorkshire** (1987) 85 Cr App R 143). Perhaps the broadest ranging power available is the common law power of arrest for breach of the peace, or to prevent an imminent breach of the peace. Fenwick suggests that this power is so broad, and so 'breathtakingly imprecise' that it makes the protection afforded to the right to protest in statute almost irrelevant. It is right to say that the power gives an individual officer considerable discretion to decide that a breach may occur and therefore make a pre-emptive arrest. However, the courts do make it clear that only a person creating a threat should be arrested (**Beatty v Gilbanks** (1882) LR 9 QBD 308), and that it is necessary to show the threat is immediate (**R (Laporte) v Chief Constable of Yorkshire** [2006] UKHL 55). The power should not be used indiscriminately and disproportionately (**Laporte**).

The Student Union have no obligations prior to the planned assemblies, but have failed to provide adequate notice of the procession and should reconsider the date in order to comply with their legal obligations. As organisers, they should be aware that they will be liable for the failure of protestors to comply with any conditions imposed. The police have considerable powers to control any disorder which arises during the event.[13]

[12]It isn't necessary to outline the differing requirements for each offence.

[13]The conclusion should briefly summarise the advice given, and demonstrate how each aspect of the question has been addressed.

✓ Make your answer stand out

- By considering in more detail the broad scope of powers of arrest available to the police, particularly in respect of breach of the peace. It could be argued that this places a potentially significant limitation on the freedom of the Student Union to conduct an effective protest.

- By expanding your argument to consider the impact of the discretion afforded to the police on Convention rights. There is a great deal of academic comment about this issue. Useful articles include Fenwick, H. 'Marginalising human rights: breach of the peace, "kettling", the Human Rights Act and public protest' [2009] PL 737 and Stone, R. 'Breach of the peace: the case for abolition' [2001] 2 WebJCLI.

- When discussing the case of *Austin*, you could consider whether or not the ruling is likely to survive, following more recent decisions concerning ss 44–47 of the Terrorism Act (see Chapter 9 for detailed discussion).

! Don't be tempted to...

- Reproduce large sections of statute in your answer. Try to summarise the key points that apply to the problem. Some universities allow you to take a statute book into your exam and some unconfident students do copy whole chunks of legislation into the answer. This is never a good strategy. You need to show your examiner that you understand the provisions, and to do this you need to be able to explain the law in your own words.

- Ignore powers that the police have in addition to those set out in the Public Order Act 1986. This question is not limited in this way; you are asked to address all the powers available to deal with disorder. You must, therefore, note the common law powers in respect of breach of the peace, and you should also mention the Highways Act.

Question 3

The creation of offences of aggravated trespass, and the use of civil injunctions have led to a situation where greater weight is given to the rights of businesses than to the right to protest.

Discuss.

Answer plan

→ Explain the rights at Arts 10 and 11.

→ Distinguish between protest, and disruptive action.

→ Explain the need to balance the rights of competing interest groups.

→ Assess the effect of s 68 CJPOA.

→ Consider the use of injunctions under the Protection from Harassment Act 1997.

Diagram plan

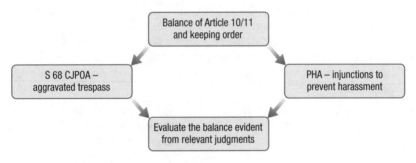

A printable version of this diagram is available from www.pearsoned.co.uk/lawexpressqa

Answer

[1]By referring to the two separate interests (business and protest), the examiner is asking you to consider the balancing act that the judiciary have to perform when considering Convention rights and by raising this in the introduction you demonstrate that you have understood the question.

Freedom of expression, association and assembly are expressly protected by the European Convention on Human Rights at Arts 10 and 11. These rights are considered central to the democratic process, which should tolerate and encourage the expression of minority views. There are limits upon such freedoms, however, as any government may legitimately seek to keep order and ensure that individuals can go about their business without fear of criminal interference.[1] Article 11 protects only peaceful assembly; therefore, there is no protection for violent protest.

[2]This question asks for a discussion of provisions in the Criminal Justice and Public Order Act, and civil injunctions. An explanation of the main statutory controls on protest demonstrates knowledge and gives the discussion some helpful context, but must be brief.

[3]It is always a good idea to give an illustrative example of the law in operation as this will provide support for the point raised, and show that you really understand the issue.

[4]You need to keep returning to the balancing exercise conducted by the courts, as you have identified this as the central issue. All the points you discuss should be related to the central argument.

[5]It will be difficult to obtain good marks for this question without a reasonably detailed knowledge of some key cases, as you must show how the courts have addressed the balance to be struck between competing interests.

In the United Kingdom, despite numerous statutory and common law provisions which entitle the state to control public processions, and assemblies, the basic right to engage in political protests of this type is supported. The Public Order Act 1986 provides the key legislative framework, and although the police have powers to impose conditions on processions or static assemblies in public places, the assumption appears to be that they should be permitted to proceed save in the most extreme circumstances.[2] For example, s 11 states organisers of a procession must give notification, but they are not required to seek permission. Only where there is a grave risk to public order that cannot be addressed by the imposition of conditions can the police make an application for a ban (s 13).[3]

The position is, arguably, more complex when the aim of a protest is not simply the expression of a view, but rather, to disrupt or prevent others from engaging in lawful activity. Here, there has been a tension between civil and criminal sanctions which can be invoked to curb direct action and protest, and the duty imposed on the court to uphold convention rights by the Human Rights Act 1998. The courts are asked to strike a balance between the rights of competing interest groups.[4]

The Criminal Justice and Public Order Act 1994 introduced measures to address problems caused by protestors who sought to enter land or premises and disrupt activity by criminalising 'aggravated trespass', and has been utilised to prosecute individuals and groups engaged in protests regarding, *inter alia*, foreign policy in Iraq, experimentation on animals, and genetically modified crops. The case of **R v Jones** [2006] UKHL 16 involved defendants who trespassed on to military bases with the intention of disrupting activity, to protest against involvement in the war with Iraq.[5] The defendants sought to argue that the conflict was an 'aggressive war', and therefore illegal under international law. If there was no 'lawful' activity taking place, it followed that there could be no intention to commit the offences outlined in s 68. The House of Lords were not prepared to entertain the argument. Lord Hoffmann plainly considered that the argument was simply an attempt to gain further publicity during the court case; a form of protest through litigation. The majority of case law decided regarding s 68 has rejected a claim that interference with the activities of others is justifiable. It is submitted that this is not contentious, as the offence seeks to

[6]Having considered the case law under s 68, the discussion needs to return to the central theme, whether the balance between competing interests has been struck appropriately.

[7]The question does not explicitly specify the Protection from Harassment Act but reference to injunctions implies you should discuss it.

[8]Here, a detailed knowledge of case law will is key, as this will help you to identify a relevant aspect of civil law and this will be rewarded.

[9]The use of the contrasting cases is helpful here as it allows the answer to examine the key argument, which is how the courts have attempted to balance business interests and article rights. You must ensure, though, that you use the case law to help you draw some conclusions about the development of the judicial approach.

[10]If you can, it is worth revising a few short quotes such as this one, which neatly encapsulate an idea.

protect the rights of individuals going about their lawful business, and therefore the legislation falls squarely within the qualifications permitted by Arts 10 and 11. Civil disobedience may, or may not, have a moral or philosophical justification in any given instance, but there appears to have been no compelling legal excuse promulgated by the protestors in these cases.[6]

More controversial is the use of civil injunctions to restrain or prevent protest under the Protection from Harassment Act 1997.[7] The Act was designed to address the problem of 'stalking', and permits a civil injunction to be granted where a course of conduct creates harassment, alarm or distress. Breach of the injunction is a criminal offence. There have been a series of cases involving protests about animal experimentation, in which civil injunctions have been obtained to restrain the activities of both individuals and groups.[8] In an early case, **Huntingdon Life Sciences Ltd v Curtin** (1997) *The Times*, 11 December, the judge refused to allow the act to be used to injunct a group, stating that it could not have been Parliament's intention that the statute would be used to suppress public protest. However, later cases have sanctioned the use of the Act to restrain the activities of protestors, including placing limitations on protesting at a laboratory save at specified times in the case of **University of Oxford v Broughton** [2004] EWHC 2543 (QB). In the latter case, the judiciary were clearly mindful of the need to balance the competing rights of protestors with the Art 8 rights of employees and contractors of the university. A recent decision was more supportive of the rights of protestors, and refused to allow an injunction to prevent protestors outside a facility using megaphones, wearing blood spattered clothing and masks **(Novartis Pharmaceuticals UK Ltd v Stop Huntingdon Animal Cruelty** [2010] HRLR 8).[9] It was held that whilst there could be occasions when protest crossed a line and became harassment; opinions that some find offensive should nevertheless be able to be expressed. As was said in **Redmond-Bate v DPP** [1999] Crim LR 998: 'Freedom only to speak inoffensively is not worth having.'[10] The courts continue to take a dim view of civil disobedience when this infringes upon the rights of others.

It is hard to see why the right to protest should extend into the curtailment of the liberties of others, by allowing protest to prevent individuals or companies carrying out their business. It is important, however, that the right to protest, and to protest robustly, is supported and upheld. If this does not occur, then there is a danger that the interest and opinions of businesses and corporations will be afforded undue weight in any debate, and those of minority groups may not be heard. This was a point stressed in the judgment of the European Court of Human Rights in **Steel and Morris v United Kingdom** (2005) 41 EHRR 22, in which it was held that refusing to grant the applicants legal aid to defend a libel action instigated by McDonalds infringed Art 10. The public interest demands that those 'outside the mainstream' can disseminate information and ideas. It is submitted that the judicial approach in response to s 68, and the Protection from Harassment Act, has sought to strike an appropriate balance by supporting the right to air controversial opinions, but preventing behaviour that unduly interferes with the lawful activity of others.[11]

[11]It is important to conclude by offering a view regarding the central argument. There is no 'correct' answer, as such, but you should ensure that the conclusions you reach are supported by the evidence provided in your argument.

✓ Make your answer stand out

- By considering the implications of the use of the Protection from Harassment Act in more detail. Is it appropriate that it has been utilised to deal with public protest, when this was not the problem Parliament had in mind? You should refer to the discussion of the use of the Act in Fenwick, *Civil Liberties and Human Rights* (4th edn, 2007) London: Routledge Cavendish, pp. 787–98 for a detailed analysis of the issue.

- By incorporating academic comment in your answer, as well as assessment of relevant case law. This will add weight to your arguments. Fenwick is an excellent starting point, as is Stone, *Textbook on Civil Liberties and Human Rights* (8th edn, 2010), Oxford: Oxford University Press.

! Don't be tempted to...

- Talk generally about powers to restrain protest; this question is focused on two particular provisions. You should not attempt this question if you have focused your revision on the application of the Public Order Act 1986. 'Question spotting' is a dangerous revision strategy. Students who expect this topic to be dealt with by a problem scenario focusing on the POA will be in trouble if forced to attempt this question!

- Attempt this question without knowledge of a range of cases that illustrate how the courts approach protests that impinge on business interests. Without this, you will not be able to obtain good marks as your answer will lack analysis.

❓ Question 4

'Trainers not traffic' is the name given to an event that takes place once a month in Fetcham City Centre, to protest against pollution caused by too much traffic. The participants, all joggers, congregate outside the Town Hall on the last Friday of the month, and at 5pm set off jogging for one hour. They take up as much room on the road as possible, to disrupt the traffic. Sunil organised the first event, and pays for a notice in the local paper inviting people to attend. The route is never decided in advance, as whoever jogs the fastest decides where to go.

One Friday, as the joggers congregate, the police hand out flyers which state: 'This is an illegal procession, because no notice has been given. Therefore, taking part is a crime.'

One of the joggers, a law student, says this is rubbish, and the event goes ahead. After 20 minutes, the police arrest Sunil.

The following day, several joggers climb over a wall into the local authority bus garage, and chain themselves to a bus. They are carrying placards that state 'Pollution is a crime. Prevent crime'. It is several hours before the chains are cut and the buses can set off. All the protestors are arrested.

The next day, 20 joggers congregate on a patch of land outside a privately owned coach garage and shout at coach drivers as they arrive for work. The police are called but decide not to attend. Several coach drivers are too frightened to go into work, and a considerable amount of money is lost. The coach company is considering whether or not to take legal action against the police for failing to act, and to prevent the protestors from attending again.

Consider the legality of the activities described, and whether the police have acted properly.

Answer plan

→ Outline the notice requirements in s 11 of the Public Order Act.

→ Analyse the legality of the police actions, and consider the case of *Kay*.

→ Assess the legality of the protest at the bus garage, in the light of s 68 CJPOA.

→ Discuss the conduct of the assembly at the coach depot.

Diagram plan

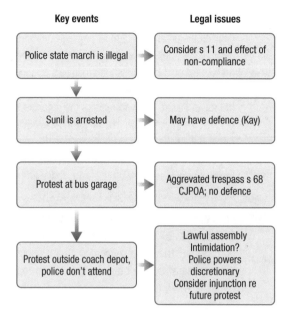

Key events

Legal issues

Police state march is illegal ➡ Consider s 11 and effect of non-compliance

⬇

Sunil is arrested ➡ May have defence (Kay)

⬇

Protest at bus garage ➡ Aggrevated trespass s 68 CJPOA; no defence

⬇

Protest outside coach depot, police don't attend ➡ Lawful assembly Intimidation? Police powers discretionary Consider injunction re future protest

A printable version of this diagram is available from www.pearsoned.co.uk/lawexpressqa

Answer

This scenario deals with the freedom of individuals and organisations to engage in forms of protest. Articles 10 and 11 of the European Convention of Human Rights protect the rights of expression, and assembly, in recognition of the fact that tolerating protest and dissent is seen as one of the hallmarks of a democracy. It is accepted, however, that a state may have legitimate reason to limit these rights, and the permitted qualifications are listed within the convention. In order to advise the joggers, it will be necessary to consider the restrictions on protest contained in the Public Order Act 1986 (POA), the Criminal Justice and Public Order Act 1994 (CJPOA), as well as civil sanctions created by the Protection from Harassment Act 1997 (PHA).[1]

[1]The facts of this problem raise issues about several different legal provisions. Setting them out in the introduction shows the marker that the key issues have been identified.

The monthly event in Fetcham City Centre is a procession, as defined in **Flockhart v Robinson** [1950] 2 KB 498 as 'a body of persons moving along a route'. The Public Order Act 1986 imposes obligations on the organisers of most processions including those which are designed to publicise or show support for a campaign, as is the case here.[2] Section 11 requires the organisers of such processions to give written notice to the police, six days in advance, including details of the route. Failure to do so renders the organisers liable for a criminal offence. The flyer distributed by the police, however, does not accurately reflect the legal position. Section 11 requires the organisers of particular processions to give notice, but failure to do so does not render the procession itself unlawful. Those in the procession are not committing an offence simply by taking part.[3]

Following the decision in **Kay v Commissioner of Police of the Metropolis** [2008] UKHL 69, Sunil may be able to deny liability for an offence.[4] That case concerned an analogous event, the monthly 'critical mass' cycle ride in London which took place on the last Friday of every month at a specific time, with no particular route. The House of Lords were only asked to consider whether or not the event was 'customary' and therefore exempt from notice provisions at s 11. Lord Philips also made a number of *obiter* statements regarding the applicability of notice requirements to such events. The case turned on whether or not a procession with a route that varied each week could be considered to be customary. It was held that despite a variable route, each monthly event shared sufficient common features to be able to state that it was a common event. Therefore, Sunil may be able to argue that the 'Trainers not traffic' events are exempt from the notice requirements at s 11.[5]

Further, Lord Philips rejected the submission that, unless customary, it would be impossible to arrange a procession of this type that did not have a planned route. The submission was based on the proposition that s 11 imposes a requirement to give notice of the route, and criminal liability if a different route is taken. This was, in the view of Lord Philips, 'draconian'. It would seem, then, that the event was lawful, and Sunil will have an arguable defence.

The position of the joggers who enter the bus garage is less certain. It is likely that the bus garage is private land, and therefore, entry will constitute civil trespass. Section 68 of the CJPOA creates an offence of 'aggravated trespass', committed by entry onto private land with the intention of disrupting or obstructing lawful activity. Here, the offence appears to be made out. It would appear that, based on the posters, the joggers may seek to argue they were acting in order to prevent a crime, but there is no precedent which would support this.[6] Although s 3 of the Criminal Law Act 1967 authorises 'public defence' to prevent criminal activity, **Blake v DPP** [1993] Crim LR 586 rejected a similar claim on the basis that the section was designed to excuse conduct involving a degree of force. It will also be difficult to point to a particular criminal offence alleged against the owners of the bus garage. Similar arguments were explored in detail, and comprehensively rejected, by the House of Lords in **R v Jones** [2006] UKHL 16, who declined to support direct action as a form of legitimate protest where this involved interference with the lawful activities of others. Therefore, the joggers will be liable for the offence of aggravated trespass and do not appear to have a defence.[7]

The protest outside the garage appears to take place on public land, and will therefore constitute an assembly as defined at s 16 of the Public Order Act.[8] There is no requirement to give notice of an assembly. Once called, the police could impose conditions on the conduct of the assembly if satisfied that these are necessary to combat a serious risk of public disorder, damage to property, disruption to the life of the community, or if the purpose of the gathering is to intimidate others. The police choose not to take action despite the fact that the protestors are shouting at drivers. The coach company may seek judicial review of this decision, on the basis that the police did not exercise their discretion correctly.[9] This is unlikely to succeed because, first, there may not be grounds to impose conditions on the assembly due to the abuse; as the case of **Police v Reid** [1987] Crim LR 702 is authority for the fact that 'intimidation' is more than 'mere discomfort'.[10] Secondly, the courts are unwilling to interfere with police discretion, as evidenced in **R v Chief Constable of Devon and Cornwall ex parte Central Electricity Generating Board** [1982] QB 458, where the courts refused to criticise an operational decision not to police a demonstration.

It would be open to the company to seek an injunction under the Protection from Harassment Act 1997 to restrain future protest, but the authorities do not provide support in these circumstances, as this protest is unlikely to be considered to be harassment. The decision in **Novartis Pharmaceuticals UK Ltd v Stop Huntingdon Animal Cruelty** [2010] HRLR 8 upheld the right to protest outside a facility in bloodstained clothes, with megaphones, despite the fact this would cause some offence. Despite the inconvenience caused to the company, this would appear to be a legitimate protest.

To summarise, it appears that the actions of the joggers in the original event, and outside the coach garage, are lawful. However, those who enter the bus garage and physically prevent the company from conducting business will be liable for aggravated trespass.

✓ Make your answer stand out

■ By discussing whether or not the police could arrest the joggers for obstruction of the highway, including a discussion of *Hirst and Agu* v *Chief Constable of West Yorkshire* (1987) 85 Cr App R 143. That case suggested that the courts have been willing to accept that protest may be a legitimate use of the highway. Although this is not the key issue raised by the question, a thorough answer should note all matters of relevance.

■ When discussing the protest outside the coach company, outline the powers of arrest under ss 4 and 5 of the Public Order Act, and the common law power to prevent a breach of the peace. This would show a comprehensive knowledge of the available powers.

■ By including academic comment to expand the discussion. You could consider the assessment of the use of s 5, POA as a restraint on free speech in Geddis 'Free speech martyrs or unreasonable threats to social peace – "Insulting" expression and section 5 of the Public Order Act 1986' [2004] PL 853.

! Don't be tempted to...

■ Ignore the detail you are given in this question. All the information you are given will be included for a reason. Therefore, consider the significance of every piece of information. For example, the examiner has told you the precise wording on the placards used. This is because you are being invited to consider cases in which protestors sought to argue they acted in the legitimate prevention of crime.

■ Fail to explain your reasoning fully. Students often make the mistake of thinking that because a particular argument cannot succeed, there is no need to address the issue. Here, you are told that the coach company are considering legal action. It is clear that there is no basis for judicial review here, but you need to show the examiner how you have reached that conclusion in order to get full credit for this point.

❓ Question 5

Peter is obsessed with healthy eating, and considers that feeding burgers to children is criminal. He begins a campaign to protest about a burger van that parks near to a school. Peter and his friend Layla go and stand near the van every day at lunch time, holding posters showing depictions of clogged arteries and ambulances. They don't say anything, but stay and hold their pictures every day. The van owner, Toby, is sure that the pictures are putting some of the children off. He calls the police, who attend, tell them that they must not use the pictures of arteries. The next day, Peter and Layla attend, and hold banners saying that junk food kills. The police arrive and ask Peter and Layla to disperse from the area, as their activities are causing people to be distressed.

Peter and Layla do leave, but return the following week. As they are holding their protest, several of Toby's friends arrive to buy lunch. The friends begin to shout abuse at Peter and Layla, who do not respond. A large crowd begins to gather, and the police are called. Peter and Layla are arrested, and when they ask why, they are told it is to prevent a breach of the peace.

Advise Peter and Layla.

Answer plan

→ Define 'assembly' using the Public Order Act 1986, as amended by the Anti-Social Behaviour Act 2003.

→ Consider whether conditions imposed are proportionate, or justifiable.

→ Define the power of arrest to prevent a breach of the peace.

→ Discuss whether or not redress is available to Peter and Layla.

Diagram plan

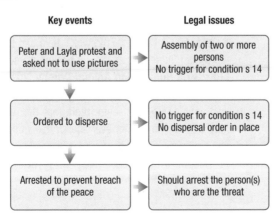

A printable version of this diagram is available from www.pearsoned.co.uk/lawexpressqa

Answer

This scenario raises questions about the powers that exist at statute and common law to regulate protests and assemblies. The right to protest is seen as an important component of a democracy, and as such, freedom of expression and assembly are protected by Arts 10 and 11 of the European Convention of Human Rights. However, these rights are subject to qualification, as a state will need to balance the freedoms of individuals to protest against the need to preserve order and prevent disturbance. The police invoke a number of statutory and common law measures to control the protest staged by Peter and Layla and it will be necessary to evaluate whether or not these discretionary powers have been fairly and correctly utilised.[1]

[1] The introduction shows the marker that the answer is not simply going to describe the law, but evaluate the issues in the scenario.

The Public Order Act 1986 gives the police powers to regulate a public assembly, defined at s 16 (as amended by the Anti-Social Behaviour Act 2003) as a gathering of two or more persons in a place which is wholly or partly open to the air.[2] A public assembly is, *prima facie*, lawful; but the senior police officer on the scene may impose conditions on the conduct of the participants if satisfied that there is a risk of serious disorder, serious damage to property, serious disruption to the life of the community, or if the purpose of the assembly is to intimidate others (s 14). It is therefore possible for the police to impose a condition on Peter and Layla, but, in this scenario, it is difficult to see how this could be justified as there do not appear to be any of the 'trigger' risks outlined in the statute.[3] It could be argued that the pictures are 'intimidating' but this would appear to be unsustainable given the authority of **Police v Reid** [1987] Crim LR 702, which held that intimidation involves more than 'mere discomfort'. In **Novartis Pharmaceuticals UK Ltd v Stop Huntingdon Animal Cruelty** [2010] HRLR 8 the right to protest against vivisection by standing in bloodstained clothes was upheld. It would seem, then, that the condition should not have been imposed. However, there appears to be little that Peter and Layla can do to seek redress. If conditions are known about far enough in advance, then judicial review could be sought. Retrospectively, this is of little assistance.[4]

[2] The ability to answer this question correctly rather depends on being aware that the powers to regulate an assembly under the Public Order Act apply, even though there are only two people present.

[3] This is a good point to make, as students often simply state that conditions can be imposed, without considering whether or not there are grounds to do so.

[4] The question asks for advice to be given to Peter and Layla, so the answer needs to set out the law, but also to consider what, if anything, they are able to do.

The following day, it is equally difficult to see how the order to disperse can be said to amount to a reasonable exercise of police powers. The conditions which could be imposed under s 14 can include a limitation on the duration of the assembly so, arguably, a condition to disperse could be considered lawful. However, the same concerns exist in relation to the absence of 'trigger' risks. Section 30 of the Anti-Social Behaviour Act 2003 gives a power to order the dispersal of two or more persons if an officer reasonably believes their presence is likely to cause intimidation, harassment, alarm or distress to a third party.[5] The power only exists when a senior officer has authorised the use of dispersal orders in an area. The authorisation must be in writing, and can not be for longer than six months. The authorisation must be publicised, by publication in a local newspaper and/or notices posted in the area. The use of dispersal orders to remove protestors has been sanctioned in **R (Singh) v Chief Constable of West Midlands Police** [2006] EWCA Civ 1118, where protestors were ordered to leave a theatre. On the facts outlined in this scenario, no authorisation appears to have been made. Again, it is difficult to see how redress can be obtained.[6]

An officer has powers at common law to prevent a breach of the peace. This can include a power of arrest, but also encompasses preventative powers falling short of arrest (confirmed in **Moss v Mclachlan [1985] IRLR 76** and **R (Laporte) v Chief Constable of Gloucestershire** [2006] UKHL 55). It would appear that these common law powers are potentially broad. It was stressed in **Laporte**, however, that such powers only arise where a breach of the peace is imminent. There is no suggestion in the scenario that there is any such immediate threat.

The following day, Peter and Layla are arrested to prevent a breach of the peace. It does seem that, on this occasion, the officers may have good reason to believe that a breach of the peace is imminent, due to the growing, hostile, crowd.[7] The police are entitled, at common law, to make an arrest to prevent a breach of the peace. There is a line of authority that suggests that the police should seek to arrest the source of the threat. The point was made in **Beatty v Gilbanks (1882) LR 9 QBD 308**, but reiterated in **Redmond-Bate v DPP [1999] Crim LR 998** which appears to be somewhat analogous with the facts here.[8] The case concerned a preacher, whose

[5]Knowledge of provisions contained in statutes other than the Public Order Act will be rewarded here.

[6]Again, you need to note whether or not there is anything that can assist Peter and Layla.

[7]You should explain why the second situation can be differentiated as the examiner has included these facts so that you will comment on them.

[8]It would suffice to refer to *Beatty* v *Gilbanks*, but an ability to recognise a case with similar facts is helpful because this allows you to draw more accurate conclusions about how the law will be applied to the facts of the scenario.

actions attracted a hostile crowd. She was arrested, and this was judged to be unlawful as the threat did not come from her. The case of **Bibby v Chief Constable of Essex** (2000) *The Times*, 24 April, which followed, sought to give clarification. The judgment stressed that there must be a clear, imminent threat arising from the conduct of the arrested person, and further, that the conduct must be a violation of the rights of others. None of these conditions appears to be satisfied here, as it seems clear that Peter and Layla are acting lawfully. Therefore, the arrest appears to be unlawful, and to give rise to a claim that their Art 10 and 11 rights have been unjustly interfered with.[9] A claim for wrongful arrest, and false imprisonment, should be considered.[10]

[9]Where you are able to reach a clear conclusion about the legal position, you should do so as this shows confidence in applying the law.

[10]This is the only part of the scenario that seems to offer a possibility of taking action to Peter and Layla, so this should be highlighted. You don't need to include any detail about the process of making a claim, it is enough to recognise that it is a possibility.

Since the Human Rights Act came into force, a series of judicial decisions have stressed the need to protect these rights. The burden will be on the police to demonstrate that the arrests were necessary and proportionate, and constituted the least possible degree of interference with the rights of Peter and Layla.

It would seem that Peter and Layla have acted lawfully throughout. Peter and Layla complied with unjustifiable conditions, and an unlawful order to disperse. However, there does not appear to be any possibility of seeking redress. They may wish to consider civil action in respect of the final arrest as this would appear to be unlawful.

 Make your answer stand out

- By discussing whether or not the use of graphic pictures could constitute 'harassment, alarm or distress' sufficient for an offence under s 5 of the Public Order Act 1986. The broad scope of this power could be considered. The matter has been considered in a number of cases that you could consider, including *Percy* v *DPP* [2001] EHWC Admin 1125. In that case, the conviction for s 5 was overturned, but on the grounds that the reasoning at first instance was flawed; leaving open the possibility that conduct considered to be deliberately insulting could constitute an offence. Comment on this, or similar cases, shows that you have a detailed knowledge of authorities relevant to the problem.

- You could draw links between the matters raised in relation to s 5 and recent judicial decisions on the use of injunctions to restrain protest (consider the *Novartis Pharmaceuticals* case), in which a more robust defence of the right to cause offence can be seen. This would demonstrate confidence in drawing parallels between cases dealing with different legal provisions.

Question 6

The powers to restrain public assemblies and processions contained in the Public Order Act 1986 are so broad that it cannot be said that there is a freedom to protest in the United Kingdom.

Discuss.

Answer plan

→ Outline the reasons why protest is worthy of protection.

→ Explain the incremental development of public order legislation.

→ Consider the broad reach of statutory and common law powers.

→ Discuss cases in which protest has been supported, and constrained.

→ Consider the relationship between public order legislation and the ECHR.

Diagram plan

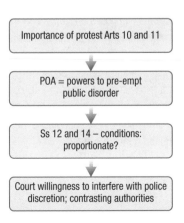

Importance of protest Arts 10 and 11

↓

POA = powers to pre-empt public disorder

↓

Ss 12 and 14 – conditions: proportionate?

↓

Court willingness to interfere with police discretion; contrasting authorities

A printable version of this diagram is available from www.pearsoned.co.uk/lawexpressqa

Answer

The freedom to protest is often said to be a necessary constituent of a democratic state. Public protest can enable minority or dissenting views to be aired, therefore encouraging debate to take place. Protest can allow people to participate in democracy in between elections, and can lead to policy change. For example, mass protest against the planned community charge led to the policy being abandoned. Protest can lead to public disorder, and it is therefore necessary to ensure that measures are available to control and contain assemblies and processions. This tension is recognised in the European Convention of Human Rights, which permits infringement on the rights of association and expression for the legitimate purpose of preventing disorder and crime. Any infringement must be proportionate in achieving the aim. It will be argued that the broad scope of legislative and common law powers in the United Kingdom has the potential to unduly infringe the right to protest. The approach of the judiciary has not been consistent in determining whether the exercise of the powers is proportionate.[1]

[1] The issue of proportionality is crucial to a consideration of whether or not the powers available to curb protest, and therefore, it should be raised in the introduction.

The Public Order Act 1986 is not the only means available to curtail and control protest, but provides the main statutory framework.[2]

[2] The question has asked you to focus on the POA, so you should not be diverted by listing all the other measures which exist, but it is worth telling the examiner that you are aware of them.

The Act gives the state powers to pre-empt public disorder, and creates specific criminal offences to allow individuals to be arrested if disorder occurs. The argument will focus on the effect of the pre-emptive powers, as it is here that there is the greater potential to curb the rights of individuals to engage in peaceful protest.[3]

[3] It probably is not possible to consider the powers of prior restraint, and the offences in the Public Order Act in detail, so it is useful to indicate an awareness of both, and giving a reason for restricting the debate in this way.

Section 11 imposes obligations on the organisers of processions to provide notice to the police of, *inter alia*, the date, time and route of a procession. This enables the police to plan an appropriate strategy to manage events,[4] and s 12 allows conditions to be imposed on a procession as necessary to control the risk of serious public disorder, serious damage to property, or serious disruption to the life of the community. Conditions may be imposed in advance, or as required during the event.

[4] This comment shows that you not only know the content of the legislation, but understand its purpose.

The requirement to give notice does not apply to customary events, or funeral processions. The possibility of spontaneous protest remains, as the notice requirement does not apply if it is not reasonably practicable to comply. It should be noted that the requirement is to inform the police of an event, rather than to obtain permission.[5] Therefore, whilst the organisers are potentially criminally liable if notice is not given, the march itself is not rendered illegal and participation is not an offence. **Kay v Commissioner of the Police for the Metropolis** [2008] UKHL 69[6] considered whether a monthly event with no specified route was 'customary' and, on the facts, held that it was. However, the Lords took the opportunity to consider the position if a new event was planned with no particular route. Section 11 imposes a duty to include details of the route. The Lords considered that the Act could not be interpreted as implying that the organisers of an event would be criminally liable, as this would be a 'draconian' interference with the freedom of assembly and inconsistent with the convention.

Section 13 allows the police to make an application to the relevant local authority for a ban on all, or on a class, of processions in an area for a period of time not exceeding three months. A ban is only permissible if no conditions are suitable to meet the risks identified at s 12. This power, however,[7] has the potential to curb legitimate protest as a ban may affect any procession in an area including those which pose no identifiable threat. There is little case law on the point since 1986, but authorities concerned with a similar power in the Public Order Act 1936 held that there was no breach of Arts 10 and 11, as it is open to an organisation to apply to vary a banning order.[8]

There is no requirement to give notice of an assembly; however, conditions may be imposed on any gathering of two or more persons, to manage the same risks as outlined in s 12.

The discretion afforded to the police to impose conditions on processions and assemblies certainly holds the potential to infringe the freedom to protest, as it is conceivable that conditions could operate to substantially reduce the impact of an event. There

[5]This is an important point to make, and one that is often overlooked. This fact allows you to argue that the POA is not as draconian as the question suggests and gives balance to your answer.

[6]This is a useful case to cite, as it is an instance of the court upholding the right to protest.

[7]You should make the point that an application for a ban will only be successful in these circumstances; students often suggest that the police can use s 13 to ban processions, which is incorrect.

[8]Here, you show the examiner that you have the ability to consider decisions on a different subject to form a hypothesis about the likely judicial approach. This shows skills of analysis and reasoning.

[9]This case provides a contrast to the attitude of the court shown in *Kay*, so inclusion of both supports the point made in the introduction, that the judiciary have been somewhat inconsistent in upholding the article rights.

is, arguably, no effective mechanism to challenge the imposition of conditions. In the case of conditions imposed in advance of a procession, or upon a recurring assembly, then it is possible to seek judicial review. This affords little assistance during an event. In **Austin and Saxby *v* Commissioner of the Police for the Metropolis** [2005] EWHC 480, it was held that both s 12 and s 14 allow for the imposition of conditions which have the effect of bringing a protest to an end.[9]

[10]This is an important point, as the use of discretionary power arguably needs to be carefully regulated by the judiciary to ensure that individual freedoms are upheld.

It is the degree of discretion afforded to the police that is, perhaps, of greatest concern when considering the effect of the Public Order Act on individual freedoms.[10] In the case of **R (Brehony) *v* Chief Constable of Greater Manchester** [2005] EWHC 640, the courts held that a decision to impose a condition requiring an assembly to move from the city centre was legitimate, as it posed a risk of disruption to Christmas shoppers. This was, it was held, proportionate to the aim of preventing 'serious disruption to the life of the community', which suggests the courts are unwilling to interfere with the operational decisions of police authorities.

[11]As your central argument is that judicial protection for the right to protest is inconsistent, you need to be able to use contrasting authorities.

It is possible to find instances in which the judiciary have been more robust in upholding the right to engage in protest.[11] In **Police *v* Reid**, it was held that a condition imposed on an assembly outside an embassy was disproportionate. The police argued it was necessary as the protestors were shouting at individuals entering the building, and the assembly therefore was for the purpose of intimidating others. The courts held that intimidation was more than 'mere discomfort'.

The authorities dealing with ss 11–14 of the Public Order Act are, to some extent, contradictory. In cases such as **Police *v* Reid**, or **Kay**, the courts have declared the fundamental importance of the right to protest. In **Austin and Saxby**, and **Brehony**, it could be argued that the right to protest has been given considerably less weight as the courts have been disinclined to interfere with police discretion.

[12]Your conclusion should refer directly to the statement set out in the question.

It is clear that the Act gives considerable powers to restrict public protest. The judiciary have to balance the legitimate aim of controlling disorder against the freedoms of expression and assembly. It would be an overstatement to suggest that there is no freedom to protest in the United Kingdom, but that freedom is certainly subject to considerable restriction.[12]

✓ Make your answer stand out

■ By providing a more detailed discussion of the case law concerned with regulating the use of discretionary powers. More detail could be given about the kinds of conditions endorsed in *Austin and Saxby*. This could allow for a broader debate about the role of the judiciary in supervising the executive under the Human Rights Act. If you are able to use this material to comment upon the separation of powers, then you will be showing the examiner that you can consider the topic of freedom of assembly in the context of your study of the constitution.

■ By incorporating some academic comment into your answer. There are numerous books and articles on the Public Order Act. Early criticism can be found in Bonner D. and Stone, R., 'The Public Order Act 1986, steps in the wrong direction' [1987] PL 202. More recent comment on the *Austin* case can be found in Mead, D., 'Of kettles, cordon and crowd control – Austin, Commissioner of Police for the Metropolis and the meaning of "deprivation of liberty"' [2009] EHRLR 376.

■ By expanding the discussion of the relationship between the POA and the Convention, and in particular, whether or not the HRA has had an impact on the judicial approach to protest. The case of *Kay* is particularly useful here because the judgment includes a discussion of the correct interpretation of s 11. You could use this to consider how s 3 has altered the approach to statutory interpretation.

! Don't be tempted to...

■ Simply list the powers available in the Public Order Act. Demonstrating knowledge of the provisions will not be sufficient here; this kind of question demands that you engage in analysis of how the law is applied. Weaker answers have a tendency to be overly descriptive.

■ Ignore the issue of Convention rights. Although the question does not expressly reference the Convention, the mention of the 'right' to protest should be seen as an invitation to address the point.

Freedom of expression, freedom of information

7

How this topic may come up in exams

This topic lends itself to either essay questions, or problem scenarios. Questions will tend to focus either on the ability of the individual to protect personal information from scrutiny; or upon the access to information held by the state, so you will need to be able to identify the subject-matter of the particular question. In either case, you will need to be familiar with the relevant statutory provisions and a considerable amount of case law. The topic overlaps with the study of the European Convention of Human Rights, as questions typically demand analysis of how the Human Rights Act has affected domestic law.

Attack the question

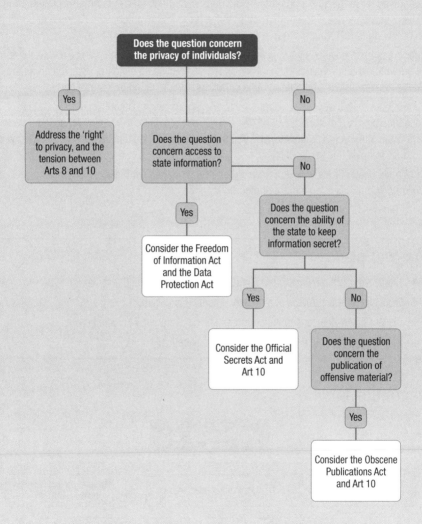

❓ Question 1

Simone Jenkins is a celebrity who presents a children's television programme. She has a lucrative career which includes advertising campaigns aimed at children. She has been interviewed for magazines and other media outlets, and has made statements condemning infidelity and drug use. For a number of months, rumours have been circulating that Simone has been unfaithful to her partner.

Simone has been advised by a relative employed by a newspaper that, next Sunday, there will be a tabloid story including an interview with an individual claiming to have had a long-running affair with her, and photographs of her seemingly taking drugs at a party.

Simone fears that, if any details about these allegations are made public, her reputation and, consequently, her career, will be damaged. She would like to know what she can do to prevent the story being published, and whether or not she should have been contacted by the paper to advise her of their plans.

Her relative does not know which newspaper intends to publish the story, or who the individual is that has supplied the photographs.

Advise Simone of any action she can take.

Answer plan

→ Briefly explain the nature of the competing rights under Arts 8 and 10.

→ Discuss the requirements of a breach of confidence claim.

→ Explore the issues concerning prior restraint with reference to recent cases.

→ Discuss the effect of a failure to give prior notification.

Diagram plan

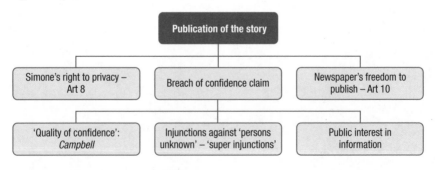

A printable version of this diagram is available from www.pearsoned.co.uk/lawexpressqa

Answer

Article 8 of the European Convention of Human Rights provides that an individual is entitled to respect for their private and family life. Article 10 protects freedom of expression. When a newspaper seeks to expose facts about an individual that the individual would rather keep private, a conflict between these Convention rights arises.[1] Simone's potential claim for injunctive relief will be considered in the light of recent decisions concerning the appropriate way to resolve the conflict of competing rights.

When untrue information is published about an individual, then that individual can seek redress through an action in defamation.[2] This may not provide a satisfactory remedy for Simone. Firstly, it will not assist if either allegation can be shown to be true, and secondly, it could be argued that any remedy given after publication is ineffective as the information is, by then, in the public domain. Therefore, Simone may wish to consider a claim for breach of confidence, and seek an injunction to prevent publication of the information.[3]

Prior to the Human Rights Act, it was clear that there was no substantive right to privacy in English law. An individual could, however, protect information through the doctrine of confidence. In order to be successful, it would need to be shown that the confidential information had been disclosed in circumstances giving rise to a duty of confidence; and that further disclosure would be detrimental to the applicant.[4] An action could restrain disclosure by third parties under the 'Spycatcher' principle (**A-G v Guardian Newspapers** (No. 2) [1990] 1 AC 109[5]). Simone would have no difficulty in arguing that information from a partner, or ex-partner, fell within circumstances creating the duty. It is well established that intimate personal relationships imply such a duty (**Argyll v Argyll** [1967] Ch 302). However, it would be harder to demonstrate a confidential relationship with the individual who had taken the photographs.

The Human Rights Act has led to developments of the law of confidence which would assist. The House of Lords confirmed in **Wainwright v Home Office** [2004] 2 AC 406 that the HRA did not introduce a right to privacy.[6] However, **Campbell v MGN Ltd** [2004] 2 AC 457 significantly reformed the law on breach of confidence, to the extent that it now incorporates the tort of misuse of private information. This may assist in restraining publication of all

[1]You will be rewarded for recognising that the discussion must take place in the context of conflicting rights, so it is worth highlighting this in the introduction.

[2]This is not a question about defamation, so there is no need to demonstrate any knowledge of this topic.

[3]This is the key issue, as it addresses the specific concern of the person seeking advice; how to stop publication.

[4]Make sure you do not spend long on outlining the previous law. Summarise the test as succinctly as possible.

[5]There is no need to give the facts of the 'Spycatcher' case; all that is required is a demonstration that you understand that it establishes a test for restraint of third parties.

[6]It is worth making this point as some students confuse the incorporation of the right to respect for private life with a right to privacy. Mention of this authority will show confidence in the subject-matter.

[7]The explanation of what is meant by 'expectation of privacy' allows the examiner to see that you can relate the law to the specific issues raised in the problem scenario.

[8]Although this is not a case about 'human rights law' per se, the balance of rights should be mentioned, as all authorities since the HRA are concerned with how this balance should be struck.

[9]This may seem like a fairly minor point, but marks will be awarded for dealing with this issue. The scenario clearly states that Simone cannot locate the source of the information, and therefore a comprehensive response should cover the issue.

the material here. Following **Campbell**, it is clear that the courts will first ask whether or not the information concerned has a 'reasonable expectation of privacy'. This test is less restrictive, as there is no need to establish the pre-existing relationship. The law is less concerned with the context in which the information was obtained than with the nature of the content. There is some authority to support the suggestion that covert photographs may attract special protection, as arguably a picture has the potential to be more intrusive and damaging than the written word[7] (**Douglas v Hello!** (No. 3) [2006] QB 125). If the information can be said to be private, then the court must ask whether this is outweighed by arguments in favour of publication, either because the material is in the public domain; or that publication is in the public interest. Here, the courts must balance the Art 8 rights of the applicant against the Art 10 rights which protect free expression in the press.[8] It appears that this will be done on a case-by-case basis and therefore the court will seek to balance the threat posed to Simone's interests against the right of the public to be informed about activities of individuals who are in the public eye.

Simone will seek an injunction to restrain publication pending resolution of a claim for misuse of private information and/or breach of confidence. There is a need for the careful scrutiny of such applications, as it is accepted that the value of news may diminish if delayed (**The Observer and the Guardian v United Kingdom** (1992) 14 EHRR 153). Here, however, the particular issues for consideration are whom the application should be made against, and how far any prohibition on publication should extend.

It is possible to seek an injunction against 'persons unknown'.[9] It is not uncommon for a celebrity to become aware that an unidentified individual possesses private information that they intend to disclose. By obtaining an injunction against an unspecified respondent, newspaper groups can be restrained from publication as third party recipients of the information under the 'Spycatcher' principle. (See, for example, **TUV v Person or Persons Unknown** [2010] EWHC 853.) Thus, Simone can seek to restrain publication of the photographs from an unknown source.

A similar situation arose in the case concerning the footballer, John Terry, who sought to prevent publication of a story concerning his affair with a team mate's partner (**John Terry (previously referred to as LNS)** *v* **Persons Unknown** [2010] EWHC 119 (QB)). Simone appears to want to suppress any mention of the story. If she were to apply for an injunction, a report of her success could arouse public speculation. Terry sought (and was initially granted) what has been referred to as a 'super injunction', restraining publication not only of the information but of mention even of the proceedings themselves. The use of such broad injunctions has been the subject of considerable academic, media and political criticism but, in any event, following **Terry**, it appears that Simone will be unsuccessful. The judge refused to renew the injunction on the basis that on the facts, he did not feel there would be an actionable claim and further, that even if there was, damage to Terry's commercial interests could be addressed by compensation. In this situation, it seems possible that the courts would determine that the freedom of the press did indeed outweigh Simone's right to privacy, as an adequate remedy exists for any harm resulting from publication.[10] Simone is not, as yet, entitled to prior notification from the press. This matter is currently being considered by the European Court in **Mosely** *v* **United Kingdom** (Application 48009/08).[11] The applicant claims that the failure of the state to impose an obligation for prior notification on the press breaches his Art 8 rights, as if notification is not given, then an effective remedy is denied as restraint cannot be obtained. It is submitted that the European Court is likely to find against the applicant, given the broad margin of appreciation afforded to the state in respect of the competing rights. It seems that Simone would be best advised to bring an action for breach of confidence and misuse of private information, and to seek an interim injunction to restrain publication. She is unlikely to be able to obtain a so-called 'super injunction', and is not able to obtain redress for the absence of prior notification.[12]

[10]Where there is a direct parallel between a reported case and the situation in a scenario, then it is worth explaining this. The aim is not to demonstrate that you know the facts, but rather, to draw some conclusions about how the precedent will be applied in the instant case.

[11]Credit will be given for reference to this matter, as it demonstrates that you have an awareness of the law as it is evolving, beyond the issues covered by the text books.

[12]As the issues have been discussed in the body of the answer, the conclusion can be a brief summation of the key points covered.

■ The *Mosely* case has been the subject of recent academic debate. You would be rewarded for examining the arguments regarding notification in more detail. Helpful comment and analysis can be found in Phillipson, G., 'Max Mosely goes to Strasbourg; Article 8, claimant notification and interim injunctions' [2009] 1 Journal of Media Law 73, and a response by Andrew Scott, [2010] 2(1) Media Law 49–65.

■ The issue of 'super injunctions' has been the focus of political attention, and a committee headed by the former Master of the Rolls has been established to consider the issue. Further discussion of this very current issue would show an ability to evaluate developing law.

■ You should make sure you keep up to date with emerging case law. You may find links to recent cases, and some commentary, via the International Forum for Responsible Media (http://inform.wordpress.com/).

! Don't be tempted to...

■ Discuss the facts of the cases. It can be particularly tempting here, as you will probably remember the details easily due to the publicity they received. Do remember that only the *ratio* is important!

■ Lose sight of the facts of the scenario. Students sometimes set out the law clearly, but do not use the points made to draw conclusions about the particular facts provided.

Question 2

'It is well known that in English law there is no right to privacy' (Glidewell J) in *Kaye* v *Robertson* [1991] FSR 62.

Assess this statement in the light of developments following the Human Rights Act 1998.

Answer plan

→ Briefly explain the traditional approach to privacy in English law.
→ Outline the effect of the HRA.
→ Assess the development of the law by focusing on major cases.
→ Consider the extension to the law of confidence.
→ Analyse how far this provides effective protection of personal privacy.

Diagram plan

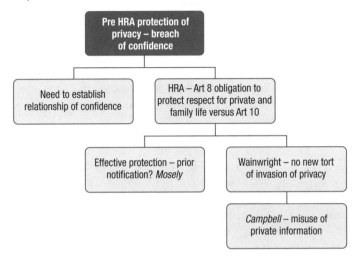

A printable version of this diagram is available from www.pearsoned.co.uk/lawexpressqa

Answer

The case of **Kaye v Robertson** [1991] FSR 62 was decided prior to the HRA, which incorporated the European Convention of Human Rights into domestic law. Article 8 protects the right to respect for private and family life. Nonetheless, in 2004, the House of Lords emphatically denied that the HRA had created a new action for invasion of privacy (**Wainwright v Home Office** [2004] 2 AC 406). It will be argued that the HRA has allowed the judiciary to provide more robust protection for individual privacy.[1]

Prior to 1998, private information could be protected in a number of circumstances.[2] First, information regarding court proceedings could be protected by way of a court order, and in respect of juvenile proceedings, the order would be made unless a successful application was made to lift reporting restrictions in the public interest. Further, an individual was able to protect personal information from dissemination if it could be established that publication would amount to a breach of confidence. It is this issue that requires discussion, as this is the area where it can be said that the HRA has had the most impact.[3] Confidence arises from a particular relationship. Often, this arises from contractual obligations. **Argyll v Argyll** [1967] Ch 302

[1] Setting out the conclusion at the start of the essay shows confidence and the ability to reach an informed view.

[2] This question asks you to evaluate how the law has changed since 2000, when the HRA came into effect. Therefore, it is essential to set out the position prior to that point.

[3] The parameters of the discussion need to be established. Here, you have stated clearly what the focus of the answer will be but, importantly, explained to your examiner why you have made that choice.

[4]These two cases are critical as they each mark a significant development in the law. In any question dealing with actions for breach of confidence, you will need to show that you recognise why they were important.

[5]You need to be able to highlight the limitations of an action for breach of confidence in order to evaluate whether the HRA has been effective in remedying any of these issues.

[6]This is a key point to make, as it will be suggested that the post-HRA balance between Arts 8 and 10 is, to an extent, dealing with the same issue.

[7]The answer highlighted the potential for 'public interest' that existed in pre-HRA actions for breach of confidence earlier, so there is no need to repeat the points here.

established that marriage was an intimate relationship giving rise to a duty of confidence. The principle developed further in **Attorney General v Guardian Newspapers** (No. 2) [1990] 1 AC 109 (the 'Spycatcher' case),[4] in which it was held that third parties who received information obtained in a confidential relationship were also subject to restraint. Hence, a measure of protection existed for celebrities, politicians, and others who wished to prevent details of their private lives being exposed in the press.

To establish an action for breach of confidence prior to the HRA, the applicant would need to demonstrate that the information had 'the quality of confidence', and was obtained in circumstances creating a duty of confidence. Further, it would need to be shown that the unauthorised use of the information would be detrimental. Thus, information already in the public domain could not be restrained.[5] It could be argued that it is in the public interest to reveal certain kinds of private information, if this exposes corruption, or hypocrisy.[6] In **Woodward v Hutchins** [1971] 1 WLR 760, the court declared there is 'no confidence in iniquity'. In that case, a celebrity who had sought publicity could not complain about coverage of his private life.

Even in cases where it was clear that a gross intrusion of privacy had occurred, in the absence of a confidential relationship, there was little effective protection. This was the situation in **Kaye v Robertson** which prompted Glidewell LJ to suggest that Parliament should review the issue.

Following the inception of the HRA, the courts, as a public body (s 6), have a responsibility to provide a remedy for an individual who can demonstrate that their Art 8 rights have been infringed. It should be noted, however, that there is a concurrent duty to uphold the protection of freedom of expression guaranteed by Art 10. In dealing with cases where restraint of publication of private information is sought, the judiciary are required to conduct a balancing exercise between the competing rights. Therefore, it cannot be said that an individual is always entitled to privacy, and indeed, it could be argued that the matters that will fall to be considered are scarcely different from those which were relevant before 1998.[7] Sebastian Coe was unable to prevent publication of details of an extra-marital affair on the grounds that, on balance, the freedom of the press and public interest outweighed his desire to keep the matter private (**Lord Coe v Mirror Group Newspapers** (2004, QBD, unreported)).

[8]It is absolutely critical to include this point as the extension to the law of confidence is, without doubt, the most significant development in this area resulting from the HRA.

[9]Campbell is the most important case in this area and must be included.

[10]Marks will be awarded here, as the answer doesn't just give the *ratio* of the case, it also explains clearly how this represents a change in the law. This shows real understanding.

[11]The question asked for consideration of the individuals right to privacy, so having shown how the law has developed, there should be an evaluation of the limitations of the protection now provided.

There is, as emphasised in **Wainwright**, no new tort of invasion of privacy. What is clear, however, is that the judiciary have felt enabled to develop the doctrine of confidence, so that it can now be said to incorporate an action for the misuse of private information.[8] The critical case is that of **Campbell v MGN** [2004] 2 AC 457,[9] concerning an action in respect of publication of photographs of her entering a drug rehabilitation unit; having previously denied taking drugs. The key distinction is that there is no longer a requirement to demonstrate a pre-existing relationship of confidence provided that it can be shown that the information carries with it a reasonable expectation of privacy.[10] This allowed Campbell to seek redress for the publication of photographs taken by a stranger. Once the threshold of reasonable expectation is passed, the courts will then consider whether or not the information is already in the public domain and, finally, whether there is a public interest in publication. It can be seen, then, that the case represents a significant extension to the legal protection for individual privacy, as it enables an action to be brought in a broader range of circumstances. The judiciary, however, have emphasised that Art 8 rights do not have primacy over those contained in Art 10 and, therefore, there will always be a careful balance to be struck.

Even where an action can be brought in confidence, on the basis that private information has been misused, this will not always provide the protection that an individual may hope for.[11] Many cases contain an application for injunctive relief to prevent publication pending the resolution of the matter. However, where the individual does not have notice of the impending publication, any action after the event will be unable to prevent the material entering the public domain. Redress is only available through complaint to the Press Complaints Commission, or by obtaining damages for breach of confidence. The matter is currently being considered by the European Court in **Mosely v United Kingdom** (Application 48009/08), where the applicant argues that, without an enforceable right to prior notice of publication, he has been denied an effective remedy. It is debatable whether the application will be successful, given the equal importance of press freedom, and the margin of appreciation granted to the state.

It is fair to say that, even before the advent of the HRA, the courts were mindful of the need to balance the rights of the individual against the importance of the freedom of the press. The incorporation of the right to respect for privacy has undoubtedly obliged the court to provide a measure of protection in a broader range of circumstances. It seems that, had **Kaye v Robertson** been decided today, the action for breach of confidence would have been successful, as the information carried the reasonable expectation of confidence outlined in **Campbell**. It cannot be said that this creates an automatic right to privacy in every case, as the courts must still balance the individual's wishes against the freedom of the press.

 Make your answer stand out

- You could expand the discussion about limits on the protection of privacy that still exist by exploring the developing stance of the judiciary in relation to 'super injunctions', and what this suggests about the appropriate balance between Arts 8 and 10. Ensure that you keep up to date with new authorities as they emerge. The UK Human Rights Blog is run by Crown Office Chambers, and provides a free updating service that should alert you to new cases: http://ukhumanrightsblog.com.

- Incorporate additional academic opinion on the law of privacy. A good starting point would be the journal *Media Law*, which often contains relevant material for this topic. Although the law has developed since publication, the textbook Feldman, D., *Civil Liberties and Human Rights in England and Wales* (2002) Oxford: Oxford University Press remains an authoritative resource.

! Don't be tempted to...

- Engage in a lengthy explanation of Convention law. You do need to explain the need to balance Arts 8 and 10 but your focus should be on application of the law in the domestic courts.

- Spend too much time outlining the law prior to the Human Rights Act. When you are asked to evaluate an area of law in light of the HRA, your examiner does require you to consider how far the Act has signalled a change; therefore you have got to outline the 'old' law but try to ensure the bulk of the answer considers the current position.

- Ignore the issue of effective remedies. Even if it is accepted that the law now does seem to protect more kinds of private information, we can see that there is debate about whether prior restraint is effective.

? Question 3

Jenna obtains a part time job as an administrative assistant with the Home Office. On commencing her employment, she was asked to sign the Official Secrets Act. She did this, but paid it little attention.

Whilst filing some documents, Jenna comes across a memorandum marked 'classified', which warns that a large number of persons who entered the United Kingdom are no longer traceable. The memorandum further states that many of these individuals originate from countries characterised by high levels of terrorist activity. Later that day, Jenna hears on the news that the Minister responsible for immigration answered a question in Parliament about security, and claimed that the tracking procedures for asylum seekers are excellent.

Jenna feels that this is highly misleading. She discusses this matter with her brother, Karl. Karl is a freelance journalist and he writes an article for the *Sunday Record*. In the week prior to publication, the paper begins to show television adverts claiming that 'insider information' from the Home Office will expose ministerial lies.

All employees in Jenna's department are told there will be an investigation into the leak. Advise Jenna of any possible consequences for her, and her brother.

Answer plan

→ Outline the main provisions of the Official Secrets Act.

→ Specify the nature of the information protected.

→ Distinguish between the obligations of, and consequences for, Jenna and Karl.

→ Consider any possible defences.

→ Briefly consider additional measures that could be taken for breach of contract, or breach of confidence.

Diagram plan

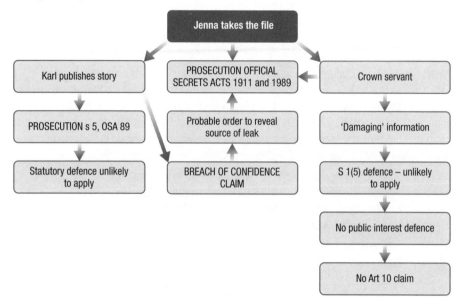

A printable version of this diagram is available from www.pearsoned.co.uk/lawexpressqa

Answer

[1]A brief introduction can show that you have been able to see all the key issues highlighted by the scenario.

[2]You should aim to summarise the purpose of the law as succinctly as you can, so that you can begin to focus on the issues relevant to the parties as soon as possible.

[3]As you have decided this is unlikely to be relevant, you should avoid spending time discussing the Official Secrets Act 1911.

[4]There is no need to give any detail about those categories that are not going to be relevant to Jenna.

Jenna and Karl may be subject to prosecution for offences contrary to the Official Secrets Acts 1911–1989. In addition, Jenna could face an action for breach of confidence and breach of contract. The Official Secrets Act 1989 does provide some defences, and the efficacy of these will be considered.[1] The liability of the parties will be considered separately, as there is variance between their positions.

The Official Secrets Acts aim to protect the interests of the state by preventing the unauthorised disclosure of information held by various government departments.[2] Section 1 of the 1911 Act remains in force, and prohibits the disclosure of information that could assist an enemy for a purpose prejudicial to the state. This is a serious offence, and is generally concerned with activities that could be classified as espionage. It is unlikely that Jenna will be prosecuted under the 1911 Act.[3] The 1989 Act categorises types of information that are protected, from security and intelligence (s 1), defence (s 2), interests abroad (s 3) or criminal investigations (s 4). It seems likely that the information regarding asylum seekers could be categorised as information concerning security and intelligence.[4]

As Jenna is a Crown servant, she may face prosecution for an offence under s 1(3). In order to be liable, it will be necessary for the Crown to prove that the information meets the 'harm' test; it must be shown that it is, or is likely to be, 'damaging'. Damage is not further defined in the Act; however, it appears likely that this will be straightforward for the Crown. The case of **Chandler v DPP** [1964] AC 763 was concerned with s 1 of the 1911 Act but, in that case, it was held that it was for the government to determine what constitutes the 'interests of the state'. This appears to suggest that the judiciary are likely to defer to executive determinations of harm. The statute does afford Jenna with a defence under s 1(5) if she is able to prove that she did not know or have reason to believe that the disclosure was damaging.[5] On a literal interpretation, this imposes a reverse burden of proof upon the defendant. This has been held to be contrary to the provisions of Art 6(2) of the European Convention of Human Rights, as it infringes the right to a fair trial (**R v Keogh** [2007] 1 WLR 1500). Section 3 of the Human Rights Act will be utilised to read the provision as conferring only an evidential burden. If Jenna is able to raise some evidence that she did not know the information was damaging, then it will be for the Crown to disprove that assertion. Given that the memorandum was marked as 'classified', and she has confirmed awareness of her obligations by signing the Act, it is probable that the defence will fail.[6]

Jenna may wish to argue that she disclosed the information because it was in the public interest.[7] It may seem desirable that a public servant who uncovers evidence that Parliament has been misled should be entitled to act as a 'whistleblower'. Under the 1911 Act, Sarah Tisdall was prosecuted and imprisoned for disclosing information to journalists. She had done so as she believed that a Minister had made false statements to the Commons. The case, and that of **R v Ponting** [1985] Crim LR 318, caused considerable disquiet and, arguably, led to the 1989 Act. The statute does not, however, provide any defence of public interest. This was confirmed in **R v Shayler** [2003] 1 AC 247, in which the House of Lords confirmed that the 1989 Act provides a mechanism for reporting concerns to a superior who may authorise disclosure (s 7), and this would have been the correct procedure. Nor can Jenna argue that a prosecution would infringe her Art 10 right to freedom of expression, a point also dismissed in the **Shayler** litigation. Article 10

[5]As you are asked to advise Jenna and explore possible defences, you do need to spend time setting out the relevant legal principles and applying them to the facts, even if it might seem obvious that they will not apply. A diligent lawyer will carefully examine all the options to ensure that the client is properly advised.

[6]You will be rewarded for being able to reach a clear conclusion about the likely application of the law to these facts.

[7]The question explicitly states that Jenna feels the information is misleading, which is an invitation to discuss whether or not there is a 'public interest' defence.

is a qualified right, and infringement is permitted if necessary for national security.

[8]Here, the answer demonstrates an awareness that proceedings in this area are concerned with matters that are not strictly legal, as there is a broader, political, implication.

Jenna does not appear to have any defence available to her. Her best hope is that the Crown may feel that the adverse publicity that could accompany any trial outweighs the need for a prosecution.[8] Katharine Gunn was prosecuted under the Official Secrets Act in 2003 after disclosing information obtained in the course of her employment with the *Observer* concerning an American request to the United Kingdom to assist in surveillance of foreign diplomats. She intended to argue that she had the defence of necessity, on the basis she acted to prevent an illegal war. It is clear, following **Shayler** (above), that there was no prospect of success. Nevertheless, the Crown offered no evidence, as it appeared that the airing of the matter in court would have been damaging.

The Crown will wish to prevent publication of the material. The most straightforward means will be to seek an injunction for breach of confidence as the material was obtained in circumstances imposing a duty of confidence. An action can be brought against the paper, and it is by this means that the Crown will be able to determine that Jenna is the source of the information. Although s 10 of the Contempt of Court Act allows a journalist to protect their sources, this can be overridden in the interests of national security. It was through such an action that Tisdall was identified; **A-G v Guardian Newspapers** (No. 2) [1990] 1 AC 109.[9]

[9]A good answer will be able to show the connection between actions against the newspaper and investigation of the source of the leak.

[10]Although you are advising Jenna, you were asked to address the implications for her brother so you must address the possible offences under s 5.

Both Karl, and the proprietors of the newspaper, will be liable for an offence contrary to s 5 of the 1989 Act, which makes it an offence for a person who receives classified or confidential information to further disclose it.[10] There is a requirement to prove that the disclosure was made with relevant mens rea, that the defendant knew, or had reason to believe, the information would be damaging. Fenwick suggests that this may afford some degree of protection for journalistic freedom, as it could feasibly be argued that the journalist took the view that disclosure was in fact beneficial to the public interest (Fenwick, H., *Civil Liberties and Human Rights* (4th edn) Routledge-Cavendish 2007, p. 603). There are as yet no authorities to confirm this view and nor does it seem that there is special protection afforded to the Art 10 rights of the press when issues of security are engaged. In **Attorney General v The Times** [2001] 1 WLR 885 an injunction was refused, with regard paid in the judgment to Art 10, but in that case, the primary reason to allow publication was that the information was already in the public domain. That is not the case here, and therefore the authority does not assist Karl.

[11]The conclusion briefly summarises the advice given, demonstrating that you have applied your knowledge to answer the specific questions asked.

Jenna and Karl both face prosecution under the Official Secrets Act 1989 in respect of the disclosure of the information. Karl will be unable to protect Jenna's identification as the source of the information. The Human Rights Act does not offer any solace for either party and there do not appear to be any arguable defences.[11]

✓ Make your answer stand out

- By expanding the discussion of the relationship between the Contempt of Court Act and Convention rights. A good discussion of this topic can be found in Stone, R., *Civil Liberties and Human Rights* (8th edn, 2010) Oxford: Oxford University Press.

- By engaging in a more critical analysis of the 'harm' test which is applicable to the s 1 offence. It has been argued that the test is potentially broad in scope and lacks definition. See the criticisms of the Act contained in Fenwick, H. and Phillipson, G., *Media Law* (2006) Oxford: Oxford University Press, pp. 923–48. This would demonstrate an awareness of the academic arguments raised by the facts in this scenario. You must make sure that you do not stray too far from the objective of advising the parties. So, for example, in this instance you may incorporate reference to the criticisms raised by Fenwick and Phillipson that 'damage' is so poorly defined that any disclosure Jenna makes could be interpreted as 'damaging'.

- By exploring the issues raised in the *Shayler* litigation regarding Art 10 in more detail. Similar issues were addressed in the case of *Attorney General* v *Blake* [2001] 1 AC 268, in which the House of Lords declined to determine whether s 1 was too widely drawn. Reference to additional cases, where relevant, shows familiarity with the subject material.

! Don't be tempted to...

- Discuss the historical development of the law. This question does not require you to consider the reasons why the 1989 Act came into existence. You need to be applying the law which is relevant, and drawing conclusions what is likely to happen to Jenna and Karl.

- Engage in a lengthy discussion of s 1 of the 1911 Act. It can be tempting to show the examiner that you have remembered everything about the topic, but you will get better marks for focusing on the law relevant to the parties here.

- Making statements about what is likely to happen to the parties without providing support from the authorities. Whilst you would be given a mark for noting that there is no 'public interest defence', more credit will be awarded for stating that this proposition of law is confirmed in the *Shayler* case.

Question 4

'Unnecessary secrecy in government leads to arrogance in governance and defective decision-making … People expect much greater openness and accountability from government than they used to …' White Paper, *Your Right to Know*, Cm. 3818.

To what extent has the Freedom of Information Act 2000 succeeded in creating open government?

Answer plan

→ Outline the aims of the Act.

→ Identify the categories of information available and discuss the process of making a request.

→ Assess the impact of the Act with reference to particular examples.

→ Draw conclusions about the effectiveness of the legislation in meeting its aims.

Diagram plan

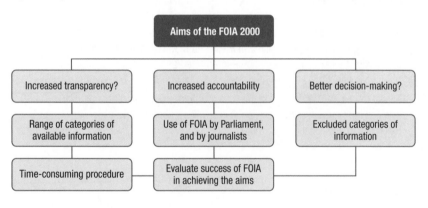

A printable version of this diagram is available from www.pearsoned.co.uk/lawexpressqa

Answer

The Labour Party made a manifesto commitment to increase open government prior to election in 1997. In December of that year, the White Paper *Your Right to Know: White Paper on Freedom of Information* (Cm. 3818, London: HMSO) was published, and this led to the Freedom of Information Act 2000, fully implemented in 2005. The Act allows the public rights of access to information held by public bodies, subject to certain exceptions and limitations. Perhaps the most notorious use of the Act thus far has been in respect of requests made concerning expenses claims made by MPs, leading to the scandal in 2009. It will be argued that whilst the Act may have led to greater transparency, the effect upon the process of government decision-making has been minimal.[1]

[1] Here, the answer suggests that a fairly complex argument is going to be developed, drawing a distinction between openness, and better government.

The Data Protection Act 1998 granted individuals access to information held about them to ensure accuracy. The Freedom of Information Act, however, conferred a broader right of access to information held by a range of public bodies including local and central government, Parliament, the police, schools and colleges, and the NHS. The Act aimed to increase transparency and accountability, improve the decision-making process of government, and also to increase public trust and participation in government.[2] Worthy and Hazell have argued that the Act has succeeded in achieving the first of these aims, but has not increased participation or trust in government, or impacted upon the decision-making process (Worthy, B. and Hazel, R., 'Assessing the performance of freedom of information' (2010) 27(4) Government Information Quarterly 352).

[2] In order to evaluate the impact of the Act, it is necessary to show that you understand the purpose of the legislation.

Requests for information must be made in writing, and the recipient must respond within twenty days. Public authorities are not obliged to disclose all information that is requested.[3] Certain classes of information are subject to an absolute exemption (including, for example, information concerning the formulation of government policy (s 35), or information relating to security matters (s 23)). The Act also exempts other kinds of information if disclosure is likely to prejudice specified interests (this includes information which may prejudice the economy, law enforcement and criminal investigations). Further, a request may be refused on the grounds that the information is, or will be, available by other means (ss 21–22), or if the cost of providing the information is excessive (s 11).

[3] The question asks for discussion of the effect of the legislation. It is necessary to demonstrate understanding of how the law operates but this can be done in a brief paragraph.

[4]Many answers will focus on the use of the Act by members of the public (and journalists), but a recognition of the potential use by Parliament recognises the constitutional position of the legislature in ensuring government accountability.

[5]When dealing with an area of legislation that has not generated a great deal of case law, it is important to make sure that illustrative examples of the law in operation are included.

[6]This is a key point in the argument that is being developed, suggesting that the impact of the Act is, in fact, fairly minimal.

[7]This shows a fairly detailed level of current awareness and also suggests that the Act is not as significant as is sometimes suggested which helps point towards the eventual conclusion.

[8]There is very little case law in this area, so there will be credit given to an answer that demonstrates knowledge of any available authorities.

The Act is overseen by the Information Commissioner, who will adjudicate any appeal against a decision to refuse a request for disclosure. The Information Commissioner can issue an enforcement notice, and decisions of the Information Commissioner are subject to appeal either by the person making the request, or the body which holds the information.

The Act has been utilised to a limited extent by Parliament as a mechanism for obtaining information held by government.[4] Worthy and Hazell have found that parliamentary questions remain the primary method for Members to obtain information; with approximately five times more tabled questions than freedom of information requests in any session. Nevertheless, the Act has provided a means to obtain information where the answers to questions have been unsatisfactory or evasive. For example, the All Party Parliamentary Group on Extraordinary Rendition sought data regarding the movement of individuals across boundaries, following perceived reticence in response to parliamentary questions.[5]

The most extensive use of the Act has been by journalists, who represent the vast majority of requesters. It is well known that the MPs' expenses scandal of 2009 was triggered by freedom of information requests made by an investigative journalist, Heather Brooke. It should be noted, however, that the utility of the Act is undermined by the procedure attendant on making a request. The 20-day response time may well mean that by the time information is received, the currency of an issue has faded so that it is no longer newsworthy.[6] This is magnified when the initial response is a refusal to release the information; necessitating a lengthy appeal process. Heather Brooke made her first request for information regarding receipts in 2005. Her investigations certainly generated considerable publicity for the issue, and the release of limited information, but the scandal finally broke when the full details of the claims for additional costs allowance was leaked from a Whitehall source.[7] More recently, the Court of Appeal has overturned a refusal of a request made in 2005 (**BBC v Sugar [2010]** EWCA Civ 715).[8] This gives some support to an assertion made by a number of respondents in the study conducted by Hazell *et al.* that the appeals process is utilised by public bodies to delay the release of information and indeed, deter some from pursuing an action. A report by the Campaign for Freedom of Information (2009) states that the average request takes almost 20 months to be concluded. The cost of legal action is feasibly a real bar to members of the general public.

[9]At this point, having discussed the effect of the Act on transparency, it is appropriate to draw a 'partial' conclusion before moving on to a different part of the argument.

It can be seen then, that the Act has allowed access to a broad range of information, and has led to a degree of increased transparency and accountability. The limitations on the types of available information and the lengthy nature of the process have meant that the impact is perhaps less than was anticipated.[9]

One of the aims of the Act was to increase public participation in the process of government. It is difficult to see how this has been achieved. Relatively few requests are made by members of the general public. It may be that the release of information obtained by the media has increased public awareness of government issues; however, the White Paper also indicated that the decision-making process would be improved.[10] Conversely, a concern expressed by Ministers during the passage of the legislation was that the decision-making process would be impaired. It was suggested that the fear of having to disclose information would deter civil servants from providing information to Ministers, thus hindering the process of full and frank debate. In the event, ss 35–36 restrict access to all information regarding the formulation of policy and other information is subject to the harm test. Thus, it seems clear that the Act has had no impact on the manner in which government decisions are made.

[10]The quote in the question raises the issue of the decision-making process, so a good answer will consider not only access to information, but the effect of the legislation on how government operates.

It was also hoped that public trust in the process of government would be improved. Given the scale of the public anger following the release of information regarding expenses, it is clear to see that this objective has not been achieved. Rather, the efforts made to obstruct access to the information led to a perception of secrecy; this was not assisted by the parliamentary time given to a Private Member's Bill proposing amendments to the Act which would have excluded much of the detail regarding individual MPs' expenses.

[11]The conclusion can be brief as it simply summarises points made throughout the answer as the argument developed.

The Freedom of Information Act has allowed details regarding the machinery of government to be obtained. It cannot be said, however, that the Act has led to open government, as a result of restricted access to much information and the unwieldy appeals process.[11]

✓ Make your answer stand out

- By refering to a broad range of illustrative examples. As the law is fairly recent, there is not a great deal of case law authority to draw on. A really good source of information (where much of the material referred to here can be found) is the work of the Constitution Unit at UCL, headed by Professor Robert Hazell. Publications can be found on line at www.ucl.ac.uk/constitution-unit.
- By using what case law there is to support your arguments. A good starting point is the discussion of the topic in Bradley, A. and Ewing, K., *Constitutional and Administrative Law* (15th edn, 2010) London: Pearson, pp. 283–8, which outlines the key authorities to date. This will show your examiner that you have a good knowledge of this developing area of law.

! Don't be tempted to...

- Simply set out the legislative provisions in detail. The bulk of the marks here are awarded for analysing the impact of the law on the operation of government. You do need to show that you understand the key provisions of the act, and, in particular, the existence of exemptions. Try to provide a brief summary or overview so that your answer can then address the central topic.
- Ignore the wording of the quotation provided. The question requires you to consider the impact of the Freedom of Information Act on the workings of government, but the quote also suggests that openness leads to better decision-making and you should address this aspect of the question. This can be a small point, as in this answer, which states quite briefly that the decision-making process is unaffected.

❓ Question 5

Julian is the editor of an internet magazine that publishes stories and photographs in a monthly, online edition, available on subscription. One month, the magazine includes a 'photo-story' involving a group of nuns engaging in sexual acts in a church. Mrs Greenhouse has a 19-year-old son who subscribes to the magazine, and she finds the story on the family computer. Mrs Greenhouse, a devout Catholic, is outraged, and also concerned that her younger children could have read the material.

The matter is reported to the police, and Julian is arrested and later released on bail whilst the Crown decides whether to press charges.

Mrs Greenhouse also informs the local paper, which publishes a story stating that Julian is a 'depraved pornographer' who must be imprisoned.

Consider the legal implications of these events.

Answer plan

→ Explain the relevant provisions of the Obscene Publication Act and the Criminal Justice and Public Order Act 1994.

→ Identify the fact that blasphemy is irrelevant.

→ Outline the provisions of the Contempt of Court Act 1981.

→ Discuss the effect of Art 10 on domestic provisions.

Diagram plan

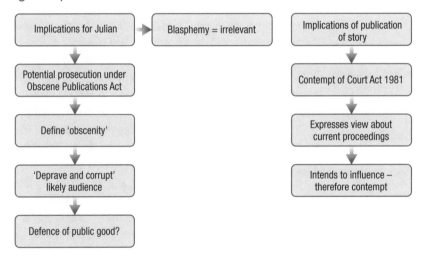

A printable version of this diagram is available from www.pearsoned.co.uk/lawexpressqa

Answer

[1]Although the question is focused on domestic law, any discussion of freedom of expression must take account of Convention law. A brief explanation of the qualified right at the outset demonstrates an awareness of the appropriate context for the discussion.

Freedom of expression is protected under Art 10 of the European Convention of Human Rights. The right to freedom of expression is qualified, and therefore restrictions are permitted in domestic law.[1] There are numerous restrictions on speech and expression in the United Kingdom; of relevance here are those concerning the dissemination of obscene material, and the reporting of court proceedings. Julian may be subject to criminal proceedings under the Obscene Publications Act 1959. The editor of the newspaper may be found to be in contempt of court.

The Obscene Publications Act 1959 makes it an offence to publish an obscene article. The Criminal Justice and Public Order Act 1994 makes it clear that 'publication' incorporates the electronic distribution of material.[2] The online magazine will be considered to have been published. Julian may, therefore, be subject to prosecution for an offence under s 1 of the 1959 Act. First, it will need to be determined whether or not the material is 'obscene' within the terms of the Act. If the jury feel that it is, Julian may wish to argue that notwithstanding its obscene nature, publication is justifiable.[3]

Section 1(1) provides that an article is obscene if it will tend to 'deprave and corrupt persons who are likely, having regard to all relevant circumstances, to read, see or hear the matter contained or embodied in it'. This definition is rather imprecise. It is clear that the fact the material may be shocking, disgusting, or 'loathsome' is not sufficient to satisfy the definition (**R v Anderson** [1972] 1 QB 304). It must be shown that the material is likely to 'deprave and corrupt', as confirmed in **R v Martin Secker and Warburg** [1954] 2 All ER 683.[4] The fact that Mrs Greenhouse found the material shocking and offensive is not, then, enough to render it obscene. The test will be whether or not a significant number of people who come across the article would be depraved, and corrupted.[5] The intended and actual audience for the online magazine may well be relevant. From the facts provided it seems that the material is restricted by the need to subscribe to see the content of the magazine,[6] which may assist as it does not appear to be aimed at children, as was the case with the infamous 'Oz' magazine (the subject of the matter of **R v Anderson**. It would not, however, be a defence for Julian to argue that the intended audience are already regularly exposed to similar material (**Shaw v DPP** [1962] AC 220), or even that the intended audience are already corrupt (**DPP v Whyte** [1972] AC 489). Mrs Greenhouse fears that her younger children could have seen the material but, given the need to subscribe to view content, it seems likely that the jury would find that children are not the intended, or likely, audience. Whether or not the material is obscene will be a question of fact for the jury to determine.[7]

If the story is deemed to be obscene, Julian may wish to claim that the publication is for the 'public good'; a defence under s 4 of the Act.[8] It is permissible for expert evidence to be called regarding the artistic or literary merits of the work, as occurred in the (unreported) trial

[2]This is a small point, but shows detailed knowledge of a range of legislation.

[3]A brief summary of how the law will be applied to the facts of the scenario is useful, and helps to ensure the answer remains focused on the problem.

[4]There are numerous cases concerned with the definition of obscenity; the answer needs to include at least one to demonstrate that mere offensiveness is not sufficient.

[5]Here, the answer demonstrates an understanding that 'obscenity' is dependent not just on content, but how it is received.

[6]All the facts given in a problem scenario will be relevant, and marks will be awarded for recognising why the information regarding subscription was included.

[7]The answer must keep referring to the facts of the scenario and here, an effort is made to draw some conclusions about how the law that has been outlined may be applied.

[8]A good answer will explore not only the possible charges, but also any defences; this is required for a full evaluation of the legal implications.

regarding *Lady Chatterley's Lover*. Again, following the evidence, this is a question for the jury to decide; however, the defence of 'public good' will be interpreted narrowly. In the case of **DPP v Jordan** [1977] AC 699, it was argued that the publication of pornography was for the 'public good' due to the supposed therapeutic benefits of such material. The judge did not allow the argument and confirmed that the 'public good' is confined to art, literature and science.

[9]The question expressly mentions religion, so this point needs to be mentioned but don't waste time explaining law that is no longer relevant.

It is stated that Mrs Greenhouse is a Catholic, and it may be that the religious content of the story is one of the reasons for her outrage. The Criminal Justice and Immigration Act 2008 (s 79) abolished the offence of blasphemy, so there can be no action taken in respect of this element of the story.[9]

[10]There are issues raised here regarding the feasibility of restricting access to material in the United Kingdom that is available on the internet, but it is not possible to deal with them in the time allowed and therefore the focus of the answer remains on obscenity law.

Julian may, then, be the subject of prosecution. He will not be able to argue that the Obscene Publication Act 1959 is an infringement of his Art 10 rights. This point was settled in **Handyside v UK** (1976) 1 EHRR 737. The right is qualified, and Art 10(2) permits restriction for the protection of 'public health and morals'. The European Court will afford the domestic state a wide margin of appreciation in determining what constitutes 'morals', even if the material is readily available in other jurisdictions.[10]

[11]A comprehensive answer must consider the issues raised by publication of the newspaper article, even though the bulk of the problem is focused on Julian's liability.

The publication of the story in the newspaper could make the editor liable for an action for contempt of court.[11] The Contempt of Court Act 1981 prohibits the publication of material that would tend to interfere with the course of justice in particular legal proceedings (s 1). The proceedings must be 'active' (s 2), which would be the case here as Julian has been arrested in connection with an offence. The court would consider whether the reporting created a 'substantial risk of prejudice' to the case (**Re Lonhro plc and Observer Ltd** [1989] 2 All ER 1100). The courts have to balance the risk of prejudice to the right to a fair trial, against the right to freedom of expression. The purpose of this article would appear to be to express opprobrium about Julian's behaviour which would appear to be prejudging the outcome of the case, and therefore, contempt. It would be possible to avoid liability if the editor were able to demonstrate the story formed part of a discussion in 'good faith' of matters of public interest (Contempt of Court Act, s 5) but this does not appear to be the case from the facts given here.[12]

[12]The facts given are quite clear, and therefore a confident answer will briefly acknowledge the potential defence before dismissing it.

It seems that both Julian and the editor of the newspaper are likely to face proceedings. The outcome of Julian's case will depend upon the view taken by the jury and without more detail about the material, it is hard to estimate the verdict. It would seem, however, that the editor will be liable for contempt of court.

 Make your answer stand out

- By analysing the approach of the European Court of Human Rights in addressing freedom of expression, and exploring in more detail how the margin of appreciation is applied. There is a useful discussion of the approach of Strasbourg in Fenwick, H. and Phillipson, G., *Media Law* (2006) Oxford: Oxford University Press, pp. 462–7.

- By incorporating reference to the case of *R* v *Perrin* [2002] EWCA Crim 747, in which it was confirmed in the domestic courts that the test for obscenity is sufficiently precise for the purpose of Art 10(2). This shows your examiner that you are familiar with a broad range of cases, and the effect that this may have upon the persons in the scenario.

- By considering whether or not Julian would have any action in defamation in respect of the comments made about him in the newspaper. You could deal with this fairly succinctly and should make the point that if Julian is convicted of an obscenity offence, the paper may well be able to claim the defence of truth in any libel action.

> ! **Don't be tempted to...**
>
> ■ Explain in detail the 'old' law relating to blasphemy. You are asked to address the legal implications of these facts, and there are no marks available for exploring principles which will no longer have any impact on the parties. The question specifically mentions Mrs Greenhouse's religion and, as all facts in a scenario are mentioned for a reason, you are being invited to mention blasphemy. You will be rewarded for having the confidence to assert that it is not relevant.
>
> ■ Fail to address the legal implications which may arise for the paper. Weaker students will fail to recognise that the examiner has asked for all implications to be addressed, and will concentrate on possible actions against Julian. It is important to ensure that you consider the impact of the events on all the parties.
>
> ■ Concentrate only on obscenity law. This question highlights the danger of 'topic spotting' as a revision technique. Students who have concentrated on the Obscene Publications Act, but have failed to revise the Contempt of Court Act will be unable to advise all the parties here.

Question 6

'The court recalls that freedom of expression constitutes one of the essential foundations of a democratic society and that the safeguards to be afforded to the press are or particular importance. Protection of journalistic sources is one of the most basic conditions for press freedom.' (*Goodwin* v *UK* (1996) 2 EHRR 123 at 39)

Discuss the impact of the Human Rights Act on the protection afforded to journalistic sources in the United Kingdom.

Answer plan

→ Outline the provisions of the common law Contempt of Court Act 1981, s 10.

→ Briefly address the approach of the courts prior to the HRA.

→ Explain the influence of the ECHR on recent authorities.

→ Identify additional relevant statutes.

Diagram plan

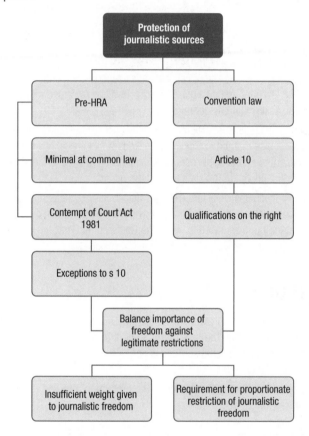

A printable version of this diagram is available from www.pearsoned.co.uk/lawexpressqa

Answer

The Human Rights Act 1998 incorporates the European Convention of Human Rights into domestic law. As the courts are a public body (s 6), the judiciary are required to ensure that Convention rights are upheld. Domestic law has recognised the need to allow journalists to protect their sources, with protection offered by the Contempt of Court Act 1981. Article 10 protects freedom of expression, and the jurisprudence of the European Court suggests that particular weight is given for the need for press freedom.[1] It will be considered how far domestic provisions were compliant with the Convention, and whether or not the HRA has signalled any significant change.

[1] The introduction demonstrates an awareness of the relevant Convention article, and the domestic legislation that needs to be discussed.

Investigative journalism has an important role to play in a democracy, as it can expose corporate or government wrongdoing. Journalists often rely on sources within an organisation for information, and it is perhaps self-evident that individuals may be unwilling to speak to the press if they could not be certain that their identity would remain secret.[2] This position remains unaffected by the Freedom of Information Act, as information held by private companies is not subject to its provisions, and there are numerous exemptions applicable to government information.

[2]It is important to explain why the issue of the protection of sources is considered to be important.

The threat to a journalistic source can arise in an action for breach of confidence, where the applicant seeks an injunction to restrain publication, and an order for disclosure of the source of the information.[3] At common law, there was little protection. In **British Steel Corp v Granada Television** [1981] AC 1096, the Court of Appeal judgment acknowledged the need for the 'free flow of information', but nevertheless refused to countenance the existence of journalistic privilege. The disquiet caused by this case led to the Contempt of Court Act 1981.

[3]Reference to the law on confidence demonstrates an awareness of when s 10 of the Contempt of Court Act will be used.

Section 10 of the Act states that a journalist will not be liable for contempt due to a refusal to name a source unless the court feels disclosure is necessary in the interests of justice, national security, or to prevent disorder or crime. Therefore, it can be seen that the Act creates a presumption against disclosure.[4] The circumstances in which disclosure may be necessary will be considered in turn.[5]

[4]As well as setting out the law, you need to be able to explain the effect of the statutory provision.

[5]Here, a clear structure is set out.

The issue of national security was considered in the case of **A-G v Guardian Newspapers** (No. 2) [1990] 1 AC 109. The case concerned Sarah Tisdall, a civil servant who had leaked information regarding the movement of nuclear missiles that exposed the tactics used by a Minister to keep the matter from discussion in the House of Commons. The Attorney General sought an order for disclosure against the *Guardian* newspaper. The *Guardian* defended the application, arguing that the matter concerned politics, rather than national security. The newspaper was successful at first instance. On appeal, the court held that the matter did concern national security, as a civil servant prepared to impart confidential information may in future disclose matters directly affecting security.

The case of **X v Morgan Grampian** [1991] 1 AC 1 considered the interpretation of 'interests of justice'. The defendants resisted disclosure on the basis that the term referred to the administration of justice in particular proceedings. The court gave the term a broad interpretation, stating that the interests of justice include helping persons to exercise legal rights, and protect themselves against legal wrongs. Further, the court had to consider whether it was 'necessary' to make the order. Lord Bridge stated that the gross breach of confidentiality by the employee and the financial risk to the company outweighed the public interest value of the informa-

[6]This is a useful point, as it shows how before the HRA, the Contempt of Court Act had a fairly limited effect on the protection of sources.

tion. Arguably, given that almost all leaks will involve a breach of confidentiality and some financial risk to the plaintiff, it is difficult to see how s 10 was being applied to afford better protection for journalistic sources.[6] Indeed, when the matter was considered by the European Court, it was held that whilst the interests of justice were a permissible restriction upon Art 10 rights, the order was dis-

[7]The issue of proportionality is crucial. As the answer will explore this in more detail it is worth highlighting here.

proportionate and failed to give due weight to the need to ensure press freedom (**Goodwin v UK** app (65723/01) [2008] All ER (D) 113 (Jan)).[7]

The incorporation of Convention rights into domestic law has meant that the judiciary must seek to protect Art 10 rights. It is fair to say that the reasons for disclosure in s 10 mirror, and are perhaps less restrictive, than the qualifications upon the right contained within Art 10(2).[8] **Goodwin** highlighted the disparity between the balancing act enacted domestically, and the more stringent test of proportionality required by Strasbourg. Since the HRA came into force in 2000, the courts have had to address the issue on a number of occasions. Most notable has been the litigation surrounding documentation leaked in respect of a proposed takeover of the company Interbrew. The company sought injunctive relief to restrain publication and, at the same time, sought to recover leaked documents and the source of the leak from a range of media organisations. The company argued that the media companies should not be able to rely on s 10 as the interests of justice exemption applied, and argued that necessity arose due to the propensity of the leak to damage the share market. The Court of Appeal ordered disclosure, and argued that the motivation of the source was very significant as it must have been malicious: for profit or for spite[9] (**Interbrew v Financial Times** [2002] EWCA Civ 274). The media outlets refused to comply with the order and the matter was referred to Strasbourg (**Financial Times Ltd v United Kingdom** [2010] (App. 821/03)). The ECtHR

[8]It is important to recognise that the Convention allows for the possibility of the kinds of restrictions that have been discussed; the key issue is whether or not the domestic courts apply these tests in a manner proportionate to the importance of the right.

[9]This is an example of when a small amount of detail about the facts makes the ratio of the case easier to explain.

ruling echoed the earlier ruling in **Goodwin**. Again, the court found that disclosure orders could be within the tolerance granted under s 10(2), but that the focus on the motive of the source could not be the main determinant, and failed to give due weight to the important aim of preserving the freedom of the press.

[10]It is useful to point out that the impact of this case has yet to be felt, as it shows an awareness of the fact the law is in a continual process of development.

This is the first time that the domestic approach to the protection of sources has been scrutinised at Strasbourg since the HRA came into force and it remains to be seen what effect the judgment will have on future litigation.[10] Thus far, however, it appears that the HRA has not fundamentally altered the position, as the domestic courts still seem willing to tip the balance in favour of commercial interests rather than the need to preserve journalistic freedom.[11]

[11]Here, the question is addressed directly and a clear answer provided. Credit will be given for reaching a firm conclusion.

 Make your answer stand out

- By showing an awareness of recent academic commentary. This is quite a specialised area, but you can find relevant material in the journal *Communications Law*.
- Journals can also keep you up to date with developing case law. For example, comment on the decision regarding confidential sources in the case *Sanoma Uitgevers BV* v *The Netherlands* appeared in the above journal before it was reported: (2010) 15(4) Comms L 124–5). Inclusion of analysis of recent authorities will show that you are engaged with the subject and able to make use of developing law.

! Don't be tempted to...

- Explain in any detail the operation of the law of confidence, as this is not the focus of the question. No marks will be awarded, for example, for setting out the law in *Campbell* or other key decisions.
- Simply describe the key cases. As well as explaining how the law has evolved in the United Kingdom, your answer must remain focused on analysing how effective the HRA has been in forcing the domestic courts to conduct a more stringent balancing act between competing rights.

Police powers

8

How this topic may come up in exams

Problem scenarios are a common way to examine this area of the syllabus. You will need to ensure that you are familiar with the major provisions of PACE, and the associated codes of practice. You should also be able to outline the possible consequences of police misconduct, and explain the means by which evidence can be excluded from a criminal trial. Essay questions may require evaluation of the safeguards against the misuse of discretionary powers. This area of the syllabus may overlap with human rights, and you should be prepared to evaluate the compatibility of police powers with Convention rights (particularly Arts 5, 6, and 8).

Attack the question

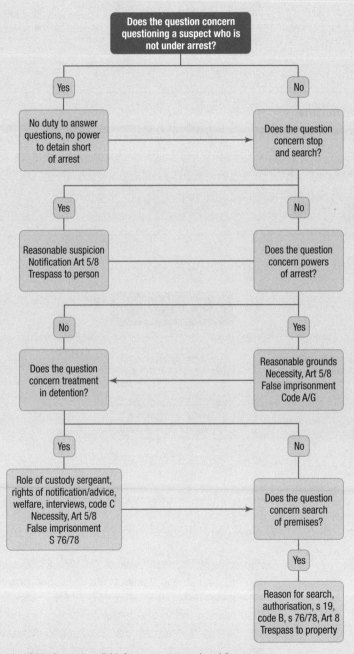

Does the question concern questioning a suspect who is not under arrest?

Yes → No duty to answer questions, no power to detain short of arrest

No → Does the question concern stop and search?

Yes → Reasonable suspicion Notification Art 5/8 Trespass to person

No → Does the question concern powers of arrest?

Yes → Reasonable grounds Necessity, Art 5/8 False imprisonment Code A/G

No → Does the question concern treatment in detention?

Yes → Role of custody sergeant, rights of notification/advice, welfare, interviews, code C Necessity, Art 5/8 False imprisonment S 76/78

No → Does the question concern search of premises?

Yes → Reason for search, authorisation, s 19, code B, s 76/78, Art 8 Trespass to property

A printable version of this diagram is available from www.pearsoned.co.uk/lawexpressqa

Question 1

The approach taken by the courts in applying ss 76 and 78 of PACE arguably endorses unlawful behaviour on the part of the police, and provides no remedy for the suspect who is treated unlawfully.

Discuss.

Answer plan

➜ Explain the meaning of ss 76 and 78, and highlight the distinction between the sections.

➜ Outline the circumstances in which s 76 is applied, and assess the effect of s 76(4).

➜ Analyse the exercise of the discretion under s 78 with reference to case law.

➜ Identify alternative remedies for the suspect.

➜ Draw a conclusion about the approach taken by the judiciary.

Diagram plan

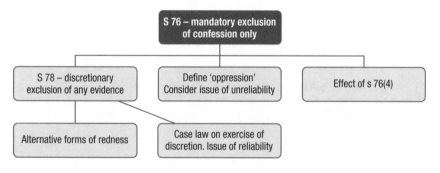

A printable version of this diagram is available from www.pearsoned.co.uk/lawexpressqa

Answer

The Police and Criminal Evidence Act 1984 (PACE) regulates the use of police powers to investigate crime. Sections 76 and 78 set out circumstances in which the court may exclude evidence from criminal trial as a result of conduct during the investigation. Section 76 deals with the exclusion of confession evidence, whilst s 78 is broader and can be invoked to exclude confession

[1]This part of the introduction reassures the examiner that the answer will take an analytical approach to the subject.

or non-confession evidence. Case law suggests that, in exercising discretion, the primary concern of the court is the reliability of evidence, rather than the conduct of officers.[1] It will be suggested that this is the correct approach, and suspects can seek redress through other channels.

Section 76 imposes an obligation on the court to exclude confession evidence in one of two circumstances. First, the court must exclude the evidence if the confession was obtained by oppression. Secondly, the evidence must be excluded if it was obtained as a result of things said or done which, in the circumstances existing at the time, render the confession unreliable. Exclusion is mandatory if either of these conditions are met. Section 76(8) states that 'oppression' in this context includes torture, inhuman or degrading treatment, and the use or threat of violence. In **R v Fulling** [1987] QB 426, the court held that the use of the word 'includes' demonstrates that this list is not exhaustive,[2] and provided a broader definition; including the exercise of authority in a 'burdensome' or 'harsh' manner as well as 'unreasonable or unjust burdens'.[3] Whilst, as Fenwick argues, it would be possible to interpret 'wrongful' in this context as 'unlawful', the courts will not exclude confession evidence simply because there has been a breach of the codes of conduct. It is clear that for exclusion under this head it must be shown that the misconduct was serious, and that there was bad faith. Even though some might maintain the bar is set too high, arguably the section does firmly discourage the police from obtaining confessions by oppressive or intimidating means; to do so could jeopardise prospects of conviction if the evidence is kept from the jury. However, as Bradley and Ewing note, s 76(4) provides that any evidence discovered as a result of the confession can still be admitted, and further, the confession itself can be admitted if it is relevant to demonstrate that the defendant expresses himself in a particular way.[4] Perhaps then, as Bradley and Ewing state '[t]he fruit of the poison tree appears to be edible in English Law.'[5]

Section 78 allows the exclusion of any evidence in a criminal trial where the court considers that 'having regard to all the circumstances, including the circumstances in which it was obtained' admission would have an adverse effect on the fairness of the proceedings. Here, the court acts at its own discretion.[6] On the face of it, the powers conferred by provision are wider; the legislation

[2]Fulling is an important authority that clarifies the meaning of the statute, and it should be included.

[3]Although there is no need to include quotations, inclusion of words from the judgment is a quick and simple way to illustrate what was meant by the decision.

[4]It is important to make reference to s 76(4), as it shows how the exclusionary provisions are limited.

[5]If you are able to include a memorable phrase such as this, the answer will seem very confident. .

[6]You do need to make the point that exclusions under s 78 are discretionary; this demonstrates a thorough knowledge of the difference between the two sections.

[7]The answer should set out the differences between the two provisions.

[8]*Khan* should be included. When outlining these cases, you should highlight the conduct of the police but avoid lengthy explanations of the facts.

[9]There are lots of cases that could be used to demonstrate that the courts often admit evidence obtained illegally. You should try to use a few examples to reinforce the argument, but, apart from *Khan*, it doesn't really matter which cases you cite.

[10]*Keenan* deals with a slightly different aspect of the point, as it is specific to breaches of the codes of conduct. It should be cited, as the 'significant and substantial' test is important.

[11]The introduction set out a very clear position. The answer should acknowledge that there is a different view that could be taken.

[12]This is the crux of the argument that is being advanced, and needs to be carefully explained.

applies to all types of evidence and, in considering fairness, there is no requirement to show bad faith.[7] Confession evidence which cannot be excluded under s 76 could theoretically be excluded under s 78. However, case law demonstrates that the courts seldom invoke the power to exclude physical evidence even where the circumstances in which it was obtained amount to serious illegality by the police. The leading authority comes from the case of **R v Khan** [1997] AC 558. The prosecution case rested on evidence obtained by illegal surveillance.[8] The House of Lords held it was proper to admit the evidence even though the police actions were probably in breach of the defendant's Art 8 rights. Other examples of evidence being admitted despite unlawful behaviour by the police include secretly recorded incriminating statements (**R v Chalkey** [1997] EWCA Crim 3416), and evidence obtained from illegally retained DNA (**A-G's Reference** (No. 3 of 1999) [2000] UKHL 63.[9] In the case of **R v Keenan** [1989] 3 All ER 598, it was held that where there has been a breach of the rules under PACE, the court should consider first whether the breach was 'substantial or significant',[10] and only then continue to assess the impact of the breach in the particular circumstances of the case.

It may appear the courts do indeed send a signal to the police which endorses unlawful behaviour whilst investigating criminality through the reluctance to exercise their discretion. It could be suggested that the courts, as an emanation of the state, must insist on due process.[11] On this view, the courts have a duty to maintain the standards expected of the police, and to punish those who fail to meet them by making sure they cannot benefit from illegal behaviour. Undoubtedly, though, there is a difficult balance to be struck. PACE was implemented to provide safeguards for the public by setting down clear standards of conduct, and ss 76 and 78 were intended to form part of the protection against the abuse of police power. However, the courts are wary of endorsing an acquittal where there is clear evidence pointing to guilt. The courts have sought to strike the balance by focusing primarily not upon the manner in which the evidence was collected, but on whether or not as a result the evidence has been rendered unreliable.[12] The first concern of the court then, is to determine the guilt or innocence of the accused, and it is not part of the judicial role to police the police. If, however, the police conduct has led to evidence that could result in a miscarriage of justice, then the courts will not countenance reliance upon it. This position is understandable. It would be disturbing if in a case such as **A-G's Reference** (No. 3 of 1999), a rapist had been allowed to walk free despite DNA evidence proving guilt.

[13]You should highlight the mechanisms that are available to obtain redress, but do not spend time explaining these as this is not the focus of the question.

Sections 76 and 78 are not the only safeguards against unlawful treatment. Where breaches of PACE or the codes of conduct have occurred, complaint can be made to the IPCC. In the most serious cases, this could result in criminal prosecution of the officer(s) involved. Alternatively, where police behaviour constitutes a tortious wrong, redress can be sought in the civil courts.[13] In conclusion, it is right to say the courts have not used ss 76 or 78 as a means of punishing police misconduct or providing remedies for the citizen. The provisions exist to ensure that miscarriages of justice do not occur, and to allow the courts to insist on reliable evidence.

✓ Make your answer stand out

- By referring to ECtHR decisions in this area. Consider *Schenk* v *Switzerland* [1988] 13 (EHRR) 242 in which it was held that it was for the national courts to determine admissibility of evidence. Admission of illegally obtained evidence does not necessarily breach Art 6.

- By expanding the discussion of the procedure which applies to s 76. The case of *R* v *Bhavna Dhorajiwala* [2010] EWCA Crim 1237 confirms that, once a representation is made to the court that a confession *may* have resulted from oppression, then it shall not be admitted unless the Crown can prove that it did not. You should use this point to reinforce the distinction between s 76 and s 78. This would show detailed knowledge of PACE, and an ability to keep abreast of case law.

- By reinforcing the point that the role of the court is not to police the police. You could cite *R* v *Smurththwaite and Gill* [1994] 1 All ER 898, in which Lord Diplock stressed that the criminal court is not there to exercise a disciplinary role over the police.

! Don't be tempted to...

- Include general information about PACE, or the codes. That is not relevant here. There is no need to demonstrate that you know the different aspects of procedure governed by the codes, for example.

- Explain in detail the facts of the cases referred to. You do need to highlight how evidence was obtained to illustrate the argument about the courts reluctance to use s 78, but that is all.

❓ Question 2

PC Binner is on foot patrol when he sees a group of three youths standing on a street corner. He instinctively feels that they look suspicious. He approaches the youths, and asks what they are up to. One of the youths, Silvio, begins to walk away.

PC Binner takes hold of Silvio by the elbow and says 'we'll see about that when I search you'. Silvio punches the officer in the chest. PC Binner uses his radio to call for assistance, and handcuffs Silvio. He then goes through Silvio's pockets, and finds a tablet loose in his trouser pocket. A police car arrives and PC Binner places Silvio in the back of the car, and Silvio is taken to the police station.

On arrival, the custody sergeant books Silvio into custody at 9pm. Silvio asks 'why am I here?' PC Binner tells Silvio he has been arrested for dealing drugs. Silvio immediately asks for a lawyer and is told this will be arranged. He is placed in a cell.

PC Binner asks the custody sergeant for permission to search Silvio's address. The custody sergeant calls for the duty inspector, who authorises the search. PC Binner and a colleague search Silvio's flat. No drugs are found, but a large quantity of car radios are seized.

At midnight, Silvio is told he can wait for a lawyer, or be interviewed immediately. He decides to be interviewed. In interview he is asked to explain about the car radios, and admits that he stole them. He insists that the tablet found is an aspirin.

Silvio is charged with assaulting a police officer and with theft. However, a friend of his who is studying law has told him that he will be able to have the case thrown out because of PC Binner's actions.

Advise Silvio.

Answer plan

- → Consider the legality of asking questions in the street.
- → Outline the requirements of ss 1–3 of PACE and consider legality of the search.
- → Assess the legality of the arrest, and consider if this provides a defence.
- → Briefly consider the search of premises.
- → Consider the applicability of s 78.

Diagram plan

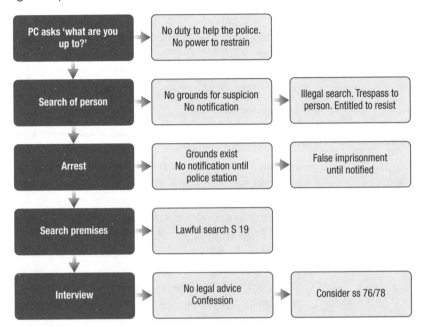

A printable version of this diagram is available from www.pearsoned.co.uk/lawexpressqa

Answer

The validity of the police actions needs to be assessed in order to advise Silvio of any options available to him. It appears that the stop and search, and initial arrest, were unlawful. This may provide Silvio with a defence to the charge of assaulting a police constable. It is unlikely that he will be able to avoid the consequences of the theft as the interview is likely to be admissible.[1]

[1] The introduction avoids repeating the facts of the scenario, and instead, demonstrates that the key issues have been understood.

On being approached and questioned by PC Binner, Silvio is lawfully entitled to walk away. It is a long-established principle that, as stated in **Rice v Connolly** [1966] 2 All ER 649, there is no general duty to assist the police.[2] Therefore, unless the circumstances are covered by a specific statutory provision (for example, the duty to give details under the Road Traffic Acts), the police have no power to detain a person for questioning falling short of the power to arrest. Accordingly, Silvio should be advised that the officer has no lawful authority to take hold of him by the elbow, and that this may constitute a battery at common law.[3] The facts of **Collins v**

[2] *Rice* v *Connolly* is the leading authority here and it is important to include the case.

[3] The answer must use the authorities to provide specific advice regarding the facts of the scenario.

[4]You should note the similarity with *Collins* v *Wilcock* but you don't need to rehearse the facts. It is useful to remember the wording from the judgment which stresses the minimal degree of contact required for the offence.

Wilcock [1984] 3 All ER 374 were similar, and are authority for the proposition that 'the slightest touch can constitute a battery'.[4] Therefore, arguably, Silvio is entitled to use force to defend himself from the unwarranted interference with his person. **Kenlin v Gardiner** [1967] 2 WLR 129 confirms that a person can resist an unlawful detention. However, Silvio should be advised that the level of force used here may not be proportionate.[5]

[5]Take care not to be diverted into a discussion regarding criminal law. There is no need to consider the elements of private defence in any detail here.

PC Binner states his intention to search Silvio. There are no grounds disclosed in the scenario that would give rise to the power to search. Section 1 of the Police and Criminal Evidence Act authorises a police officer to stop and search if he has reasonable grounds to suspect that the person is in possession of one of the specified items (stolen goods, offensive weapons, fireworks, or items made or adapted for use in criminal damage). We are not told whether or not PC Binner suspects that Silvio is in possession of such articles, however, the facts do not disclose any reasonable grounds for any such suspicion. The Codes of Practice, Code A 2.2, makes it clear that suspicion must be based on objective factors, and cannot arise purely on the basis of personal factors such as age, appearance or previous convictions. We are not told of any objective basis for the officer's concerns. The subsequent search is illegal as it is not justified, and in addition, the notification requirements of ss 2 and 3 do not appear to have been complied with.[6]

[6]The facts of the scenario are very clear, and credit will be given for providing unambiguous advice in these circumstances as it shows confidence.

[7]Again, it is possible to give very definite advice here.

The initial arrest is unlawful, as PC Binner does not advise Silvio of either the fact of, or the grounds for arrest as required by s 28 PACE.[7] The case of **Christie v Leachinskey** [1947] 1 All ER 567 made it clear that failure to inform a person of the fact and reason for arrest renders it illegal.[8] The more recent case of **Lewis v Chief Constable of the South Wales Constabulary** [1991] 1 All ER 206 demonstrates that an illegality can, in effect, be 'corrected' when the detainee is properly notified. It seems that Silvio is notified once at the police station. Although detention after unlawful arrest constitutes an actionable false imprisonment, any claim would be limited to the time period prior to notification as from that point, the detention is rendered lawful.[9]

[8]Despite the fact that s 28, PACE deals with the same issue, the case remains good law, and is usually cited.

[9]It is important to consider any remedies that Silvio may have, as this would form part of the advice to a client.

Once in custody, Silvio's treatment is governed by statutory provisions and Code C. The custody sergeant is responsible for ensuring that Silvio's detention is necessary, and for ensuring that his welfare and his rights are protected. It is his responsibility to ensure that Silvio is advised of his rights, including the right to have some-one notified of his arrest (s 56, PACE) and of his right to free legal advice (s 58). We are not told whether or not the sergeant complies with this, only that Silvio makes a request for legal representation. Equally, it is not clear whether or not a lawyer is ever contacted. If this has not occurred then this will be a clear, and potentially signifi-cant, breach of PACE.[10]

Before considering the effect of such a breach, it is worth noting that the search of premises appears to be lawful. Section 18 of PACE provides for the search of premises occupied or controlled by a person in custody for evidence connected with the offence for which he has been arrested.[11] Although the extent of the search must be limited to that which is necessary for the nature of the items sought, s 19 (as amended) makes it clear that it is permis-sible for the officers to seize any items discovered in the course of the search that they reasonably believe are connected with any offence. The seizure of the car radios is, therefore, legitimate.[12]

During the course of the interview, Silvio admits the offence of theft. He may seek to have the confession evidence excluded at any subsequent trial,[13] under either s 76 or s 78 of PACE. Section 76 provides for such exclusion if the confession was obtained by oppression, or if it was obtained in consequence of things said or done which, in all the circumstances, would render it unfair if admit-ted. On the facts provided, neither of these conditions appears to be met. Section 78 allows for the exclusion of any evidence (includ-ing confessions) if, having regard to all the circumstances in which it was obtained, it would be unfair to admit it. In this case, Silvio may seek to argue that either the initial illegal stop and search, or the denial of legal advice would render the confession unfair. Whilst both these breaches are serious, the authorities suggest that the courts are unwilling to exclude evidence unless it appears to be unreliable (see, for example, **R v Khan** [1997] AC 558.[14] Therefore, Silvio should be advised that an application under s 78 is unlikely to succeed and that therefore, contrary to the advice of his friend, the case will proceed.

In summary, it appears that the police have acted unlawfully. Silvio may wish to consider claims in tort for trespass to the person, and false imprisonment.[15] The illegal search and arrest may afford Silvio a defence to the charge of assaulting a police constable. It is doubtful that confession evidence would be excluded in this instance, as it would seem the reliability of the evidence is unaffected.

✓ Make your answer stand out

■ By including additional authorities in the answer. You could cite *DPP* v *Blake* [1989] 1 WLR 432 as part of the discussion regarding the illegal search, or any number of cases concerning the application of s 78. Whilst you should only include authorities where they are relevant, you will certainly be rewarded if you can provide an authority for as many propositions of law as you can.

■ By using recent case law to reinforce the fact that Silvio is likely to have a defence to the charge of assault PC. You could cite *R (Michaels)* v *Highbury Corner Magistrates' Court* [2010] Crim LR 506, in which the Divisional Court stressed that the notification requirement of s 2 will be strictly enforced. In that case, a conviction for obstructing a police officer was set aside. You could demonstrate an ability to use analogous cases to form conclusions about the outcome of a scenario.

■ By discussing the potential remedies in more detail; in particular, the answer does not address the potential for a formal complaint through the IPCC. It would be useful to show that you are aware of this procedure, as it would demonstrate that you are familiar with all aspects of this topic.

! Don't be tempted to...

■ Show the examiner that you have revised all aspects of PACE. For example, many students will give detail about how and when powers to search premises may arise under s 17 or s 32. More credit will be given for demonstrating an ability to recognise that s 18 is the one which is relevant here.

■ Discuss the requirements of the criminal law. It is fairly common for students to make the mistake of thinking it is helpful to outline what the Crown would have to prove to obtain a conviction for theft. There are no marks available for demonstrating knowledge of the components of criminal liability. You must ensure your answer focuses on the public law aspects of the scenario.

Question 3

Powers afforded to the police to investigate crime fail to provide adequate safeguards for the human rights of the suspect.

Discuss.

Answer plan

→ Outline the main statutory sources of police powers to search, arrest and detain.

→ Identify those that will be the focus of discussion; access to legal advice, search and arrest.

→ Explain the Convention rights which are engaged and assess the domestic and European approach to the use of police powers.

→ Draw conclusions that the HRA imports sufficient safeguards.

Diagram plan

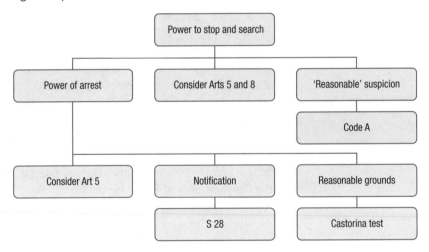

A printable version of this diagram is available from www.pearsoned.co.uk/lawexpressqa

Answer

The police have extensive powers to investigate crime, and it is clear that powers of search, arrest and detention have the potential to interfere with the liberties of the citizen. Many of these powers are authorised by warrant, and are therefore subject to the scrutiny of the court. The police also have extensive discretion to detain persons at statute and common law; some of these provisions will be considered to evaluate the level of protection given to the individual suspect.[1] The Police and Criminal Evidence Act 1984 (PACE) remains the main source of police powers, and, together with the Codes of Practice, gives guidance on how discretion should be exercised. It will be suggested that the domestic law has only been partially successful in ensuring that the rights of the suspect are upheld during the investigation process. The European Convention of Human Rights has the potential to afford more robust protection. The discussion will focus on powers to stop and search and powers of arrest.[2]

A number of statutory provisions confer a power to stop and search individuals in particular circumstances (for example, the Misuse of Drugs Act 1971), but the broadest and most commonly used power is contained at s 1 of PACE. Section 1 allows an officer to search on reasonable suspicion that the individual is in possession of stolen or prohibited articles. Sections 2 and 3 set limits on the extent of a search in public place, and Code A 2:2 gives some guidance about what constitutes 'reasonable suspicion'. It is unlikely that a search under s 1 would be deemed to be a breach of Art 5 (deprivation of liberty) or Art 8.[3] The domestic courts addressed the issue in **R (Gillan) v Commissioner of Police for the Metropolis** [2006] UKHL 12. The case concerned powers under s 44 of the Terrorism Act, but it was held that a brief search would not be of sufficient seriousness to constitute interference with either Arts 8 or 5. The European Court took a different view, certainly in respect of Art 8. It was held that the public nature of the search could constitute a breach, and having reached that decision the Court did not feel it necessary to address Art 5. Accordingly, a search under s 1 is, in principle, capable of engaging Art 8 following **Gillan and Quinton v United Kingdom** [2009] ECHR 28. However, the rationale for finding that s 44 searches were a breach of Convention rights was that the power could not be said to be 'prescribed by law' due to

[1] It is helpful to establish the parameters for the discussion in the introduction. The use of discretionary power should be the focus as the court can only review how such a power has been exercised after the fact.

[2] As the answer cannot deal with the totality of police powers, you should make clear what areas of the law you intend to concentrate on.

[3] As the question refers to human rights, it is essential that the answer evaluates each power in light of the European Convention of Human Rights.

[4]By drawing a distinction between the powers in the TA 2000 and the PACE power, the answer is able to demonstrate a sound grasp of the legal reasoning used in evaluating Convention rights.

[5]It is important to make note that not every loss of physical freedom will amount to a deprivation of liberty.

[6]There is no need to list the statutory provisions here, as the effect can be explained without doing so.

[7]Despite the fact that it could be argued that the HRA has affected the ruling in this case, it should be the starting point for the discussion as it is still considered to be a crucial authority.

[8]Although *Wednesbury* unreasonableness has not been explained here, it is clear from the way the terminology is used that the meaning is understood.

[9]This is a useful authority to include and allows the answer to show how the law has developed over time.

[10]It is important to use the term 'proportionality' as this is central to ECtHR jurisprudence.

the breadth of application. The power in PACE will be lawful as it is narrower in focus, and requires reasonable suspicion.[4] Any interference with Convention rights will fall within the permitted qualifications for the recognised purpose of preventing crime.

There is some doubt about the efficacy of the test for 'reasonable suspicion', as, although Code A sets out some parameters and makes it clear that suspicion must not be based on discriminatory factors, at 2:3 provision is made for a search based on suspicious behaviour without specific intelligence.

The arrest of a suspect will, of course, remove their freedom. This will not be a breach of Art 5, however, as the Convention permits lawful arrest and detention to bring an individual before a court on reasonable suspicion of having committed an offence.[5] The Serious Organised Crime and Police Act 2005 amended PACE, and broadened the power of arrest. The distinction between 'arrestable' and 'non-arrestable' offences has been removed. A power of arrest arises in respect of all crimes as long as the arrest is 'necessary' for one of the reasons set out at s 24(5). It should be noted that the permitted reasons are drafted broadly enough to incorporate almost all circumstances.[6] The officer must, again, have reasonable suspicion that the individual has committed an offence. The domestic courts considered the requirements prior to the Human Rights Act in **Castorina v Chief Constable of Surrey** [1988] NLJ 180[7], which held that a 'mere hunch' would not suffice, and that the decision to arrest should be in accordance with **Wednesbury** principles. It appears that very few arrests would be held to be **Wednesbury** unreasonable,[8] leaving little room to challenge an officer's exercise of discretion. The European Court has imposed a more stringent interpretation by holding that there should be a standard that would satisfy an objective observer (**Fox, Campbell and Hartley v UK** (1991) 13 EHRR 157). The HRA now requires the domestic courts to give effect to convention rights. The case of **Cumming v Chief Constable of Northumbria** [2003] EWCA Civ 1844 considered the matter and left the test largely unaltered, save that in order to be unlawful the decision must be one no officer would reasonably take in light of the impact on the suspects liberty.[9] This does, at least, suggest a requirement to consider the proportionality of arrest,[10] and indeed, this is now specified in the revised codes published in 2009 (code G).

[11]This is a good case to cite, and the incorporation of the words used in the judgment stresses the fact that the rights of the suspect in this instance are seen to be paramount.

According to s 28 of PACE, the arrested person must be informed of the fact of, and reason for, arrest. This placed the ruling in **Christie v Leachinskey** [1947] AC 573 on a statutory footing. Failure to do so renders the arrest unlawful. This was confirmed more recently in **Edwards v DPP** [1993] Crim LR 854 in which the court stressed the 'constitutional significance'[11] of the requirement in protecting against the possibility of arbitrary arrest. Thus, the arrest was held to be unlawful as the officer provided an invalid reason, notwithstanding the fact that other, relevant, reasons palpably did exist. The European Court considered the issue in **Fox** (above) and felt that the reasons must be given promptly and clearly, but need not be particularly detailed.

Powers of search, and of arrest, must be subject to proper scrutiny and control to ensure that citizens are not subject to arbitrary and unwarranted interference with their liberty. The statutory framework introduced by PACE aimed to provide clear guidance on the exercise of discretionary powers. This did provide a measure of protection and set some clear and fixed boundaries, for example, in respect of the extent of a public search. Where a decision fell to be determined on 'reasonable' grounds, the courts appeared reluctant to interfere with the judgment of the officer concerned. There must of course be a balance between the rights of the suspect, and the need for the police to operate for the public good.[12] The Human Rights Act imposes a duty on the police to give consideration to the Convention rights of the suspect and to act in a manner which is proportionate. It is submitted that this has led to more robust protection for the rights of the suspect.

[12]It is important to highlight this fact, as the court is required to find the appropriate balance.

✓ Make your answer stand out

- By including academic comment to support the argument regarding the power of arrest. The change to the power of arrest was discussed by R. Austin, in 'The new powers of arrest: plus ça change: more of the same or major change?' [2007] Crim L R 459.

- By making more use of case law from Strasbourg. Of particular relevance here would be the case of *S and Marper* v *UK* [2008] ECHR 1581, in which it was held that the retention of DNA by police was an infringement of Convention rights. It could be argued that the domestic law fails to give sufficient protection to the rights of the suspect, particularly in light of *R (on the application of GC and C)* v *Commissioner of the Police for the Metropolis* [2010] EWHC 2225 (Admin), in which it was held that the domestic courts were entitled to ignore the ECtHR ruling. You could demonstrate to your examiner that you are confident with the material by assessing the conflict of these decisions.

- The above case is also interesting as it appears to be in conflict with a recent line of authority in which the judiciary have considered themselves bound by Strasbourg (see, for example, *Manchester City Council* v *Pinner* [2010] UKSC 45). You will be rewarded for acknowledging the complexity of the subject-matter.

! Don't be tempted to...

- Address too many issues. You cannot expect to incorporate discussion of every power that the police have to investigate crime. Students who try to do this will inevitably deal with matters in a superficial and descriptive way. More marks will be given if you focus on a few areas and engage in a more in depth analysis.

- Focus solely on the provisions of PACE, without considering how the powers relate to Convention rights. It will not be sufficient, for example, to say that an arrest is an interference with the right of liberty. You will need to be able to explain that the Convention right is qualified, and permits infringement for a lawful purpose.

❓ Question 4

Tim suffers from anxiety, and takes medication for this. He has a job delivering pizzas. On his first night, he is asked to take some pizzas to an address. When he arrives, he is approached by uniformed police officers. They advise him that they wish to search him as they have information that he is carrying drugs. Tim is taken to the side of the road and his coat is searched. The pizza box is opened and found to contain a bag of cannabis. Tim is told he is being arrested on suspicion of supplying class B drugs.

Tim arrives at the police station at 10pm. He is cautioned again, and told of his rights. He asks for a solicitor during interview, and to ring his mother. The sergeant explains that a solicitor will be called, but that he can not speak to his mother. Tim tells the sergeant that he needs to take his medication at midnight. The sergeant tells him not to worry as he will not be there long.

Tim is placed in a cell. The sergeant authorises a search of his address. This takes place at 2am, and nothing is found. At 3am, Tim is told that he can be interviewed. He asks where the solicitor is, and is told that the solicitor cannot attend until 5am, but could speak to him on the phone. Tim agrees, and again, tells the sergeant he needs his medication. He is told he can wait to see a doctor, which will be the next day, or get the interview over with.

Tim speaks to the solicitor shortly after 3am, and by this time he is very anxious and distressed. He tells the solicitor he knows nothing about the drugs, and that he feels very unwell. The solicitor advises him to make no comment.

Tim begins the taped interview by saying 'no comment' to all questions. The officer repeatedly tells him that he knows he was dealing drugs, and will keep on asking him until he admits it. Eventually, Tim says 'yes, I did it'. The interview is terminated and he is charged with the offence.

Advise Tim.

Answer plan

→ Briefly explain that both search and arrest are lawful.

→ Identify the rights that Tim has whilst in custody, particularly s 56 and s 58 of PACE.

→ Consider the role of the custody sergeant in protecting the welfare of the suspect.

→ Discuss whether or not the telephone consultation is sufficient.

→ Outline the effect of ss 34–37 of the Criminal Justice and Public Order Act 1994 and consider the effect of Tim's decision to stay silent.

→ Assess whether or not the confession is admissible.

Diagram plan

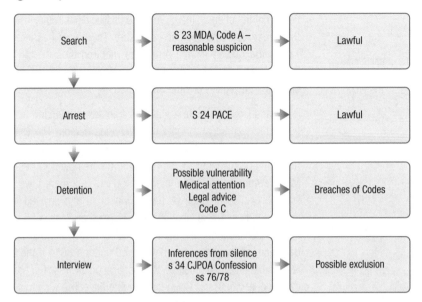

A printable version of this diagram is available from www.pearsoned.co.uk/lawexpressqa

Answer

[1]This is the key issue that arises as a result of Tim's experiences, and therefore the introduction makes it clear that this has been understood.

Tim has confessed to committing an offence, despite the fact that he claims to have had no involvement in it.[1] Although his initial arrest and detention appears to be lawful, there are some concerns regarding his treatment in custody. As a result, the evidence obtained may be deemed to be unreliable.[2]

[2]There is no need to summarise the facts of the scenario: instead, the introduction should highlight the legal issues that are suggested.

The first issue is the search. The search is regulated by s 23(2) of the Misuse of Drugs Act 1971,[3] which empowers an officer to detain and search any person reasonably suspected to be in possession of a controlled drug. Guidance concerning reasonable suspicion is given by the Codes of Practice issued under the Police and Criminal Evidence Act 1984 (PACE). Code A makes it clear that there must be an objective basis for the suspicion. This is unproblematic, as the facts state that the officer is acting in response to specific intelligence.[4] The search appears to be conducted lawfully, as we are told it is restricted to outer clothing (PACE s 2).

[3]Problems commonly focus on the powers contained in s 1 of PACE, so credit will be given for recognising that a different statutory provision is utilised here.

[4]You must ensure that as well as explaining relevant law, you apply it to the facts provided.

Section 24 of PACE (as amended) entitles an officer to arrest without warrant any person reasonably suspected of committing a criminal offence, provided that the arrest is 'necessary' for one of the purposes specified at s 24(5). These include facilitation of investigation of the offence; therefore it seems likely that in this instance, the arrest would be deemed necessary. The officer has informed Tim of the reason for the arrest, as required by s 28 of PACE. Provided he has been properly cautioned, there are no grounds to challenge the legality of either the search, or subsequent arrest.[5]

PACE and Code C create a statutory framework intended to safeguard the welfare and rights of a detained person. The Custody Officer is the person who must authorise detention, and ensure that the rights of suspects are protected. Tim's treatment in detention raises a number of concerns and it appears that there have been some breaches of Code C. Tim is cautioned and advised of his rights, and is told he cannot speak to his mother. Section 56 states that an individual has the right to have someone informed of their detention; although this can be delayed under s 56(2) if there are reasonable grounds to believe that notification will result in harm to evidence, or witnesses. Given the fact that the police wish to search Tim's address, there could be grounds which justify delay. The delay must be authorised by an officer of the rank of inspector or above, however, and further, the reason for delay must be explained to the detainee. It does not appear that the delay has been properly authorised, or explained.[6]

[6] Having noted that there may be a justifiable reason for delay, students often fail to consider whether or not the correct procedure has been followed, so credit will be given for recognising this point.

Tim is entitled to free legal advice whilst in custody (s 58). Once the detainee has requested legal advice, they must not be interviewed until this has occurred. The entitlement is not necessarily to have a solicitor present in interview, merely to receive advice.[7] Therefore, the telephone call is sufficient as it will then be for the solicitor to determine if attendance is merited.

[7] This is a point that is often missed so inclusion demonstrates a thorough knowledge of the area.

Tim suffers from anxiety, and it appears that he tells the custody officer about his condition. He certainly advises him that he will require medication. The Codes of Practice state that any person who is a juvenile, mentally disordered or 'otherwise mentally vulnerable' (C 3.15) must be attended at the police station by an appropriate adult. It could be argued that a diagnosis of anxiety does not render someone 'mentally vulnerable', but this is a point that should certainly be raised, given concerns regarding the reliability of the confession that follows.[8] If the custody officer has any suspicion that Tim would be vulnerable, he should be treated as

[8] The answer should recognise that this is a debatable point, and that it is not possible to reach a firm conclusion on the information available.

216

such (C 1.4), and therefore it is suggested that failure to secure an appropriate adult constitutes a further breach.

[9]Conversely, there is no ambiguity on this point and it is possible to make a definite statement about the fact of a breach, which shows confidence in understanding the legal implications of the scenario.

Tim has indicated that he needs his medication. Failure to provide medical attention in these circumstances is a clear breach.[9] Paragraph 9.5 requires the custody officer to obtain clinical attentioned for any detained person suffering from a physical illness, even if this has not been requested.

[10]This part of the problem raises two issues: inferences from silence and exclusion of confession evidence. You must ensure that the answer deals with both.

During the interview, Tim initially makes no comment. He is entitled to exercise his right to silence, however, ss 34–37 of the Criminal Justice and Public Order Act (CJPOA) state that a court may draw an adverse inference if an individual fails to mention when questioned matters which they wish to rely on in defence.[10] This may be of concern for Tim, as it seems that, in a future trial, he would wish to provide an innocent account. Early case law suggested that reliance on legal advice would not prevent an adverse inference being drawn (**R v Condron and Condron** [1997] 1 WLR 827). In **Beckles v UK** [2004] EWCA Crim 2766, however, it was held that no inference should be drawn if the suspect reasonably relies on legal advice to remain silent. It is submitted that it is unlikely that any inference would be drawn in these circumstances.[11]

[11]It is important to include *Beckles*, as this is the authority that provides Tim with assistance.

At trial, it will be in Tim's interests to ask that the confession evidence be excluded. According to s 76 of PACE, the court must exclude the evidence if satisfied that it was obtained through oppression, and has discretion to do so if it is felt that the confession was made in circumstances that could render it unreliable. The leading case is **R v Fulling** [1987] QB 426, which makes it clear that oppression should be given an everyday meaning. Repetitive hostile questioning can be oppressive (**R v Paris** (1992) 97 Cr App R 99), but this will be a question of fact and degree for the court to determine.[12] It is submitted that the circumstances surrounding the confession are sufficient to render it unreliable, as it would seem that Tim has been denied medical attention. Following **R v Delaney** [1989] Crim LR 139, the court may well feel that, given concerns about Tim's anxiety, the discretion should be exercised in his favour. Indeed, it seems likely that an argument could be made to exclude the interview evidence in its entirety under s 78 of PACE.[13] The court may do so if it considers that, in all the circumstances, it would be unfair to admit it. Cumulative breaches of PACE may lead to exclusion (**R v Keenan** [1989] 3 All ER 598); the key consideration for the court will be whether or not the evidence is reliable.

[12]The answer should note the difference between the first test (for oppression), and the second test of reliability. It is not possible to reach a firm conclusion in respect of the first without further information about the content of the interview.

[13]Marks will be given for recognising that s 78 may also apply here.

Tim has no grounds to complain about his initial arrest, but may wish to consider lodging a complaint in respect of the breaches of the codes of practice which occurred whilst in detention. Of these, the failure to obtain medical advice is the most serious, and this may well have impacted upon the quality of evidence obtained by the police in interview. As a result, this may be excluded at any subsequent trial.

✓ Make your answer stand out

- By discussing the applicability of Art 6 to this case, and addressing some of the case law concerning the impact of ss 34–37 CJPOA on procedural fairness. Consider, for example, *Condron* v *UK* (2001) 31 EHRR 1. This would show the examiner that you can set the facts of the scenario in the broader context of human rights law.

- By explaining the available remedies in more detail and highlight the fact that a breach of the Codes of Practice can not, in and of themselves, give rise to an action in tort (s 67(10) PACE), as this will demonstrate that you have detailed knowledge of the relevant statutory provisions. Remedies are an aspect of police powers that are often overlooked.

- By incorporating a discussion of the efficacy of the Independent Police Complaints Commission. You could note that Liberty have raised concerns regarding complainants who lack mental capacity, which is clearly relevant to this scenario (www.liberty-human-rights.org.uk/pdfs/policy09/liberty-s-response-to-the-consultation-on-the-ipcc-s-proposed-statutory-guid.pdf).

! Don't be tempted to...

- Speculate about why Tim made the confession. The facts give no indication of this, and therefore you should only consider whether or not there are grounds to exclude it. Often, students are diverted into discussing hypothetical situations which are not highlighted in the scenario. It is important to focus on the information that has been provided.

- Confuse the provisions of the Code with those in the statute. A common mistake is to say that the police have the power to stop and search under Code A. This is incorrect: the statute gives the power, and the Code stipulates the manner in which it should be exercised.

❓ Question 5

PC Tomlin has been asked to investigate reports of a young woman with short blonde hair approaching pedestrians in the city centre and obtaining money by deception, by pretending she needs the train fare home. PC Tomlin is on duty in plain clothes, when he sees a young woman whose hair is hidden by a hat. The young woman approaches an old lady and tries to speak, but the old lady continues walking. PC Tomlin suspects this may be the person he is looking for, and decides to arrest her. He approaches her, saying, 'Right, you, you've got some explaining to do.'

The young woman, Penny, says 'get lost' and starts to walk away. PC Tomlin takes hold of her arms. She begins to struggle violently and strikes PC Tomlin before he is able to restrain her. He then tells her she is under arrest for assaulting a police constable in the lawful execution of his duty, and attempting to obtain property by deception.

Once at the police station, the custody officer on duty agrees that PC Tomlin can search her home address for evidence relating to the deception offence. In the breadbin, PC Tomlin discovers a bag containing a small amount of powder which later tests positive as cocaine. Penny is later charged with possession of a class A drug, and with assaulting a police constable.

As she is leaving the station, she tells PC Tomlin that she intends to take legal action against him.

Advise PC Tomlin of the legality of his actions and the likely outcome of proceedings against Penny.

Answer plan

→ Outline the issues raised: arrest, and search of premises.

→ Discuss the initial arrest, and the possible consequences for PC Tomlin and Penny.

→ Consider the legality of the search of premises and in particular the effect of this on future proceedings.

→ Conclude by summarising the implications for PC Tomlin, and the likely outcome for Penny.

Diagram plan

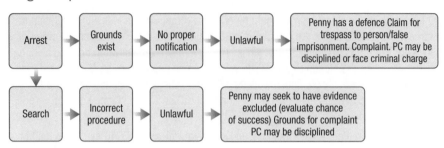

A printable version of this diagram is available from www.pearsoned.co.uk/lawexpressqa

Answer

The police are empowered to interfere with the liberty of the citizen for the purpose of preventing and detecting crime, and to keep the peace. Police powers are mainly governed by the Police and Criminal Evidence Act (PACE), as amended, and the associated Codes of Practice. If PC Tomlin has exceeded his powers, then this may lead to a complaint or even tortuous action. In addition, there may be implications for any charges that Penny faces.[1]

[1]This question requires the answer to advise the police officer as well as the suspect, so the introduction should reassure the examiner that this will be done.

PACE (as amended by the Serious Organised Crime and Police Act 2005) sets out the circumstances in which a police officer is able to arrest an individual without a warrant. Section 24 authorises an arrest in circumstances where the officer has reasonable grounds to suspect that an individual has committed an offence, provided that the arrest is necessary. From the facts provided, PC Tomlin may well be able to demonstrate that he had the requisite level of suspicion.[2] The Codes of Practice give some guidance on the issue. Code A, paragraph 2.2 makes it clear that there must be some objective basis, and at 2.3 sets out that there need not always be specific intelligence as an individual's conduct may give rise to suspicion.[3] The authorities suggest that it will not be particularly difficult for an officer to establish reasonable grounds for suspicion. The leading case (prior to the Human Rights Act), **Castorina v Chief Constable of Surrey** [1988] NLJ 180, confirmed the need for some objective basis, although this could be slight. The European Court of Human Rights has, in a number of judgments, stressed the need for reasonable grounds as protection against arbitrary arrest

[2]The answer should note that a lawful arrest requires both grounds and necessity, and these issues must each be addressed.

[3]This is an important part of the Code to note, given the facts of this particular problem in which it appears that it is Penny's conduct that is the basis for suspicion.

(see, for example, **O'Hara v UK** (2002) 34 EHRR 32). Post-HRA, it was held in **Cumming v Chief Constable of the Northumbria Police** [2003] EWCA Civ 1844 that the officer must consider the reasonableness of arrest in light of the importance of Art 5 rights but, nonetheless, the test still relies on the concept of **Wednesbury** irrationality; therefore the court will only question the exercise of discretion where the decision is one that no officer could have arrived at.[4] Penny's conduct, observed in light of the information regarding the crimes committed, is likely to justify reasonable suspicion. The arrest must also be 'necessary' for a purpose specified at s 24(5). It is likely that PC Tomlin will be able to claim that in this case, there was a need to arrest to facilitate prompt and effective investigation of the offence.[5]

Although PC Tomlin may justify the arrest, it is, nevertheless, likely to be considered to be unlawful. Section 28 of PACE states that an individual must be informed of both the fact of arrest and the reason for it.[6] No particular form of words is required (**R v Brosch** [1988] Crim LR 743),[7] but it must be clear to the suspect that they have been arrested. Even if PC Tomlin had been in uniform and therefore identifiable as an officer, it is submitted that the words used are not an unambiguous explanation that an arrest is taking place.[8] This can only be compounded by the fact he is in plain clothes and seemingly makes no attempt to identify himself. Further, Penny is not informed of the grounds for arrest. This is an obligation imposed by PACE, and also by Art 5(2) of the European Convention of Human Rights.[9] **Fox, Campbell and Hartley v UK** (1990) 13 EHRR 157 stressed the importance of the requirement, as an individual must know the reason for detention in order to be able to challenge it.

PC Tomlin's conduct means that Penny has a defence to the charge of assaulting a police officer in the execution of his duty. As the arrest is unlawful, the use of force to restrain Penny is also illegal. She is entitled to use proportionate force to defend herself against an unjustified threat.[10]

Penny states that she intends to take legal action, and it would appear that there are grounds for a civil claim for trespass to person and false imprisonment.[11] If successful, damages could be awarded. Following **Thompson v Commissioner of Police for the Metropolis** [1997] 2 All ER 762, aggravated damages may

[4]This case should be cited, and the test will need to be explained in order to demonstrate the basis for deciding that the officer is justified here.

[5]As this is straightforward, the issue can be dealt with briefly.

[6]Credit will be given for noting that a lawful arrest must be procedurally correct as well as justifiable.

[7]Students generally cite *Christie v Leachinskey* when discussing the requirement to be informed of arrest. This is a better authority to use here, to support the contention that there is problem with the words used.

[8]You have outlined the legal requirements in some detail, but you must go on to apply the law to the facts of this scenario.

[9]Marks will be available for recognising the role of the European Convention of Human Rights here.

[10]There is no need to engage in a detailed discussion of the principles of criminal law: simply noting that police misconduct may give rise to the possibility of a defence is sufficient.

[11]As well as recognising areas of police misconduct, the answer must address the potential consequences as this is specifically required by the question.

be awarded if the arrest occurred in 'humiliating' circumstances. Although PC Tomlin would not be personally liable, a finding against the force would almost certainly result in disciplinary proceedings.[12] Penny may also consider making a complaint either to the Chief Superintendent, the Police Authority, or the Independent Police Complaints Commission. Complaints are now governed by the Police Reform Act 2002. PC Tomlin should be advised that an investigation could result in disciplinary actions, and the matter could be referred to the Department of Public Prosecutions to consider whether criminal charges are appropriate.

[12]You should explain what the possible implications for the officer might be.

If the arrest and subsequent detention are unlawful, this has further implications for the legality of the search. Section 18 of PACE confers a power to search, without warrant, any premises occupied or controlled by a person who is under arrest. The search must be for evidence in relation to the offence in question. Authorisation is required by an officer of the rank of Inspector or above. The custody sergeant is not able to give permission. The search of Penny's flat would have been unlawful even if the initial arrest had been conducted properly.[13] The evidence against her in respect of the cocaine has, then, been obtained as a result of an unlawful search. Penny will doubtless seek to have that evidence excluded at trial. Section 78 of PACE gives the court discretion to exclude any evidence if, in all the circumstances, including those in which it was obtained, admission would have an adverse effect on the fairness of proceedings. Whilst 'significant and substantial' breaches of PACE and the Codes may justify exclusion (**R v Keenan** [1989] 3 All ER 598), the authorities seem to suggest that the court will be more concerned with the reliability of the evidence. This was confirmed in **R v Khan** [1996] 3 All ER 289, in which evidence obtained as a result of unlawful surveillance was admitted.[14] It is submitted that the evidence is unlikely to be excluded here, as the fact of the illegal search will not prevent Penny accounting for the presence of the drugs if she is able to do so.

[13]It is important to note the procedural requirements of s 18: the need for proper authorisation is often overlooked.

[14]This is a very important point to note. *Khan* is the key authority to cite here as it gives a clear indication that the evidence is unlikely to be excluded.

To conclude, Penny will have a defence to the charge of assaulting a police constable. She is unlikely to be successful in an application to exclude the evidence obtained as a result of an illegal search. PC Tomlin should be aware that she has a number of potential claims in tort: trespass to person and property, and false imprisonment. She may make a formal complaint. He may face disciplinary actions, and even criminal charges in respect of the use of force.[15]

[15]The conclusion should summarise the key points that answer the questions asked.

✓ Make your answer stand out

- By considering the search in more detail, and addressing s 19 of PACE, which would authorise seizure of items not the subject of the initial search. The point could be made that this is a broad power, which, makes it difficult to argue that s 78 will be used to exclude evidence obtained during the search. This would show your examiner that you have detailed knowledge of the law in this area.

- By referring to some academic comment in your answer. An excellent text dealing with the search of premises is Stone, R., *The Law of Entry, Search and Seizure* (5th edn, 2005) Oxford: Oxford University Press.

! Don't be tempted to...

- Explain irrelevant law. A clear example would be the reasons why an arrest may be necessary at s 24(5). There is no need to list them all, it is better to highlight the one which is applicable to the facts. Students sometimes feel it necessary to demonstrate that they have learnt substantial amounts of law; when in fact, marks are given for the ability to identify and utilise only the relevant provisions.

- Ignore the instructions which have been given to you in the question. Here, you have been specifically advised to consider not only whether the officer has behaved lawfully, but the likely outcome of proceedings against Penny. A word of caution: this is not an invitation to write about the elements of the criminal offences charged.

❓ Question 6

Jerome is a young black male who is stopped by a uniformed officer on his way home one night. The officer asks to search him, and Jerome asks what the grounds are. The officer explains that there has been a spate of recent thefts of jewellery in the area.

Jerome replies that those are not lawful reasons and he begins to walk away. The officer takes hold of Jerome's arm, and explains he intends to detain him in order to be searched.

Jerome is then searched, and a ring is recovered from his pocket. He is arrested on suspicion of theft.

Jerome is booked into custody and his rights are explained. He declines legal advice. He is then taken to a separate room and asked to strip to his underwear so his clothing may be searched for more jewellery. Nothing is found.

An inspector authorises a search of his home address, but nothing is found.

When asked to account for the items in interview, Jerome makes no comment. He is subsequently charged with theft of the ring. His fingerprints and a sample of DNA are taken.

Jerome seeks your advice. He tells you that he feels the initial search was motivated by racist assumptions and that, accordingly, the whole case will be thrown out. He explains that the ring was a gift from a relative. He would like his fingerprints and DNA sample to be destroyed.

Advise Jerome.

Answer plan

→ Discuss the legality of the stop and search.

→ Consider the legality of the arrest.

→ Discuss the legality of the search of his premises, and of the strip search.

→ Briefly discuss the retention of DNA.

→ Consider whether an adverse inference can be drawn from interview.

Diagram plan

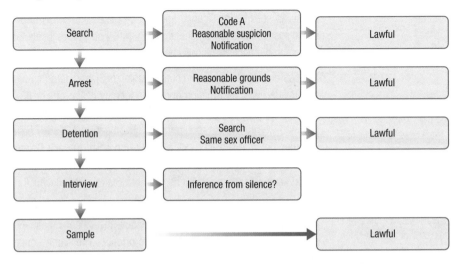

A printable version of this diagram is available from www.pearsoned.co.uk/lawexpressqa

Answer

[1]The introduction identifies the relevant legal area, and sets out the structure that the answer will use. There is no need to give a synopsis of the facts.

The police have substantial powers to investigate and prevent crime, and are required to act in a manner consistent with obligations created by the European Convention of Human Rights. The exercise of police powers is largely controlled by the Police and Criminal Evidence Act (PACE) and the associated Codes of Practice. The legality of the actions of the police will be considered, and any remedies that may be available to Jerome will be addressed.[1]

[2]The answer should give a brief summary of the relevant legal provisions for each part of the incident.

Section 1 of PACE allows an officer to detain a person in order to search them if they have reasonable grounds to suspect the individual is in possession of stolen or prohibited articles. The Codes of Practice give some guidance about what will, or will not constitute 'reasonable' grounds for suspicion.[2] Code A, paragraph 2.2 makes it clear that there must be some objective basis, and that this cannot be based on personal factors such as race, age or other stereotypical assumption. Jerome feels that the officer has stopped him because he is black, and this would constitute a breach of the Code of Practice.[3] Statistics compiled by the Ministry of Justice do show that young black men are eight times more likely to be stopped and searched than their white counterparts.[4] Nonetheless, it may be difficult to challenge the search as the officer may well

[3]Having outlined the law, the answer needs to apply the provisions to the facts of the scenario. Here, the problem raises the issue of race, so you must address this.

[4]This kind of detail shows a broad range of knowledge of the subject area.

be able to demonstrate that there was reasonable suspicion. Paragraph 2.3 of the Code states that the officer need not be acting on specific intelligence and can be based on the behaviour of the suspect. In this instance, the officer may be able to justify the search on the basis of reports concerning the thefts in the area.

The search must be limited to outer clothing (s 2), and Jerome must be provided with information about the identity of the officer (s 2) and a written record of the search (s 3). It is not clear from the facts provided whether these requirements have been met. If they have not, then the search will be unlawful (**Osman v Southwark Crown Court** (1999) *The Times*, 28 September). If the officer has acted in accordance with these provisions, then the search will be lawful.[5]

[5]The answer is careful to avoid speculating about matters that are not included in the facts.

The arrest appears to be lawful. Section 24 of PACE authorises arrest without warrant of an individual the officer reasonably suspects of involvement in a criminal offence. The same conditions regarding reasonableness apply as outlined above. Case law shows that the test is not particularly stringent; the decision must not be one that no officer could have arrived at (**Castorina v Chief Constable of Surrey** [1988] NLJ 180). The arrest must be 'necessary' (s 24(5)).[6] In this instance, it would seem the officer will be able to argue that finding the ring establishes the requisite level of suspicion, and the arrest is necessary to facilitate investigation of the offence. It appears that Jerome is informed of the fact of arrest, and the reason for it (s 28), and therefore the arrest is lawful.[7]

[6]A useful structure is adopted here, by locating the relevant area, and providing a brief summary of the law before applying the provisions to the problem.

[7]Where it is possible to reach a clear conclusion from the facts, then you should do so. Provided you have explained your reasoning, this demonstrates confidence with the subject.

Whilst in custody at the police station, Jerome is the subject of a further search. Any search in which the detainee is asked to remove more than the outer layer of clothing will be considered to be a 'strip search'. A custody sergeant may authorise such a search (Code C 4.1).[8] Provided that the search takes place in private and in the presence of male officers, this will be lawful. **Wainwright v Home Office** [2003] UKHL 53 held that a strip search of visitors to a prison did not constitute a breach of either Art 8 or Art 3 of the Convention. There do not appear to be grounds for complaint in respect of the search.[9]

[8]This part of the problem requires a fairly detailed awareness of PACE and the Codes. Credit will be given for recognising that this is a strip search, and for citing the source of the custody sergeant's authority.

[9]It is a good idea to reach a conclusion in respect of each part of the incident as it is dealt with, as this will ensure that the answer stays focused on providing advice to the client.

Jerome's address is also searched. This is permissible under s 18 of the Police and Criminal Evidence Act, which authorises search without warrant of any premises occupied or controlled by

[10]As the search is not contentious, it can be dealt with briefly.

an arrested person, for the purpose of obtaining and securing evidence connected to the offence in question.[10] The search has been authorised by an inspector. There do not appear to be any grounds to challenge the search.

During interview, Jerome chooses to make no comment. A suspect has the right to silence, however, the Criminal Justice and Public Order Act qualifies this by allowing an adverse inference to be drawn at trial if the defendant fails to mention facts during interview that he later relies on in court (s 34). The European Court has considered the matter in a number of cases, including **Condron *v* UK** (2001) 31 EHRR 1 and **Murray *v* UK** (app 18731/91) (1996) 22 EHRR 29. It has been held that the right to silence is not absolute, and an adverse inference from silence will not necessarily violate the defendants Art 6 rights.[11] An adverse inference was not permissible where the suspect has been denied access to legal advice (**Murray**). Here, it appears that Jerome did have the option to speak to a solicitor, and it may be that this will allow an inference to be drawn. The court will not be entitled to draw an inference of guilt if silence at interview is the only evidence against the defendant, but Jerome should be advised that his decision to remain silent may have repercussions for him if the case comes to trial.[12]

[11]Credit will be given for demonstrating familiarity with the decisions of the ECtHR on this point.

[12]It is very important for the answer to return to the facts of the scenario. Sometimes, as here, it is not possible to definitively predict the outcome and credit will be given for recognising that further information about the evidence available would be needed.

The police are empowered to take fingerprints and a DNA sample by s 61 and 65 of PACE respectively. There is some doubt about whether or not these samples can be retained in the event that Jerome is acquitted. Section 82 of the Criminal Justice and Public Order Act 1982 amended PACE to allow for the retention and use of such samples, but this provision was held to violate Art 8 in **S and Marper *v* UK** (2008) 48 EHRR 50. The ECtHR held that the provisions were too widely drawn to fall within any margin of appreciation that can be applied. The Crime and Security Act 2010 reduced the period of retention of samples for persons who are not convicted to six years and the coalition government has pledged further reform.[13]

[13]This discussion shows a breadth of knowledge about the developing law: it is important to keep it fairly brief to avoid straying too far from the task of advising the client.

Jerome may feel that the grounds for the initial stop and search were flawed, but it will be difficult to demonstrate this as the officer is likely to be able to establish sufficient grounds for reasonable suspicion. From the facts provided, it appears that there will be no grounds to challenge the legality of the police actions.

Make your answer stand out

- Considering the Convention rights engaged by the stop and search; mention could be made here of the effect of the decision in *Gillan* v *UK*, and a distinction drawn between the facts of that case and more focused power contained in PACE. This would show that you are aware of current developments in the law and that you recognise that interference with Convention rights is permissible provided it is for a legitimate, legally prescribed purpose.

- By incorporating more recent case law regarding the notification requirements. *Osman* has now been confirmed in the more recent case *R (on the application of Michaels)* v *Highbury Corner Magistrates' Court* [2010] Crim LR 506. This would demonstrate knowledge of more recent developments which may not have reached your textbooks.

- Incorporating further comment regarding the suggestion made by Jerome that the initial search was racially motivated. There is considerable academic discussion of the issue; see, for example, Bowling, B. and Phillips, C., 'Disproportionate and discriminatory: reviewing the evidence on police stop and search' (2007) 70(6) Modern Law Review 936–61. However, you should continue to stress that this will be difficult to prove as the search results in the seizure of material which will justify the search. This will demonstrate that you have read around the subject.

! Don't be tempted to...

- Speculate about whether or not Jerome is telling the truth about the gift of the ring. This is irrelevant. The only reason for including this fact is to make it clear the client wishes to maintain a plea of not guilty.

- Explain the sections of PACE that are relevant without then assessing how they may apply in this case. There will be marks awarded for recognising the key statutory provisions, but a good answer will need to be able to engage in an analysis of how the law will be applied.

Counter-terrorism measures

How this topic may come up in exams

This is a topic that is increasing in popularity in law schools, as the wealth of legislation and case law touches on many other areas of the syllabus. There is a clear overlap with the study of the Human Rights Act and Convention law and this will almost certainly need to be included in response to every question. Alternatively, questions may require consideration of anti-terrorism legislation and the operation of the rule of law, or the separation of powers. There is scope for either problem scenarios or essay questions. The law concerning this topic is evolving rapidly, so it is important to be aware of new judgments or legislative proposals.

Attack the question

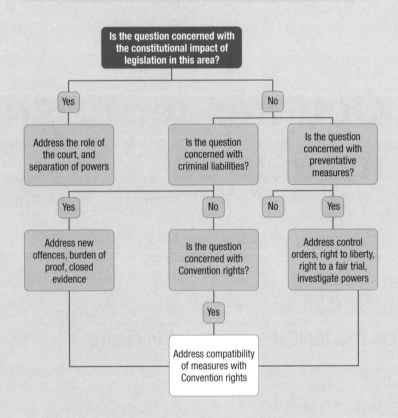

Question 1

The legislative response to terrorism has brought the executive and judicial arms of the state into a conflict which threatens the separation of powers.

Discuss.

Answer plan

→ Briefly outline the doctrine of the separation of powers.

→ Explain the history of judicial deference to executive decisions.

→ Focus the discussion on key cases concerning terrorism.

→ Assess the impact of the HRA on the judicial approach to terrorism.

→ Analyse the extent to which the doctrine remains in force.

Diagram plan

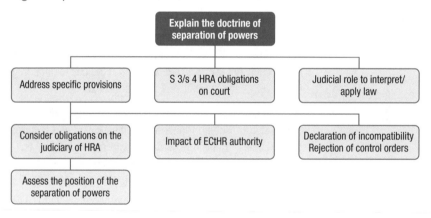

A printable version of this diagram is available from www.pearsoned.co.uk/lawexpressqa

Answer

The doctrine of the separation of powers is recognised as a key feature of the UK Constitution. According to the doctrine, the three branches of government have separate roles and responsibilities, and operate a system of checks and balances to prevent the arbitrary use of power by any organ of the state. The threat of international terrorism has led to a series of high profile cases addressing the

[1]The introduction has shown awareness of the key elements of the question, and signalled to the examiner the direction that the argument will take.

[2]The answer needs to demonstrate understanding of the doctrine of the separation of powers, but this is not the main focus of the question so there is a need to be brief.

[3]This is an important point, as anti-terrorism measures certainly concern national security, so the traditional approach of the judiciary needs to be examined in order to evaluate whether there has been a change.

[4]There has been a lot of legislation in this area, and the answer cannot possible consider all the measures. It is important to pinpoint those measures that will be the basis for the discussion.

[5]As the argument will suggest that the HRA has affected the judicial approach to 'national security', a brief explanation of the relevant part of the legislation is required.

[6]This is an important point, as the case law on the area is not, in fact, focused on liberty, but the legality of the derogation.

compatibility of legislation with commitments under the European Convention on Human Rights. It will be argued that the Human Rights Act imposes an obligation on the judiciary to take a more robust approach to matters affecting the liberty of citizens. To suggest this threatens the separation of powers is to overstate the case. Conversely, the willingness of the judiciary to scrutinise executive action could be seen as evidence of the strength of the doctrine.[1]

The doctrine of the separation of powers, the sovereignty of Parliament and the rule of law are seen as the theories that underpin the organisation of the state. Using these models, the role of the judiciary is to apply legislation made by Parliament, and to ensure that the executive uses discretionary powers lawfully.[2] The judiciary have, however, traditionally been unwilling to interfere with executive policy in sensitive areas, in particular, national security.[3] In the seminal **GCHQ case (Council of Civil Service Unions v Minister for the Civil Service** [1985] AC 374), the court asserted the right to review the exercise of prerogative power, but accepted that areas of 'high policy' would remain 'non-justiciable'.

Legislation conferring powers on the state to prevent and control terrorism is, of course, concerned with matters of national security. The discussion will focus on Part IV of the Anti-Terrorism, Crime and Security Act 2001, now repealed, and the control order regime introduced by the Prevention of Terrorism Act 2005.[4]

The Human Rights Act 1998 has incorporated the European Convention of Human Rights into domestic law and requires all public bodies to act in accordance with convention rights.[5] The courts are required to interpret all legislation in accordance with those rights 'in so far as it possible to do so' (HRA, s 3). If such an interpretation cannot be found, then a declaration of incompatibility can be made (s 4). Part IV of ATCSA made provision for the indefinite detention without trial of foreign nationals suspected of involvement in terrorism. The individuals concerned could not be deported to their country of origin, as there was a risk that they could be subject to torture or inhuman and degrading treatment; therefore deportation would be a violation of the government's obligations under Art 3. The UK government accepted that the provisions were an infringement of the right to liberty, but had applied a derogation from Art 5 in accordance with Art 15; due to the state of emergency posed by the threat of terrorist action.[6]

[7]This is a crucially important case, and should be included in the answer as, arguably, it marked a real shift in the relationship between the judiciary and the executive.

[8]The judgment in this case is complicated, and credit will be given for the ability to summarise the key points clearly.

The matter fell to be considered by the House of Lords in **A v Secretary of State for the Home Department** [2004] UKHL 56.[7] The Lords accepted that a state of emergency existed justifying the derogation, in accordance with the conventional acceptance of executive judgment on such matters. However, Convention jurisprudence emphasises the need for proportionality, and their Lordships found that the measures were disproportionate, and further, discriminatory; as they applied only to foreign nationals.[8] A declaration of incompatibility was made. The case is highly significant, as it signalled a readiness to review executive actions in areas previously considered to be non-justiciable.

[9]As this question is concerned with the relationship between the judiciary and the executive there is no need to give detail about the nature of control orders.

The offending legislation was repealed by the Prevention of Terrorism Act 2005, which created the system of control orders, used to monitor individuals within their own homes.[9] The system of control orders has been analysed for Convention compatibility in a number of cases. As Walker has pointed out, although the initial cases considered Art 5 and the acceptable limitations on liberty, the more contentious matters have related to the compatibility of the regime with Art 6 rights to a fair hearing (Walker, C., 'The threat of terrorism and the fate of control orders' [2010] Public Law 4–17). Hearings concerning control orders routinely rely upon 'closed' evidence; material that cannot be disclosed to the individual concerned due to security or intelligence risks. Such material is dealt with by a 'special advocate' appointed to represent the interests of the individual. In **Secretary of State for the Home Department v MB** [2007] UKHL 46, the majority held that special advocates could, in principle, counter the risk of procedural unfairness in all but the most exceptional of cases. The matter was considered again in **Secretary of State for the Home Department v AF** (No. 3) [2009] UKHL 28, which followed a determination in Strasbourg that such procedures violated Art 6 (**A v UK** [2009] ECHR 301). Lord Hoffmann regarded that decision as wrong, but the majority appeared to accept that they were bound by judgment; as Lord Rodger remarked: 'Strasbourg has spoken, the case is closed.'[10] As a result, the government is considering whether to revoke existing control orders, or make further evidence available to achieve the required degree of fairness. (Human Rights Joint Committee *Counter-Terrorism Policy and Human Rights (Sixteenth Report): Annual Renewal of Control Orders Legislation 2010*).

[10]It is not essential, or even expected, that students will include many direct quotations in examination answers but a short phrase is useful to include as it makes the answer appear confident, and also neatly expresses the fact that the judiciary appear to feel that they are bound by the European Court of Human Rights.

It can be seen, then, that the Human Rights Act has empowered the judiciary to engage in consideration of matters previously considered to be within an area of executive competence.

[11]Having explored the judicial response to anti-terrorism measures, the answer needs to return to the issue of the separation of powers.

The structure of the Human Rights Act, however, limits the extent to which these developments can be seen as an alteration to the separation of powers.[11] As McKeever points out, the judiciary can criticise policy, and indeed legislation, but are powerless to change it (McKeever, D., 'The HRA and anti-terrorism in the UK: one great leap forward by Parliament but are the courts able to slow the steady retreat that has followed?' [2010] Public Law 110–39). A declaration of incompatibility does not affect the validity of legislation; following the judgment in **Secretary of State for the Home Department v AF** (No. 3), the individuals remained in detention until ACTSA was repealed by the legislature.[12] Similarly, despite the ruling that the procedure for obtaining control orders is flawed, they remain in force unless and until the executive instigates change.

[12]This is an important point to make, as the HRA was drafted to preserve Parliamentary supremacy.

The readiness to address executive decision-making in these cases can be seen as evidence of the strength of the doctrine of separation of powers, as the judiciary operate to check the use of executive powers. The preservation of Parliamentary supremacy, however, ensures that the basic shape of the constitution remains unchanged.

✓ Make your answer stand out

■ By discussing in more detail how judicial review of anti-terrorism measures forms part of a system of checks and balances to prevent the arbitrary exercise of power. This could make reference to some of the theorists who have commented on the separation of powers. The last chapter in Vile, *Constitutionalism and the Separation of Powers* (2nd edn, 1998) Indianapolis: Liberty Fund Inc provides an overview of the changing role of the judiciary.

■ Staying up to date. It cannot be stressed enough how quickly this area of law develops. Check important judgments and recent academic comment so that you can include matters that are not yet in the textbooks. The journal *Public Law* is a good starting point and should be checked regularly.

■ Expanding the discussion regarding the decision in *Secretary of State for the Home Department* v *AF (No. 3)* [2009] UKHL 28, and in particular the fact that the court feel bound by the ECtHR. This could be contrasted with the decision in *R (GC and C)* v *Commissioner of the Police for the Metropolis* [2010] EWHC 2225 (Admin), in which the courts appeared to prefer a more traditional approach to parliamentary supremacy. This could show an ability to address the complexities of the argument.

! Don't be tempted to...

■ Attempt to outline all 'terrorism' legislation that has been enacted since 2000. If you do this, you will end up with an answer that lists a lot of law, but which includes little analysis. The answer should concentrate on one or two provisions that allow for analysis of the relationship between government and the judiciary.

■ Spend too much time explaining the structure of the constitution and the meaning of the separation of powers in general terms. Discussion of the doctrine must be focused on the issue of anti-terrorism measures. Weaker answers tend to approach this question as if it were a question about constitutional doctrines.

❓ Question 2

Jamal attends most of the public events held at his local community centre. One evening, he attends a public lecture entitled 'Global politics: a new vision'. The event has been organised by a group called 'Freedom through Fear'. Although he has no real interest in politics and knows nothing about the organisation, he decides to attend as he thinks it will be more interesting than staying in and watching television. On arrival, Jamal is told he needs to register, by writing his name and email address on a list. He does this.

Jamal is shocked by the speaker, who advocates suicide bombing, and by the leaflets he is handed, which contain graphic images of the damage caused by explosions in urban areas and poetry glorifying the mayhem. After the meeting, he rushes home, and puts the leaflets in a drawer.

Over the next few months, Jamal receives numerous emails from Freedom through Fear, inviting him to meetings, and sending him links to websites. He does not look at the websites, but does forward the links to his cousin, who is writing a dissertation on international terrorism.

Five months later, Jamal is arrested. He is told it is because he is on a membership list for an illegal organisation.

Advise Jamal of his liabilities under anti-terrorist legislation, and any defences he may have.

Answer plan

➜ Outline the main offences which may have been committed.

➜ Consider the application of the statutory defences.

➜ Discuss the nature of the burden of proof.

➜ Summarise the liabilities.

Diagram plan

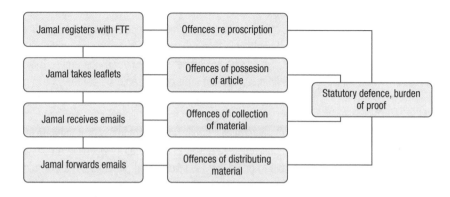

A printable version of this diagram is available from www.pearsoned.co.uk/lawexpressqa

Answer

Since 2000, five statutes have been enacted with the aim of pre-venting terrorist activity, creating a total of 46 new criminal offences and granting extensive powers to investigate terrorist activity. As a result of his association with the organisation, Jamal may face a number of charges.

[1]It is important to be able to set out the statutory definition of terrorism as all of the substantive offences Jamal may be charged with will depend on the activities of the group falling within the definition.

The Terrorism Act 2000 replaced previous temporary measures to combat the threat of terrorism with permanent powers. Section 1 defines 'terrorism' as the use, or threat, of violence to influence government, the public, or a section of the public, to advance a political, religious or ideological cause. The Counter Terrorism Act 2008 amends the definition to include advancement of a racial cause. Section 1(2) makes it clear that actions for such purposes can involve violence, serious damage to property, a risk to health or safety of the public, or serious disruption to an electronic system.[1] The definition has been subject to academic and judicial criticism (see, for example, **R v F** [2007] EWCA Crim 243) due to its breadth, and the risk it may capture groups that would not previously have been categorised as terrorist. In this scenario, however, Freedom through Fear (FTF) is a group that advocates activities which would clearly fall within the scope of the definition.[2]

[2]Having outlined the definition of terrorism, the answer must ensure that the law is applied to the facts of the scenario.

[3]The problem does not definitely state that the group is proscribed, so a good answer would note that this is an assumption.

[4]Don't make the mistake of saying whether or not, on the facts, Jamal is guilty of the offence. You may indicate the view a jury is likely to take, but remember, it will be their decision.

[5]The question asks for consideration of the defences and therefore it is essential to include discussion of s 11(2).

[6]Having explained the law, the answer must make sure that this is applied to the facts of the problem.

[7]Again, it is possible to say what you feel is likely to happen, but remember that you cannot make a definite statement about the outcome.

[8]As the answer has already explained the distinction between evidential and legal burdens, there is no need to repeat the same information.

Jamal has been informed that he is suspected of belonging to an illegal organisation. This suggests that a proscription order has been made by the Home Secretary in accordance with s 3(3).[3] The Act creates offences of belonging to, or supporting, a proscribed organisation. Jamal could face prosecution for an offence under s 11 of the Act, if it can be proved he is a member of the group. This is a serious offence, carrying a maximum sentence of ten years in custody. Jamal may wish to argue that his registration on a mailing list does not amount to membership; this will be a question of fact for the jury to determine.[4] It may be relevant to discover the date of the proscription order, as s 11(2) states that he will have a defence if he is able to prove that his involvement predates the order, and he has not been involved in the activities of the group since that time.[5] Section 11(2) appears to impose a reverse burden of proof upon the defendant. This was considered by the House of Lords in the conjoined appeals **Sheldrake v DPP; Attorney General's Reference (No. 4 of 1992)** [2004] UKHL 43: it was held this was a breach of the presumption of innocence, and incompatible with Art 6 rights. Therefore, the provisions are read down using s 3 of the Human Rights Act (HRA) as imposing an evidential burden only. Accordingly, Jamal will need to provide some evidence that his involvement predated proscription, and it will then be for crown to disprove this assertion.[6] It should be noted, though, that it will be no defence for him to claim that he was unaware the group is a proscribed organisation (**R v Hundal; R v Dhaliwal** [2004] 2 Cr App R 19). Given that Jamal has received, and forwarded, emails from the group over a period of time, it seems unlikely that the jury will accept the statutory defence.[7]

Jamal may face additional charges in respect of the leaflets in his possession, and material stored on his computer. Section 57 of the 2000 Act makes it an offence to possess an article for a purpose connected with the commission of, preparation for, or instigation of an act of terrorism. Again, there is a statutory defence available, if he can prove his possession was not for one of the prohibited purposes. It seems clear that the same considerations regarding the burden of proof will apply, and it will be for the crown to prove the purpose.[8] It is unlikely that this is a charge that the Crown would pursue, following the decision in **R v Zafar, Butt, Iqbal, Raja and Malik** [2008] EWCA Crim 184, in which it was held that there must

⁹This is an important case in this situation, as the effect will be that it is harder for the Crown to prove this offence against Jamal. Therefore, it should be mentioned.

¹⁰Credit will be given for recognising that further information is required. Do not make the mistake of speculating about what material the websites may contain.

¹¹There are few authorities that are directly relevant regarding these charges, and less to discuss. Potential liabilities under TA 2006 can, then, be dealt with quite briefly.

be proof of a direct connection between possession and the perpetration of an act of terrorism.⁹

Section 58 of the Act creates an offence of collecting or making a record of material likely to be useful to persons committing or preparing an act of terrorism. Although there is no direct authority on the point, it appears this is broader than the s 57 offence, and does not require the same degree of causal connection. The case of **R v K** [2008] EWCA Crim 185, however, did provide that it is not sufficient to show that material supports terrorist activity for an offence under this section; it must be capable of providing 'practical assistance' to persons involved in such activity. Further information regarding the content of the websites is required in order to advise Jamal on this point.¹⁰

Finally, Jamal may face offences under the Terrorism Act 2006.¹¹ The Act prohibits publication of material which encourages terrorism (s 1), and the dissemination of terrorist material (s 2). Section 2 (3) makes it clear that internet activity is covered by the Act. Jamal has forwarded links to websites to his cousin, which would amount to an offence under s 2 if it can be shown that he did this either intending to, or being reckless about, encouraging terrorist activity. He may have a defence if he is able to demonstrate that the material did not have his endorsement, and that this was clear to the recipient of the information (s 2(9)). Although s 2(9) again appears to impose a reverse burden of proof, the authorities referred to above suggest that this will be read down as merely evidential. Jamal may be successful in establishing the defence given the nature of his cousin's academic studies.

To summarise, Jamal may face charges under ss 11, 57 and 58 of the Terrorism Act 2000, and s 2 of the Terrorism Act 2006. Each of the offences provides a statutory defence for Jamal and each defence purports to reverse the burden of proof. Jamal should be advised that this will be considered incompatible with Art 6 and therefore, he need only discharge an evidential burden. It is submitted that, from the facts provided, Jamal is unlikely to be convicted of offences under s 57 of the Terrorism Act 2000, or s 2 of the Terrorism Act 2006. Further information is required regarding the material in his possession in order to advise him regarding his potential liability under s 58 of TA 2000. His greatest difficulty relates to the offence under s 11 of TA 2000 as, if it can be shown he 'joined' the group, it is unlikely that he will be able to rely upon the statutory defence.

Make your answer stand out

- By considering some of the powers available to the state to seize property and freeze assets of those suspected of terrorism. Although the question will lead most students to concentrate on possible offences, there is no reason why you should not touch on these powers as well, as theoretically this could affect Jamal.

- By recognising that the law in this area changes rapidly and ensuring you are abreast of developments. At the time of writing, the Terrorist Asset Freezing Bill is before Parliament, seeking to establish a permanent legislative framework for the seizure and freezing of assets. You can, and should, check for changes in the law.

- By incorporating academic comment in support of the propositions you make. For example, there is some helpful discussion of the courts' construction of 'reasonable' excuses in respect of ss 57 and 58 in Middleton, B., 'Sections 57 and 58 of the Terrorism Act 2000: interpretation update' (2009) 73 *Journal of Criminal Law* 203–6.

! Don't be tempted to...

- Begin your answer by writing out the facts of the scenario. No marks are awarded for doing so, but this is a surprisingly common mistake. It can be hard to know how to begin the answer to a problem; the best way is to summarise the legal issues that arise.

- Speculate about facts not contained in the scenario, such as the content of websites, or Jamal's state of mind when forwarding the emails to his cousin. A good lawyer never makes assumptions about facts which are not known.

Question 3

'The UK government, in adopting anti-terrorism measures, frequently ignores the provisions and indeed goals of the regime it itself established a decade ago' (McKeever, D., 'The HRA and anti-terrorism in the UK: one great leap forward by Parliament but are the courts able to slow the steady retreat that has followed?' [2010] Public Law.

Discuss the compatibility of measures to control terrorist activity with Convention rights.

Answer plan

→ Outline the provisions that will be the focus of discussion.
→ Describe the powers of stop and search under the TA 2000.
→ Identify the Convention rights that are engaged.
→ Analyse compatibility with reference to key cases.

Diagram plan

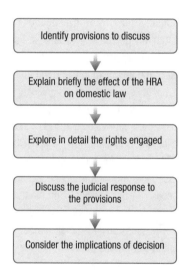

Identify provisions to discuss

↓

Explain briefly the effect of the HRA on domestic law

↓

Explore in detail the rights engaged

↓

Discuss the judicial response to the provisions

↓

Consider the implications of decision

A printable version of this diagram is available from www.pearsoned.co.uk/lawexpressqa

Answer

[1]The answer will focus on only one provision, but it is useful to demonstrate an awareness of the amount of legislation that exists in this area.

The threat posed by international terrorism has intensified in the first part of the twenty-first century, and has resulted in new measures being enacted designed to prevent attacks in the United Kingdom. Five statutes have created numerous new offences, and granted the police and other bodies extensive powers to investigate and detain persons in order to detect and control terrorist activities.[1] Many of these engage Articles of the European Convention Rights and have led to court cases assessing compatibility with the Convention, both in the domestic courts, and at Strasbourg. As it is not possible to address the Human Rights implications of all measures that deal with terrorist activity, the discussion will focus on the powers of stop and search granted by ss 44–47 of the Terrorism Act 2000 (TA), as these have been held to contravene Convention rights.

The Terrorism Act 2000 created a permanent, statutory scheme to investigate and control terrorist activity. Terrorism is defined at s 1 as the use or threat of serious violence to persons or property, designed to influence government, the public (or a section of it) to advance a political, religious, racial or ideological cause. The Act creates a number of offences, but ss 44–47 also grants the police additional powers of investigation, including powers to stop and search any person or vehicle where authorisation has been given by the senior officer in the district. The Home Secretary must be notified of the authorisation, and the duration must be no more than 28 days. These powers are a significant extension of the powers police officers have to investigate 'ordinary' offences.[2] Various measures exist which authorise searches of individuals in public, including the Police and Criminal Evidence Act 1984 and the Misuse of Drugs Act 1971. In order for such a search to be lawful, the officer must have reasonable grounds to suspect that the individual concerned is in possession of specifically prohibited articles. A s 44 search does not require the officer to have any grounds to suspect the individual is in possession of articles connected with terrorism.[3] Failure to comply with a search is an offence punishable with imprisonment. Dispensing with the need for reasonable grounds is, then, a departure from the ordinary law.

The Human Rights Act 1998 incorporates convention rights into domestic law, and requires public bodies to exercise their powers in a manner which is compatible with those rights. A stop and search in a public place may constitute interference with either the right to liberty, or to respect for private and family life. These rights are protected by Arts 5 and 8 of the European Convention of Human Rights. The right to liberty and the right to respect for one's private and family life are both qualified rights; the Convention authorises interference with the right if prescribed by law, and necessary for a specified purpose.[4] The question of whether ss 44–47 fall within the permitted qualifications has been addressed in the litigation concerning Gillan and Quinton (**R (Gillan and Quinton) v Commissioner of Police for the Metropolis** [2006] UKHL 12).

[2] It is important to highlight how the provisions differ from other powers that the police have.

[3] This is important to highlight, as the answer will show that the absence of the need for suspicion is one of the key factors that makes the legislation incompatible with the Convention.

[4] The answer does need to be able to explain what is meant by a qualified right before considering the compatibility of the legislation.

In 2003, Gillan attended an arms fair in London to engage in a peaceful protest. Quinton was a freelance journalist who attended the same event. An authorisation under s 44 was in place, and both were searched. They claimed, *inter alia*, that the searches were an unjustified interference with Art 5 and Art 8 rights. The House of Lords found against the claimants on both counts.

Lord Bingham, in the leading judgment, felt that there was no deprivation of liberty. He relied on the European Court of Human Rights decision in **Guzzardi v Italy** (1980) 3 EHRR 333, which held that the difference between restriction and deprivation was one of fact and degree.[5] Given the relatively brief period of detention, and the absence of physical restraint, he viewed the searches as a restriction. Further, even if there was a deprivation, this would be in accordance with the law and within the qualifications countenanced by the Convention.[6]

The Lords also found that, whilst the right to respect for a private and family life had been construed widely to cover various aspects of personal autonomy, a superficial search of the person was acceptable. Analogy was drawn with searches at airports, which occur routinely and without the need for suspicion.[7]

Gillan and Quinton lodged an application with the European Court of Human Rights, and judgment was delivered in January 2010 (**Gillan and Quinton v United Kingdom** [2009] ECHR 28). The ECtHR did find that the regime contained in the Terrorism Act breached Art 8 rights. The comparison with airport searches was rejected, on the basis that passengers exercise a choice to seek to board an airline; searches in the street are more coercive.[8] The public nature of the search, with the possibility of humiliation, exacerbated the interference. The court found that the searches could not be considered to be 'in accordance with law'[9] due to the 'extraordinay breadth' of the power with the absence of proper legal safeguards or means of challenging the decision to search. In the light of these findings, the court did not find it necessary to determine the issues in relation to Art 5.

In July 2010, the government was refused permission to appeal the matter to the Grand Chamber. It is submitted that the Strasbourg decision is significant, and has implications that stretch beyond the powers of ss 44–47.[10] **Austin v Commissioner of Police of the**

[5] This is a key authority to note, when addressing the ECtHR position on the right to liberty, and it should be noted.

[6] The bulk of the answer is concerned with a single case, therefore, a clear explanation of the ruling is needed. This will also allow you to compare the views of the ECtHR judges on particular points.

[7] It is worth including this point, as the ECtHR expressly rejected the assertion.

[8] This is a key point, as it is the fact that individuals can be compelled to comply with a search that makes it potentially more invasive.

[9] This phrase is important as qualifications to the right are only permissible if necessary and prescribed by law.

[10] The answer concentrates on the *Gillan* judgment, but credit will be given for demonstrating ability to asses the impact on other areas of legislation.

Metropolis [2009] UKHL 5 concerned the police tactic of 'kettling' (detaining peaceful protestors in an area, often for long periods), and found this to be a lawful exercise of common law powers to prevent a breach of the peace. Ashworth has suggested that this ruling is unlikely to stand, as the common law power may also be found not to be 'in accordance with the law', given its imprecision and scope. (Ashworth, A., '*Gillan and Quinton v United Kingdom*: human rights – article 5 – stop and search as deprivation of liberty' (2010) 5 Crim LR 415–19). Buxton has criticised the decision, arguing that the court failed to give due weight to the nature of the threat posed by terrorism in determining the limits of 'necessary' interference[11] (Buxton, R., 'Terrorism and the European Convention' (2010) 7 Crim LR 533–42). Nevertheless, the UK government has accepted that ss 44–47 must be abolished in order to achieve compliance with the judgment. The Coalition government has announced that the powers will be repealed, but it is not yet clear whether an alternative scheme will be proposed.[12]

[11]This is a useful authority to include. It is very easy to find academic opinion criticising anti-terrorism legislation, so credit will be given for including comment to balance this.

[12]Mention of the announcement shows that you are aware of new developments that are relevant to the topic.

It is clear, then, that the stop and search regime created by the Terrorism Act 2000 was not compliant with Convention rights. The Convention would permit a degree of interference with a citizen's private life, but the provisions are too broad, and indiscriminate.

✓ Make your answer stand out

- By explaining that there are other measures that have been held to contravene Convention rights; notably indefinite detention and the use of the Special Advocate procedure.

- By ensuring that you keep up to date with policy developments in this area. At the time of writing, the Coalition government is in the process of reviewing counter terrorism powers. It will impress your examiner if you are able to include information about any changes in the law that occur during your period of study. This would show that you are prepared to read around the topic.

- By incorporating a broad range of appropriate source material and commentary. In addition to academic articles and case commentary to be found in journal articles, you may wish to look at reports prepared by organisations such as liberty, or the Equality and Human Rights Commission (available online).

Don't be tempted to...

■ Attempt to deal with too many provisions in your answer. More marks will be given for in-depth analysis of one, or perhaps two, provisions. It is tempting to want to show the examiner that you have remembered every legislative provision dealing with terrorism but you must always bear in mind that marks are given for discussing the law, not for describing it.

■ Lose focus on the issue of Convention rights. Your answer must focus on compatibility with particular articles in the ECHR. It will be difficult to obtain a good mark for this question if you are not confident with Convention law and the concept of qualified rights.

? Question 4

Omar is a Pakistani national who has lived in the United Kingdom for one year on a student visa whilst undertaking a Masters degree. The intelligence services believe that he has been plotting to carry out terrorist activity, and have intercepted a number of emails which, they say, contain code words referring to bombs and explosives. Omar has made an application to renew his student visa for another year, and this has been refused under r 322(5) of the Immigration Rules, on the basis he is a threat to national security.

Omar appeals against that decision.

The security services do not wish to reveal the information they have regarding the code words used, as it is felt this would seriously undermine ongoing operations.

If Omar were to be deported, he would be arrested by the Intelligence Service of Pakistan, and there is some evidence that individuals have been subject to torture whilst in their custody. The United Kingdom has no agreement with Pakistan regarding the treatment of prisoners.

Advise the Home Secretary whether or not Omar is likely to be deported, and any other measures that could be taken to control the threat he poses. You should consider whether or not the evidence from the security services will need to be revealed.

Answer plan

→ Identify the issue relating to deportation, and Art 3.

→ Consider whether or not deportation is likely in the light of recent rulings.

→ Explain the meaning of control orders.

→ Assess the effect of 'closed' evidence in the light of recent decisions.

Diagram plan

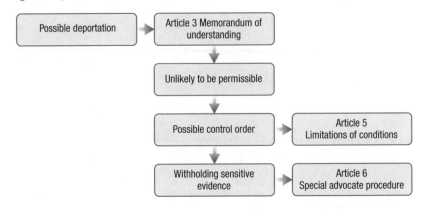

A printable version of this diagram is available from www.pearsoned.co.uk/lawexpressqa

Answer

[1]The answer demonstrates from the outset that the discussion will consider the relationship between domestic law and Convention rights.

[2]The introduction summarises the legal issues raised in the problem, which shows the examiner that the implications of the scenario have been understood.

[3]It is important to point out that there are no exceptions to the right, as this helps to explain why the problem in relation to some foreign nationals has arisen.

[4]Chahal is the most important case to cite here. The use of supporting judgments is helpful as it shows that you have detailed knowledge of the subject-matter, but is not essential.

There is no doubt that the threat posed by international terrorism requires the state to take action to protect the general public, but the measures adopted by the United Kingdom must be in accordance with obligations under the European Convention on Human Rights.[1] These obligations apply to all individuals within the jurisdiction, whether or not they are British citizens. The legality of Omar's deportation will need to be considered, as this may place the government in breach of Art 3, which prohibits torture and inhuman and degrading treatment. It may be possible to obtain a control order under the Prevention of Terrorism Act 2005 (PTA), but the proceedings may raise concerns regarding the use of closed evidence which may jeopardise Omar's rights under Art 6 to a fair hearing.[2]

Article 3 of the Convention protects the right to live free from torture, or inhuman and degrading treatment. This is an 'absolute' right, and there are no circumstances in which an infringement would be tolerated.[3] The government is prohibited from deporting an individual to a country where they face a real risk of torture or inhuman treatment, as this would be a breach of the obligations imposed on the state to uphold Convention rights. This position was established in **Chahal v UK** (1996) 23 EHRR 413, and has been confirmed in a number of cases since that time, notably **Saadi v Italy** (2008) 24 BHRC 123.[4] If there is a risk that Omar

5Here, the law is applied to the
facts of the problem, which
helps to maintain the answers
focus on the scenario.

will be subject to torture on return to Pakistan, then he must not be
deported.[5] Since 2001, the government has sought to establish a
system of formal, diplomatic assurances (memorandum of understanding) with certain states, in which it is agreed that a deported
person, if detained, would be treated humanely and offered legal
representation. It is the government's position that the memorandum of understanding is sufficient to discharge obligations under
Art 3. It should be noted that this has not been tested before the
European Court, but the Joint Committee on Human Rights has
expressed grave concerns about the enforceability and reliability of
such assurances.[6] In any event, the facts state that no memorandum of understanding is in existence with Pakistan. The situation
bears analogy with the case **Naseer v Secretary of State for the
Home Department** [2010] UKSIAC 77/2009, in which an appeal
against deportation to Pakistan was upheld in the absence of sufficient safeguards for the appellants.[7] It is unlikely that Omar will be
able to be deported if there is evidence that his Art 3 rights would
be infringed as a result.

The Home Secretary may wish to consider making a non-derogating
control order pursuant to the power granted by s 2(a) of the PTA.
This is a civil order, intended to prevent an individual from engaging in terrorist activity by the imposition of conditions limiting
movement and activity. A non-derogating control order is one containing conditions that the Home Secretary judges to be compatible
with the rights of the suspect under Art 5 (the right to liberty). The
Lords have considered the acceptable limits of restrictions that
can be made under a control order without infringement of Art 5
in a series of linked judgments: **Secretary of State for the Home
Department v MB** [2007] UKHL 46; **Secretary of State for the
Home Department v JJ** [2007] UKHL 45; **Secretary of State
for the Home Department v E** [2007] UKHL 47. Taken together
with the more recent Supreme Court Authority of **Secretary of
State for the Home Department v AP** [2010] UKSC 24,[8] these
cases provide an indication of the conditions that will be considered lawful. It is clear that a deprivation of liberty can occur
without imprisonment, and will be a question of fact and degree in
each case; the conditions should be taken together as a whole.[9] A
16-hour curfew may not, in and of itself, constitute a deprivation
of liberty. When this condition is coupled with others imposing a

6The facts refer to the
absence of a memorandum
of understanding, so you do
need to explain this issue.

7The problem scenario does
have similarities to this case
and so you should cite it.

8The series of cases cited
here are all important, and
ideally, should be mentioned.
Certainly, you should refer
to the most recent Supreme
Court authority.

9This is the crucial point to
emerge from the judgments,
and it is important to explain
this. The examples that follow
help to clearly illustrate the
principle.

considerable degree of social isolation (as was the case in **AP**), then there may be an infringement. The conditions must be viewed as cumulative, and if a curfew in excess of 12 hours is to be imposed, then the scope for further limitations on movement and association will need to be carefully considered, as was held in **MB**.

[10]As the problem specifically asks for consideration of this issue, it follows that the answer must deal with circumstances in which evidence may be withheld.

In either the appeal against deportation, or proceedings in respect of a control order, the issue of the sensitive evidence concerning the security services will need to be addressed.[10] The rules of court do allow evidence to be withheld from a party to proceedings if disclosure would be contrary to the public interest. This must be balanced against the duty of the court to ensure that the individuals Art 6(1) rights to a fair hearing are upheld. The opportunity to answer allegations is a key component of this right. The use of closed material in terrorist proceedings, then, creates a tension between the public interest and the rights of the suspect.[11] The use of such material has been approved by Strasbourg in some circumstances, provided that measures are taken to protect the rights of the individual. The PTA allows for the use of 'special advocates', who are granted access to the closed material, and appointed to represent the interests of the suspect in closed hearings. The special advocate procedure has been challenged in a number of cases. In **MB** (above), the court found that it provided an adequate safeguard in all but the most exceptional of cases. More recently, in **Secretary of State for the Home Department v AF** (No. 3) [2009] UKHL 28, the House of Lords found that they had been 'far too sanguine'[12] about the ability of the special advocate to protect the rights of the suspect, and determined that sufficient evidence must always be disclosed to the individual in order to allow them to provide instructions. The ramifications of this decision may mean that, in future cases, disclosure will be ordered, and the Home Secretary will need to balance the harm to the public interest that would result against the need to protect the public by pursuing the proceedings.[13] It is not possible, therefore, to advise with certainty that the evidence from the intelligence services can be withheld.

[11]It is not sufficient to simply explain the Special Advocate procedure: the answer should outline why the issue is contentious by explaining the requirements of Art 6.

[12]The use of short quotes can improve the quality of an answer as it shows familiarity with the judgment.

[13]This is an important point to make, as recent judgments arguably mean that the control order scheme will need to be radically changed.

It appears that deportation of Omar may place the government in breach of Art 3 of the European Convention of Human Rights. Stringent conditions could be imposed by a control order in order to contain any threat posed by him. Following **AF**, the court may order disclosure of the evidence obtained by the security services.

✓ Make your answer stand out

■ By considering the impact of ECtHR decisions on domestic law. The decisions regarding the definition of a deprivation of liberty draw on the authority of *Guzzardi v Italy* (1980) 3 EHRR 333 and you should be able to note the key provisions of that case. The Lords have accepted that it is the key authority. You could make the point that the ECtHR has not yet directly addressed the position regarding control orders.

■ By highlighting the fact that the use of control orders has diminished in recent years, arguably as a result of judicial decisions. The Home Secretary is required to report regularly to Parliament about this issue. You can find details on the Home Office website. In July 2010, the Home Secretary confirmed that there were 12 control orders in force. This will show the examiner that you are able to keep pace with the law as it develops.

■ By expanding the analysis of the special advocate procedure. An interesting discussion by an undergraduate student can be found here: Crowther, S., 'The SIAC, deportation and European law' (2010) 6(1) *Cambridge Student Law Review* 227–37. Incorporation of comment and analysis will demonstrate that you read around the subject.

! Don't be tempted to...

■ Discuss any other issues that you think could arise for Omar, either using legislation specifically concerned with terrorism, or under the general criminal law. Some students attempt to include information about potential offences concerning the possession of, or dissemination of, terrorist material. Whilst this could be an issue in respect of the material seized from his computer, there will be no marks available for considering this in any detail. This question is very specific, and spells out the issues that you must address. This should alert you to the fact that the examiner expects that you will have enough material about those issues to fill an answer.

■ Discuss the scenario without reference to convention rights. When considering whether or not the closed evidence will need to be revealed, you must be able to set the discussion in the context of the right to a fair trial. Students who attempt questions regarding terrorism without reference to human rights issues will struggle to get good marks.

Question 5

'The judiciary bears not the slightest responsibility for protecting the public and sometimes seem utterly unaware of the implications of their decisions for our society' (Charles Clark, former Home Secretary cited by the Rt Hon Lord Philips in the Gresham Special Lecture 2010).

Discuss the extent to which the judiciary have utilised the Human Rights Act to undermine legislative efforts to combat terrorism.

Answer plan

→ Outline the provisions that will be the focus of discussion: indefinite detention; closed evidence; control orders.

→ Set out a number of cases in which the judiciary have refused to approve legislative provisions dealing with terrorism.

→ Analyse the extent to which these 'undermine' government policy.

→ Consider parliamentary supremacy and the role of the judiciary.

Diagram plan

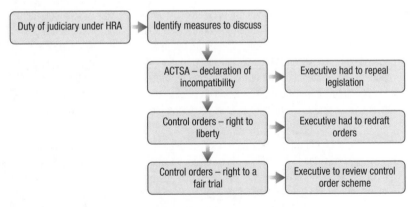

A printable version of this diagram is available from www.pearsoned.co.uk/lawexpressqa

Answer

The Human Rights Act came into force in 2000, one year before the terrorist attacks on New York demonstrated the scale of the threat posed by global extremism. The Terrorism Act 2000 had already been enacted, but further legislation followed to control and contain the threat. The United Kingdom currently has five statutes directly concerned with the prevention, investigation and prosecution of terrorism. The Human Rights Act obliges the judiciary to give effect to Convention rights when interpreting statutes. Legislative provisions concerning terrorism have given rise to a large number of human rights cases, and significant judicial decisions which run counter to the intention of the executive.[1] This discussion will focus on key decisions concerning the indefinite detention without trial of foreign nationals and the implementation of control orders.[2]

A *v* Secretary of State for the Home Department [2004] UKHL 56 considered the legality of provisions made in the Anti-Terrorism Crime and Security Act 2001, which allowed foreign nationals suspected of terrorist activity to be detained indefinitely without trial.[3] The legislation was designed to contain the threat posed by a number of individuals resident in the United Kingdom who, if returned to their country of origin, may have faced torture, or inhuman and degrading treatment. **Chahal *v* UK** (1996) 23 EHRR 413 established that, if the government returns an individual to a nation knowing that there is such a risk, this will be a breach of its obligations under Art 3. Criminal prosecution could not take place owing to the need to keep sensitive security information secret, but the individuals were felt to be a grave risk. The government felt that the risk to society posed by terrorism constituted a 'national emergency' justifying a derogation from Art 5 in respect of the detainees. Lord Hoffmann felt that the derogation was unjustified, and memorably commented: 'The real threat to the life of the nation ... comes not from terrorism but from laws such as these. That is the true measure of what terrorism may achieve.'[4]

The remaining judges felt that the circumstances did permit derogation, but all agreed that the measures in the act went beyond those strictly required by the situation and were, therefore, disproportionate.[5] A declaration of incompatibility was made in accordance with s 4 of the Human Rights Act. In reaching the

[1]The question requires a discussion of the tension between the judiciary and the executive so it is important to show that this has been understood. In addition, the introduction recognises that the HRA imposes an obligation on the judiciary.

[2]It is perfectly acceptable to limit the discussion in this way, and indeed, you should, as it is not possible to consider more than one or two areas in sufficient depth.

[3]Although there are a number of areas that can be discussed, this is a useful case to include because it is a clear illustration of the conflict between the executive and the judiciary.

[4]This is an excellent quote to include as it is a very strong and clear criticism of the legislation. If you cannot remember the wording, you should ensure that you can paraphrase the comments.

[5]The concept of proportionality is crucial to Convention jurisprudence. Use of the correct terminology demonstrates that this has been understood.

decision, the Lords rejected government submissions that it was for the executive to assess the proportionality of legislative responses to terrorism.[6] Lord Bingham stated that the role of the independent judiciary in interpretation and application of statute is 'a cornerstone of the rule of law itself'. The legislation was repealed, and replaced with the system of control orders. The case is perhaps the clearest illustration of the conflict between the judiciary and the executive in respect of measures enacted to prevent terrorist activity, but it is not an isolated example.

The control order regime, established by the Prevention of Terrorism Act 2005 to replace indefinite detention, has itself been the subject of numerous human rights claims. A control order is a civil order which imposes obligations and restrictions on the suspect to limit the risk of terrorist activity. Conditions are tailored to the individual, but commonly include curfews, electronic monitoring, geographical restrictions and limited access to communications technology. The PTA creates two kinds of orders: derogating orders made by the court, containing conditions known to be in breach of Art 5; and non-derogating orders made by the Home Secretary with conditions considered compatible with the Convention.[7] Non-derogating orders are subject to the supervision of the High Court, which must assess whether or not the Home Secretary's decision was 'obviously flawed' (PTA, s 3). A series of linked judgments considered the range of conditions applied to various individuals to assess whether or not the orders were in breach of Art 5. Some of the orders were assessed as acceptable; however, in **Secretary of State for the Home Department v JJ** [2007] UKHL 45, the majority found the orders imposed on the applicants to be incompatible with Art 5. The Lords referred to **Guzzardi v Italy** (1980) 3 EHRR 333, in which it was held that the combined and cumulative effect of restrictions could amount to a deprivation in circumstances falling short of imprisonment.[8] In reaching the decision, the Lords expressly rejected the government argument that the acceptability of the orders must be assessed in light of the serious risk posed by the individuals concerned. Lord Brown stated that such claims must be 'firmly resisted'. As a result, the government redrafted some of the orders, with less stringent conditions.[9]

More recent authorities have assessed the use of 'closed evidence' and the Special Advocate Procedure in hearings concerning control orders, as authorised by the PTA and the rules of court, and considered whether this can be compatible with Art 6 rights to a fair hearing. In **Secretary of State for the Home Department _v_ MB** [2007] UKHL 46, it was held that the Special Advocate procedure provided adequate safeguards for Art 6 rights in all but the most exceptional cases. Two years later, following the Strasbourg ruling in **A _v_ UK** [2009] ECHR 3455/05, the Lords reconsidered the issue and held that an individual must always be told sufficient information about the evidence to enable them to provide instructions to a special advocate (**Secretary of State for the Home Department _v_ AF** (No. 3) [2009] UKHL 28).[10] Lord Hoffmann, dissenting, felt that the Strasbourg decision was wrong, and could result in the destruction of the control order system which he described as an important part of the defence against terrorism. It is difficult to see how the system can continue to operate, as, if the government is required to disclose sensitive evidence, a more acceptable alternative may be to discontinue the proceedings. The Coalition government announced an urgent review of control orders shortly after the election in May 2010.

[10]Here, the answer demonstrates knowledge of how domestic law develops in conjunction with decisions reached in the ECtHR.

It is clear that the judiciary have reached decisions which have forced the executive to revisit measures enacted to combat terrorist activity. In assessing how far this should be viewed as 'undermining' the aims of government, it must be noted that the Human Rights Act charged the courts with the obligation to uphold Convention rights.[11] As Lord Philips noted in the Gresham lecture; Parliament asked the courts to protect the rights, and therefore the judiciary have a specific, democratic, obligation to do so.

[11]This is a point worth making, as arguably, the courts are doing no more than is required by statute.

Make your answer stand out

- There is scope to broaden the discussion to consider the operation of the separation of powers within the constitution. In particular, the case law could be used to show how judicial deference to executive decisions concerning 'national security' has evolved since the **GCHQ case (Council of Civil Service Ministers *v* Minister for the Civil Service** [1985] AC 374). You could refer to more recent decisions in **R (Al Rawi) *v* Foreign Secretary** [2007] 2 WLR 1219 to make the point that foreign policy is still held to be non-justiciable; but you can certainly argue that the control order cases suggest that the HRA has resulted in a clearer system of 'checks and balances' between the institutions of state.

- You could spend more time considering the ECtHR jurisprudence regarding *Chahal* and the later case of *Saadi* v *Italy* (2008) (Application 37201/06), which appears to confirm that position regarding deportation and Art 3 has not altered following 9/11.

- By incorporating a broader range of academic opinion. The following article argues that the judiciary are still extremely deferential to parliamentary supremacy: Ewing, K.D. and Tham, J., 'The continuing futility of the Human Rights Act' [2008] PL 668–93.

! Don't be tempted to...

- Engage in detailed discussion of which conditions the judiciary considered incompatible with Art 5 in the control order cases. The detail is not important, only the fact that the judiciary and the government reached different decisions.

- Ignore the effect of decisions made in Strasbourg. The judiciary are, after all, guided by precedent from the ECtHR. Failure to address this fact would result in an overly simplistic approach. It should be recognised that, since becoming a signatory to the Convention, decisions have been persuasive precedent and therefore the impact of the HRA is perhaps less dramatic than the quotation in the question suggests.

 # Question 6

'Draconian anti-terrorist laws … have a far greater impact on Human Rights than they ever will on crime.' (J. Wadham, the *Guardian*, 14th November 1999.)

Discuss.

Answer plan

→ Identify the powers created since 2000 to control terrorism.

→ Outline the definition of terrorism.

→ Consider the use of stop and search powers under s 44.

→ Explain the concerns about the use of covert surveillance.

→ Assess the impact of the Human Rights Act on legislation.

Diagram plan

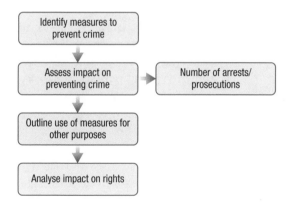

A printable version of this diagram is available from www.pearsoned.co.uk/lawexpressqa

[1]Measures to combat terrorism deal with a wide range of issues, but the question is pointing towards a discussion of provisions concerned with criminal investigation and prosecution so the introduction should establish that this will be the focus of the discussion.

Answer

Since 2000, Parliament has conferred extensive powers upon the state to investigate, contain, and prosecute individuals suspected of involvement in terrorism, in addition to those found within the normal criminal law.[1] These include measures authorising covert surveillance; powers to stop and search people and vehicles;

mechanisms to freeze assets and seize property; and control orders which can severely curtail the activities of individuals. The legislation has been the subject of academic and judicial criticism, and the viability of some measures is now in doubt as they have been declared incompatible with the European Convention on Human Rights in the domestic courts, and in Strasbourg. It is clear that the state now has a greater ability to interfere with the liberty of the citizen than ever before.

The Terrorism Act 2000 defined terrorism as the use or threat of serious violence to persons or property to advance a political, religious, ideological or racial cause. The imprecise definition has been subject to criticism, as it has the potential to cover a far wider range of groups than previous legislation; the breadth of the definition was the subject of adverse comment by the House of Lords in **R v F** [2007] EWCA Crim 243.

[2]It is worth highlighting this as the question asks for consideration of whether or not the measures are effective in preventing criminal acts.

The aim of much of the legislation is preventative, and focuses on powers of investigating and restricting the activities of individuals suspected of involvement in terrorism.[2] The Terrorism Act 2006 creates a specific offence of any act that is preparing for terrorism, punishable with life imprisonment. McKeever has noted that this represents a significant extension to the principles of the 'ordinary' law, in which an attempt is only criminal if it involves conduct which goes beyond 'mere preparation' (McKeever, D., 'The HRA and anti-terrorism in the UK: One great leap forward by Parliament but are the courts able to slow the steady retreat that has followed?' [2010] 'Public Law 110–39).[3] The Prevention of Terrorism Act 2005 authorises the making of control orders which impose severe restrictions on individuals who have not been convicted of any offence. It could be argued, however, that new, more stringent, methods are justified due to the scale of the threat to the general public of a terrorist attack.

[3]The quote refers to 'draconian' laws; the answer does need to be quite precise in highlighting why measures could be seen as more stringent than 'ordinary' law.

[4]Here, the answer provides information to support the assertion that measures are ineffective.

Fenwick has noted that 'one of the most striking aspects of ... provisions [to combat terrorism] is their under use' (Fenwick, H., *Civil Liberties and Human Rights* (4th edn, 2007) London: Routledge Cavendish, p. 1333). This is certainly the case with control orders.[4] In June 2009, a total of 38 persons were subject to control orders (noted in McKeever, 2010). In June 2010, in a written answer to a parliamentary question, the Home Secretary confirmed that just 12 orders were currently in force.[5] McKeever suggests that this

[5]Credit will be given for including material that is specific, and up to date.

[6]Consideration of the reasons for under use shows an ability to be analytical, rather than merely descriptive.

may result from the erosion of the scheme by successive judicial decisions, which mean that prosecution for offences may now be a more certain option.[6] Certainly, a key feature of the system was the ability to supervise orders on the basis of 'closed' evidence, withheld from the suspect. This was preferable to a criminal prosecution, which would be more likely to require disclosure of sensitive material to satisfy the enhanced protection afforded in criminal trials under Art 6(2). Following the decision in **Secretary of State for the Home Department v AF** (No. 3) [2009] UKHL 28, this advantage has been lost, as it was held that the suspect must be informed of sufficient evidence to enable instructions to be given to a special advocate.

Powers of stop and search authorised by ss 44–47 of the Terrorism Act 2000, however, have been used extensively. The Coalition government has announced plans to repeal the powers following the ECtHR ruling that they are incompatible with Art 8 (**Gillan and Quinton v United Kingdom** [2009] ECHR 28). A report by Human Rights Watch records that 148,000 people were stopped and searched using the power in England, Scotland and Wales in the period January–December 2009 alone. The Act allowed authorisation to be granted by a Chief Constable for stop and search to take place of any person in a specified area, without the need to have any suspicion that the individual is involved in terrorism. Many commentators have noted that the extensive use of the power has not resulted in a corresponding increase of prosecutions for terrorist related offences. Human Rights Watch note that the 450,000 searches recorded between 2007 and 2009 have failed to result in a single conviction.[7] Similar points could be made in relation to many of the offences created by the legislation. In 2005, the then Home Secretary, Charles Clarke, acknowledged in evidence to a Select Committee that over 750 arrests under the Terrorism Act 2000 had led to just 22 prosecutions.

[7]Inclusion of figures is helpful, as this provides evidence to demonstrate that the measures in question do not appear to have worked.

[8]Here, the answer directly addresses the question and reaches a partial conclusion before moving on to the next part of the argument.

It is, then, possible to argue that the powers granted to the state to combat terrorism have done little to bring terrorists to justice.[8] Fenwick suggests that the powers are 'largely symbolic' (Fenwick, 2007, p. 1333), and can be considered to be a statement of intent, an attempt to 'isolate and marginalise' particular groups within society. The extension of state power is of concern to commentators who note that, once on the statute book, legislative provisions

[9]The question requires
you to consider whether
the measures have been
effective and also the impact
on human rights. Here, the
answer moves on to address
the second part of the issue.

[10]It is important to find some
examples of inappropriate
use of legislative measures,
to avoid broad, unsupported
statements of opinion.

[11]The conclusion should
directly address the question.

may be used for a purpose not originally envisaged.[9] The Regulation of Investigatory Powers Act 2000 enables covert surveillance and communications interception, and was intended to assist the security services and similar bodies in their investigative duties. Press reports emerged in 2008 highlighting the use of the Act by local authorities investigating matters such as dog-fouling and fly-tipping (see, for example, the BBC report of 27 April 2008).[10]

McKeever notes that powers created to freeze terrorist assets were utilised by the government to protect the savings of UK citizens following the collapse of an Icelandic bank; a measure described as 'hostile' by the Icelandic government, and certainly a purpose that cannot have been contemplated by the legislature. The stop and search schemes discussed above were held to be in breach of Art 8 due to the imprecision of the power, which afforded a broad and virtually unchallengeable discretion to the police. The use of discretionary powers by the state can be of concern to the citizen, and this could be exacerbated by the fact that it seems a number of officers do not understand the limits of their powers. The *British Journal of Photography* reported that the Association of Chief Police Officers had issued a memorandum to officers confirming that there is no law against taking photographs in public places, following publicity surrounding incidents in which individuals were stopped and questioned for doing just that (*Independent*, 3 December 2009).

There is no doubt that international terrorism poses a grave and serious risk to the public, and requires effective measures to ensure protection. Broad, discretionary powers have an arguably limited effect in achieving that aim, and leave open the possibility of unwarranted intrusions into the liberty of the citizen. It does appear then, that legislation has had a greater impact on human rights than on the prevention of crime.[11]

✓ Make your answer stand out

■ By expanding the discussion of the use of the Regulation of Investigatory Powers Act. The decision in *Kennedy* v *United Kingdom* (app 26839/05) [2010] Crim LR 868 suggests that the legislation itself does not infringe Art 8. This may be a useful authority to mention and would contribute to a more balanced argument.

■ By referring to academic comment regarding RIPA. A useful discussion can be found in Loftus, B., Goold, B. and MacGiollabhui, S., 'Covert policing and the Regulation of Investigatory Powers Act' (2010) 8 *Archbold Review* 5–9.

■ Incorporating further academic comment to broaden the debate. You might consider the work of Campbell, D., 'The threat of terror and the plausibility of positivism' [2009] PL 501, which argues that it was wrong to classify the detention of terrorist suspects at Belmarsh as discriminatory. This would demonstrate that you have the ability to engage with a range of views.

❗ Don't be tempted to...

■ Include statements of opinion that you cannot support with evidence. The examples could be relevant political events, case law, or academic opinion. Sometimes students attempt a broad question like this and submit weak answers that are vague and lack content. It is important to be able to express a point of view, but remember, as a lawyer, there must always be evidence provided to persuade the examiner that the point is valid.

■ Simply describe legislative provisions and outline the rights affected. The answer must address how effective the law has been in combating terrorism and therefore, you do need to be able to draw on some factual source material in relation to, say, the number of control orders, or prosecutions for terrorist offences.

Bibliography

Allan, T. R. S (2001) *Constitutional Justice: A Liberal Theory of the Rule of Law*. Oxford: Oxford University Press

Ashworth, A. (2010) '*Gillan and Quinton v United Kingdom*: human rights – article 5 – stop and search as deprivation of liberty', 5 Crim LR 415

Austin, R. (2007) 'The new powers of arrest: plus ça change: more of the same or major change?', Crim LR 459

Bagehot, W. (1963) *The English Constitution*. London: Fontana

Barber, N. (2009) 'Laws and constitutional conventions', LQR 125

Bonner, D. and Stone, R. (1987) 'The Public Order Act 1986, steps in the wrong direction', PL 202

Bowling, B. and Phillips, C. (2007) 'Disproportionate and discriminatory: reviewing the evidence on police stop and search', 70(6) MLR 936

Bradley, A. and Ewing, K. (2006) *Constitutional and Administrative Law* (14th edn). London: Pearson

Bradley, A. and Ewing, K. (2010) *Constitutional and Administrative Law* (15th edn). London: Pearson

Brazier, R. (1999) *Constitutional Practice* (3rd edn). Oxford: Oxford University Press

Buxton, R. (2010) 'Terrorism and the European Convention', 7 Crim LR 533

Campbell, D. (2009) 'The threat of terror and the plausibility of positivism', PL 501

Campbell, D. and Young, J. (2002) 'The metric martyrs and the entrenchment jurisprudence of Lord Justice Laws', PL 399

Craig, P. (1992) 'Legitimate expectations – a conceptual analysis' 108 LQR 79

Craig, P. (1997) 'Formal and substantive conceptions of the Rule of Law: an analytical framework', PL 467

Crowther, S. (2010) 'The SIAC, deportation and European Law', 6(1) Cambridge Student Law Review 227

de Smith, S. and Brazier, R. (2008) *Constitutional and Administrative Law* (8th edn). London: Penguin

Dicey, A. (1885) *The Law of the Constitution*. London: Macmillan

Ewing, K. D. and Tham, J. (2008) 'The continuing futility of the Human Rights Act', PL 668

Feldman, D. (2002) *Civil Liberties and Human Rights in England and Wales.* Oxford: Oxford University Press

Fenwick, H. (2007) *Civil Liberties and Human Rights* (4th edn). London: Routledge Cavendish

Fenwick, H. (2009) 'Marginalising human rights: breach of the peace, "kettling", the Human Rights Act and public protest', PL 737

Fenwick, H. and Phillipson, G. (2006) *Media Law.* Oxford: Oxford University Press [241, 255]

Geddis, A. (2004) 'Free speech martyrs or unreasonable threats to social peace – "insulting" expression and section 5 of the Public Order Act 1986', PL 843

Goudkamp, J. (2008) 'Facing up to actual bias' CJQ 32

Hickman, T. (2008) 'The courts and politics after the Human Rights Act: a comment' PL 84

Home Office (1997) *Your Right to Know: White Paper on Freedom of Information* (Cm. 3818) London: HMSO

Human Rights Joint Committee (2010) *Counter-Terrorism Policy and Human Rights* (16th Report): Annual Review of Control Orders Legislation 2010

Jaconelli, J. (2005) 'Do constitutional conventions bind?' 64(1) CLJ 149

Jennings, I. (1959) *Cabinet Government* (3rd edn). Cambridge: Cambridge University Press

Jennings, I. (1959) *The Law and the Constitution* (5th edn). London: Hodder and Stoughton

Jowell, J. and Oliver, D. (eds.) (2000) *The Changing Constitution* (4th edn). Oxford: Oxford University Press

Jowell, J. (2000) 'Beyond the rule of law: towards constitutional judicial review' PL 671

Knight, C. J.S. (2009) 'Expectations in transition: recent developments in legitimate expectations' PL 15

Law Commission (2010) Report, *Administrative Redress: Public Bodies and the Citizen* (No. 322). www.lawcom.gov.uk/docs/lc322.pdf

Leopold, P. M. (1999) 'Report of the Joint Committee on Parliamentary Privilege', PL 604

Lever, A. (2007) 'Is judicial review undemocratic?' PL 280

Loftus, B, Goold, B. and MacGiollabhui, S. (2010) 'Covert policing and the Regulation of Investigatory Powers Act', 8 Archbold Review 5

Loveland, I. (2009) *Constitutional Law, Administrative Law and Human Rights: A Critical Introduction* (5th edn). Oxford: Oxford University Press

Marshall, G. (1971) *Constitutional Theory.* Oxford: Cavendish Press

McKeever, D. (2010) 'The HRA and anti-terrorism in the UK: one great leap forward by Parliament but are the courts able to slow the steady retreat that has followed?', PL 100

Mead, D. (2009) 'Of kettles, cordon and crowd control – Austin, Commissioner of Police for the Metropolis and the meaning of "deprivation of liberty"' EHRLR 376

Middleton, B. (2009) 'Sections 57 and 58 of the Terrorism Act 2000: interpretation update', 73 JCL 203

Phillipson, G. (2009) 'Max Mosely goes to Strasbourg; Article 8, claimant notification and interim injunctions', 1 Journal of Media Law 73

Schaeffer, A. (2004) 'Reasons and rationalisations: late reasons in judicial review' JR 151

Scott, A. (2010) 'Prior notification in privacy case: a reply to Professor Phillipson' 2(1) Journal of Media Law 49

Stone, R. (2001) 'Breach of the peace: the case for abolition' 2 Web JCLI

Stone, R. (2005) The Law of Entry, Search and Seizure (5th edn). Oxford: Oxford University Press

Stone, R. (2010) Textbook on Civil Liberties and Human Rights (8th edn). Oxford: Oxford University Press

Straw, J. (1994) 'Abolish the Royal Prerogative', in A. Barnett (ed.), Power and the Throne: The Monarchy Debate, London: Vintage

Sunkin, M. (2004) 'Remedies available in judicial review proceedings', in D. Feldman (ed.), English Public Law (2nd edn). Oxford: Oxford University Press

Vile, L. (1998) Constitutionalism and the Separation of Powers (2nd edn) Indianapolis: Liberty Fund Inc

Waldron, J. (1990) The Law. London: Routledge

Waldron, J. (2006) 'The core of the case against judicial review' 115 Yale Law Journal 1346

Walker, C. (2010) 'The threat of terrorism and the fate of control orders', PL 4

Worthy, B. and Hazel, R. (2010) 'Assessing the performance of freedom of information', 27(4) Government Information Quarterly 352.

Index

INDEX